ARNULFO L. OLIVEIRA MEMORIAL LIBRARY
1825 MAY STREET
BROWNSVILLE, TEXAS 78520

MEDICOLEGAL ASPECTS of CRITICAL CARE

Contributors

Alexander M. Capron
Joel E. Frader
William A. Knaus
Judith R. Lave
Rosa Lynn Pinkus
Katharine C. Rathbun
Nancy K. Rhoden
Edward P. Richards III
Deborah J. Robinson
Robyn S. Shapiro
James V. Snyder
George L. Wallace-Barnhill

MEDICOLEGAL ASPECTS of CRITICAL CARE

Katherine Benesch, JD, MPH
Attorney at Law
Adjunct Assistant Professor
of Anesthesiology and
Critical Care Medicine
University of Pittsburgh

Norman S. Abramson, MD
Assistant Professor of Critical Care
Medicine/Anesthesiology
Resuscitation Research Center
University of Pittsburgh

Ake Grenvik, MD, PhD
Professor of Anesthesiology and Surgery
Director,
Critical Care Medicine Training Program
University Health Center of Pittsburgh

Alan Meisel, JD
Professor of Law and Psychiatry
University of Pittsburgh
Schools of Law and Medicine
Of Counsel
Berkman Ruslander Pohl Lieber & Engel

Pittsburgh, Pennsylvania

AN ASPEN PUBLICATION®
Aspen Publishers, Inc.
1986

Rockville, Maryland
Royal Tunbridge Wells

Library of Congress Cataloging in Publication Data

Medicolegal aspects of critical care.

"An Aspen publication."
Includes bibliographies and index.
1. Critical care medicine—Law and legislation—United States. 2. Intensive care units—Law and legislation—United States. 3. Tort liability of hospitals—United States. 4. Critical care medicine—United States. 5. Intensive care units—United States. I. Benesch, Katherine. [DNLM: 1. Critical Care—United States—legislation. 2. Legislation, Hospital—United States. 3. Malpractice—United States—legislation. WX 33 AA1 M489]
KF3825.M43   1986   346.7303'1   86-3342
ISBN: 0-87189-292-8   347.30631

Editorial Services: Jane Coyle

Copyright © 1986 by Aspen Publishers, Inc.
All rights reserved.

Aspen Publishers, Inc. grants permission for photocopying for personal or internal use, or for the personal or internal use of specific clients registered with the Copyright Clearance Center (CCC). This consent is given on the condition that the copier pay a $1.00 fee plus $.12 per page for each photocopy through the CCC for photocopying beyond that permitted by the U.S. Copyright Law. The fee should be paid directly to the CCC, 21 Congress St., Salem, Massachusetts 01970.
0-87189-292-8/86 $1.00 + .12.

This consent does not extend to other kinds of copying, such as copying for general distribution, for advertising or promotional purposes, for creating new collective works, or for resale. For information, address Aspen Publishers, Inc., 1600 Research Boulevard, Rockville, Maryland 20850.

Library of Congress Catalog Card Number: 86-3342
ISBN: 0-87189-292-8

Printed in the United States of America

1 2 3 4 5

To all patients, families,
and health professionals
whose lives have been touched
by experiencing or treating
critical illness.

Table of Contents

Preface xi

Chapter 1— **Developing Standards of Care for Critical Care Medicine** 1
Deborah J. Robinson

Establishing Legal Standards of Care 2
Guidelines for Establishing a Standard of Care for CCM 5
Conclusion 9

Chapter 2— **Risk Management in the Intensive Care Unit** 11
Edward P. Richards III and Katharine C. Rathbun

Principles of Risk Management 11
Establishing an ICU Risk Management Program 14
Conclusion 27

Chapter 3— **Deciding about Treatment in the ICU** 31
Nancy K. Rhoden

Decisions for Competent Patients 31
Decisions for Incompetent Patients 39
Conclusion 53

Chapter 4— **Critically Ill Infants** 61
Robyn S. Shapiro and Joel E. Frader

	The Right to Refuse Treatment	62
	Pediatric Medical Treatment Decisions	65
	Medical Decision Making for the Impaired Newborn	68
	Proposed Solutions for the Impaired Newborn	76
	Conclusion	83
Chapter 5—	**The Economics of Intensive Care Units**	**87**
	Judith R. Lave and William A. Knaus	
	The Growth in Intensive Care	87
	Factors Associated with the Growth of ICU/CCU Beds	88
	The Effectiveness of Intensive Care	92
	Cost of Intensive Care	94
	Changes in the Financing Arrangements for Hospital Services	97
	Increasing the Efficiency of Intensive Care	99
	Potential for Savings	100
	Recommendations for Change in the ICU	101
	Summary and Conclusions	104
Chapter 6—	**Determination of Death**	**109**
	Alexander Morgan Capron	
	The Need for Change in Standards	110
	Translating Medical Knowledge into Policy	116
	Adopting a Legal Standard	121
	The Future	125
Chapter 7—	**Human and Environmental Factors in Critical Care: Patients and Their Families**	**133**
	G.L. Wallace-Barnhill	
	ICU Environment and the Patient	134
	ICU Psychosis	134
	Families and Coping	136
	Grief and Grieving	141
	Robert	142

Chapter 8— Human and Environmental Factors in Critical Care: Health Professionals 147
G.L. Wallace-Barnhill

The Stress Concept 147
Environment 148
Nursing Stress 149
Physician Stress 152
Standards and Staffing Problems 155
Staff Interaction 156
Legal Considerations and Ethics Committees 157
Conclusion and Recommendations 160

Chapter 9— Deciding about Life-Sustaining Treatment: The Role of Hospital Guidelines 165
Alan Meisel, Ake Grenvik, Rosa Lynn Pinkus, and James V. Snyder

The Effect of Technology 166
The Influence of Law 166
The Cost of Care 167
The President's Commission 167
Basic Principles 168
Collaborative Decision Making 169
What Constitutes "Treatment" 171
Decision Making for Incompetent Patients 172
The Presumption against Judicial Involvement 174
Advance Directives ("Living Wills") 175
The Role of the Ethics Committee 176
Writing Orders and Keeping Records 177
Conclusion 177

Appendix A— Presbyterian-University Hospital Guidelines on Foregoing Life-Sustaining Treatment 181

Index 195

Preface

Critical care practitioners face decisions involving life and death on a daily basis. Frequently they are called upon to render care or determine what level of care should be provided in highly stressful situations. Decisions in this context often have significant medical, legal, psychological, ethical, and economic implications.

This book provides guidance from various professional disciplines and presents a multidisciplinary approach to the complex medical, legal, psychological, ethical, and economic problems faced every day by the myriad health professionals, patients, and relatives who come into contact with the critical care system. It is designed as a resource and reference book for physicians and surgeons, nurses, respiratory therapists, attorneys with medical/legal practices, hospital administrators, educators, researchers, and students. The underlying assumption of the book is that critical care is a multidisciplinary specialty requiring the skills of a team of health care providers working with patients and their families for effective, timely decision making in the face of difficult treatment choices that often involve life and death.

The material presents the reader with a variety of approaches to different aspects of critical care delivery. From the legal point of view, the doctrine of informed consent and the case of Karen Ann Quinlan have spawned almost three decades of complicated and often conflicting court decisions. In response to the common law, state legislatures have passed statutes defining death, discussing the requirements of informed consent, and enacting "natural death acts." This book is not a substitute for competent legal counsel, nor can it rationalize the inconsistencies that exist in the law. It does, however, provide a comprehensive overview of the variety of areas of law essential to critical care practitioners and lawyers advising hospital-based clients. For those who work in intensive care units, the text gives a framework for analyzing complicated medical/legal issues that arise every day.

A chapter is devoted to the handling of special problems related to the care of critically ill infants. This special topic in critical care has been included because of the particular interest and difficulty in this area generated by the Baby Doe regulations promulgated by the federal government. For hospital administrators and critical care managers, there is an in-depth exploration of the allocation of limited resources—a subject that has gained increasing national significance in light of the fast-paced development of expensive medical technology and the scarcity of economic resources to provide for all of the new treatment modalities available. Practitioners, administrators, and lawyers should all be interested in the subject of risk management in the intensive care unit, one of the highest risk areas in any institution. The book also covers stress, a factor which is omnipresent in critical care settings. Finally, we have included a thought-provoking chapter on guidelines for forgoing life-sustaining treatment, a subject that institutions and critical care practitioners have wrestled with for many years.

This book attempts to address the considerations that different disciplines must take into account when making decisions on medical issues within critical care. It offers guidance and examples from those who have successfully handled critical care dilemmas. Both law and medicine in this area have changed rapidly. Neither will remain static. The reader, however, should come away with a firm foundation from which to begin to resolve the complicated problems that exist in critical care, and be prepared to deal with complex issues that undoubtedly will arise in the future.

The editors wish to thank many individuals for their assistance in the preparation of this book. One, however, stands out for his special dedication, assistance, and good-natured willingness to work. Special thanks go to John A. Magnanti, without whom this text would not have come to fruition.

Katherine Benesch
Norman Abramson
Ake Grenvik
Alan Meisel

Pittsburgh, Pennsylvania
April, 1986

Chapter 1

Developing Standards of Care for Critical Care Medicine

Deborah J. Robinson

Critical Care Medicine (CCM) and Intensive Care Units (ICUs) have become well-recognized components of modern medical care. The history of CCM and the development of ICUs began as recently as the early 1950s.[1] By the mid-80s, however, only some 30 years later, it has become common for even small community hospitals to have a variety of ICUs.[2] The degree and level of services rendered in ICUs have evolved so that today there are many specialty ICUs, where medical practice is substantially different from critical or emergency treatment provided in the past. It is now becoming clear that CCM as a medical and nursing subspecialty has found general acceptance.

In the last two decades, CCM has evolved from a medical field emphasizing resuscitative techniques and interventions for acute respiratory care to a sophisticated, broad-based multidisciplinary subspecialty recognized by the American Board of Medical Specialties (ABMS).[3] As physicians have developed new definitions for this growing subspecialty, hospitals too have developed a variety of critical care units (CCUs) and have provided special equipment and trained health personnel to support these new units. The emergence of this multidisciplinary CCM subspecialty, however, was not greeted with uniform approval by the established medical disciplines involved. Therefore, in 1985, the ABMS approved five somewhat different CCM subspecialties: Anesthesiology CCM, Internal Medicine CCM, Pediatric CCM, Surgical Critical Care, and Neurosurgical Critical Care.[4] In addition, the American Boards of Obstetrics/Gynecology and Psychiatry/Neurology have applied to ABMS for the right to certify subspecialists in CCM.

Despite the granting by the ABMS of subspecialty status to CCM, the struggle to define CCM continues. Although Emergency Medicine has become a recognized specialty, for example, there is no consensus as to exactly how it relates to Critical Care Medicine.[5] Nor is there a consensus as to the appropriate relationship between the CCM physician and the patient's attending physician, who is usually a specialist in the field of the patient's underlying disease. While this difficulty with definition is not the primary topic of this chapter it is germane to the chapter's focus and content, i.e., the appropriate legal standards applicable to CCM.

The complexity of determining how the legal system will apply standards when judging allegations of malpractice arising in ICUs and involving CCM will mirror the difficulty medicine has had in creating appropriate roles for this subspecialty. What, for example, is the duty of care required of the CCM physician as opposed to the patient's attending physician? What is the hospital's responsibility for monitoring and maintaining the complex medical equipment necessary for an ICU? The law has a tendency to lag behind technology development. Thus, it will be some time before courts are comfortable evaluating claims that allege malpractice in intensive care settings. This chapter explores the issues and policies involved in creating an appropriate standard.

ESTABLISHING LEGAL STANDARDS OF CARE

In analyzing and evaluating the evolution of Critical Care Medicine as a new subspecialty, the key legal question becomes, how will traditional tests of negligence be applied to this emerging area of medicine? This question is posed for both the medical practitioner and the institution. The law already has well-established tests for determining medical negligence (malpractice). This liability can be imposed on either the physician or the hospital or on both parties.

Traditionally, physicians have been found negligent for personal injuries sustained by their patients when those injuries are caused by physician conduct that failed to conform to the standard of care owed the patient. Hence, the benchmark in any malpractice case is the appropriate standard of care owed the patient. In determining the standard of care, courts have historically imposed on physicians the duty to provide medical care according to the customary practice in the community.[6] Theoretically, the rural physician treating a patient in a 50-bed hospital was held to a different standard of care than the physician treating a patient in a major urban teaching center. However, the development of standardized medical education and national certification requirements, as well as the ready availability of medical information, has virtually eliminated the "locality rule." In most states, physicians are judged against a national and hence uniform standard of medical practice.[7]

A physician is generally required to have the skill and knowledge commonly possessed by members of the medical profession and will be liable for harm resulting from care that falls below this standard. However, when a physician presents himself or herself as a "specialist" or as having greater skill than an "average" practitioner, and when patients are accepting treatment on this basis, the standard of care will be modified accordingly.[8] Clearly, the new subspecialties of CCM can be expected to create new standards for CCM physicians as subspecialists.

Respondeat Superior

Hospitals for their part have traditionally found themselves to be liable under a variety of legal theories. The traditional doctrine of *respondeat superior* holds the hospital liable when an employee or agent of the hospital acts negligently and injury results. This is an example of vicarious liability; the employer becomes vicariously liable for the acts of employees and/or agents. For example, a hospital can become vicariously liable for the negligent activities of its employed nurses and salaried physicians.

Most recently, hospitals have also been considered to be independently liable for negligent medical acts performed within the institution. Although a hospital itself does not render patient care, a hospital is thought to have a separate legal duty to provide for high-quality medical care in its institution. This responsibility includes the duty to properly supervise and review the quality of medical care.[9] Courts have gone on record to describe the duty of the hospital to an individual patient, e.g., as follows:

> ...If the individual looked to the hospital to provide him with medical treatment and there has been representation by the hospital that medical treatment would be afforded by physicians working therein, an agency by estoppel can be found....[10]

As agency is a question for the jury to decide, this theory exposes the hospital to almost limitless risks of liability.

Strict Liability

Another theory of liability that previously had not been applied to hospitals is "strict liability." Strict liability has evolved as liability without fault (i.e., without negligence) and is generally applied in products liability cases in which a seller is liable for all defective or hazardous products that unduly threaten a consumer's life, health, or safety. Traditionally, hospitals had not been held to be sellers or merchants of products but rather of services and therefore not subject to strict liability. In addition, there has been a great deal of discussion of public policy considerations that dictate against holding hospitals liable as sellers or merchants of products, even though hospitals are responsible for equipment provided or lack thereof.[11] This issue of liability for defective products or equipment could have a major impact on CCM and the care provided in ICUs because of the abundance of complex equipment utilized in these settings.

Legal precedent concerning a hospital's liability for the provision and use of a defective product has been evolving since the late 1970s. The Illinois Appellate Court in 1980 held that it would not impose strict liability for harm that resulted from radiation therapy treatment for cancer. The court held that

> Public policy dictates against the imposition of strict liability and tort for injuries resulting from the administration of x-radiation treatments by a hospital.[12]

However, as recently as 1984, the Alabama Supreme Court determined a hospital to be a merchant of medical supplies and equipment and held the hospital liable for harm resulting from a defective suturing needle. The court stated:

> In the course of their competition, hospitals certainly hold themselves out to the public as having special knowledge regarding the provision of medical services to patients. Inherent in this presentment is a warranty that the hospital will sell, furnish or supply patients with goods for use in the provision of medical services .... [13]

Today, the concept of the hospital as a merchant, seller, or distributor, and with this the implications for products liability suits, has spread to other jurisdictions. Thus, this is an important legal trend to monitor as health centers become more competitive and characterized as "businesses" rather than "charitable operations."

The CCM Physician as Specialist

Thus far, the courts have had little opportunity to apply traditional principles of legal liability to CCM.[14] It is clear, however, that the courts will look to both the physician and the hospital when determining an appropriate standard of care to be used to assess liability in situations involving patients treated in critical care units and/or by physicians trained in CCM. In determining physician liability the courts will consider the statements of standards applied to other medical specialists. That is, medical specialists have been expected to demonstrate and are held to a higher standard of care than general practitioners:

> One who holds himself out as a specialist must employ not merely the skill of the general practitioner, but also the special degree of skill normally possessed by the average physician who devotes special study and attention to the particular organ or disease or injury involved having regard to the present state of scientific knowledge.[15]

We can, thus, expect courts to look at CCM as a new and separate subspecialty and require higher standards of care for CCM specialists than for general practitioners. More important, and as yet, unresolved, is the question of the standards of care that will be expected of CCM physicians in comparison with other specialists (e.g., cardiologists, pulmonologists) who treat critically ill patients in the ICU.

CCM and the Hospital

Standards of care have also been established for hospitals and most states have well-developed case law which should be consulted. In general, courts will look to standards of accreditation (e.g., the Joint Commission on Accreditation of Hospitals, or JCAH), licensure laws, Medicare Conditions of Participation, and other voluntary accreditation standards.[16] For example, in its *Accreditation Manual*, JCAH includes an entire chapter on standards for Special Care Units. In addition, hospitals have a general duty to provide safe equipment and appliances for use in the diagnosis and treatment of patients. A hospital can be liable for defective equipment if it fails to exercise adequate care in furnishing and maintaining such equipment.[17] Hospitals must assure that their equipment and appliances are reasonably fit for intended use and must assume the responsibility for providing tests and inspection of instruments and equipment for determining defects. Hospitals may also find themselves liable for harm resulting from use of defective equipment even when they had no knowledge of the defect or control over design or manufacture.[18] Obviously, these considerations have broad implications for the practice of CCM, where complex technologies and medical equipment are involved.

GUIDELINES FOR ESTABLISHING A STANDARD OF CARE FOR CCM

By 1983, the AMA acknowledged the existence of 80 specialties. Of these, 52 correspond to specialty and subspecialty areas for which member boards of the American Board of Medical Specialties issue certificates. There are in addition, 25 organizations outside the ABMS that certify physicians.[19] Thus, the courts have available an abundance of guidelines to define the areas of expertise and skill of the various medical specialists. As noted earlier, the courts will refer to these models also when establishing a standard of care for CCM practice. The courts will also look to the literature and the body of knowledge that has already evolved in CCM, or other involved medical specialties.

Scope of Discipline and Training

When the ABMS initially approved the Applications for Certification of Special Competence in CCM in 1980, CCM skills and the body of knowledge defining the specialty were described in detail, including the breadth of the discipline and training required for certification. This reflected the unique development of a multidisciplinary subspecialty:

> CCM is a multidisciplinary endeavor that crosses traditional departmental and specialty lines inasmuch as the problems encountered in the critically ill patient encompass various aspects of many different specialties. The CCM physician is a specialist whose knowledge is of necessity broad, involving all aspects of management of the critically ill patient and whose base of operation is the ICU. The CCM physician must have completed training in a primary specialty and, in addition, he must have training in the CCM aspects of many disciplines to enable him: to work in concert with the various specialists on the patient care team in the ICU; to utilize recognized techniques for life support; to teach other physicians, nurses and health professionals that practice in intensive care; and to foster research. Thus, CCM is a multidisciplinary subspecialty based in the ICU, with its primary concern being the care of the patient with a critical illness.[20]

The body of knowledge that this multidisciplinary subspecialty embraces requires detailed and complex training:

> The content of the Body of Knowledge can be categorized within major organ systems for conditions which are not unique to, but common among, the critically ill patients. These categories include the CCM aspects of the following groups: 1) cardiovascular; 2) pulmonary; 3) metabolic-endocrine-nutritional; 4) renal-genitourinary; 5) obstetric-gynecological; 6) gastrointestinal; 7) hematology; 8) oncology; 9) trauma; 10) infectious disease, including infection control; 11) neurological-neurosurgical; 12) psychiatric; 13) drug

overdoses-intoxication; 14) cardiopulmonary and CNS resuscitation; 15) evaluation and certification of brain death; 16) ethical and legal issues related to ordinary versus extraordinary means of life support . . . [21]

The Role of the CCM Physician Specialist

In addition to the scope of disciplines involved, the courts must examine the role of the CCM physician specialist in the special care unit as well as the nature of his or her patient. If it is contemplated that each CCM physician will not become an independent specialist in all fields, but rather that he or she will coordinate and monitor critical care management, then the CCM physician cannot undertake the responsibility of becoming a specialist in all fields involved but rather becomes a medical manager. This role can involve direct care but in general suggests a broader role of patient coordination as confirmed by the following objectives that describe the multidisciplinary CCM subspecialist:[22]

1. To provide a high level of intensive care by coordinating when requested, several physician specialists, critical care nurses and allied health professionals (including respiratory therapists, physiotherapists, and ICU laboratory technicians) . . .
2. To offer an educational setting in which a concentrated experience in the care of the critically ill may be gained by physician trainees, medical students, and others with the active participation of CCM physician staff.
3. To provide thorough direction and education, active critical care to patients outside the ICU, e.g., cardiopulmonary resuscitation, and other life-supporting efforts in crisis situations.
4. To provide staff specialists with ICU skills for coordination and responsibility, e.g., regarding JCAH standards, budget, infection control policy, quality control of patient care, and various ICU-related committees.
5. To participate in the design and evaluation of ICU policies and procedures, standing orders, standards of care, and special equipment.
6. To provide, within the ICU, coordination, quality control, and education of ancillary services, e.g., respiratory therapy, ICU laboratories and electrical safety control.
7. To engage in clinical research for the advancement of the clinical science of CCM including cost controlling measures.

In 1985, the ABMS approved new applications by the American Boards of Anesthesiology, Internal Medicine, Pediatrics, Surgery, and Neurological Surgery to separately issue certificates of special competence in CCM to qualifying primary specialists in these five fields. This new system created five different subspecialists in CCM each with similar skills and knowledge.[23] Thus, if a court were now to look carefully at any of these new subspecialties it would need to consider both the body of knowledge that the subspecialty encompasses and the particular role the CCM physician plays in the management of the critically ill patient. If it is determined that the CCM physician preempts or replaces the attending physician and provides continuous coverage as a primary physician or as a team leader rather than a consultant, he or she should be prepared to be held to a standard of the attending specialist physician he or she replaces. If, on the other hand, the CCM physician will primarily coordinate and monitor the many specialists providing care to the critically ill patient, then he or she should expect to be held to a standard of reasonable care for a physician in such a patient management position.

Because CCM represents interdisciplinary subspecialties and because it is focused on providing care to the critically ill in a particular setting (the ICU), it cannot be evaluated without looking at the multitude of professionals who interact with the CCM physician. Each one of these professionals working in an ICU as part of the ICU team is also a primary specialist and his or her care will be evaluated as that of a primary specialist as well.

The Role of the CCM Nurse

The critical care nurse is another example of an essential professional on the CCM team. In recent years, as the need for nurses in critical care units in hospitals expanded, the nursing profession has moved to develop professional standards for critical care nursing practice. This nursing specialty has its own professional association, the American Association of Critical Care Nurses (AACN), which has developed nursing standards in this area. The AACN defines standards for care of the critically ill as "statements of quality which serve as a model to facilitate and evaluate the delivery of optimal nursing care to the critically ill."[24] These standards have become available not only as a guide to the profession, but also as a formal indicator of what the profession holds itself out to be.

A recent publication described the value of critical care standards as twofold: (1) for job performance evaluation and (2) as ongoing indicators for evaluation of critical care nursing.[25] A third, although unintended, use of such published standards is their introduction in a court of law as evidence of a standard of care. In addition to AACN standards, the critical care nursing profession has published books describing standards for critical care nursing. For example, *Standards for Critical Care* published in 1981, was the first text ever totally devoted to describing standards for critical care nursing.[26] It is a valuable tool, serving to educate the profession, to help formulate plans for ongoing patient care, and to evaluate care once delivered. At the same time, it provides further legal evidence of a uniform standard of care that can be applied in the courts when there is a maloccurrence in the ICU.

The Role of the Hospital

Although a complete discussion of hospital liability arising out of the ICU and the provision of CCM is beyond the scope of this chapter, it is clear that any analysis regarding CCM cannot exist in a vacuum but is directly related to the particular hospital's ICU service. It is very likely that the courts will look at the ICU as a patient care unit that the hospital provides for the specific management of the critically ill. As such, an ICU patient has the right to expect a certain quality of care. Hospitals now have JCAH accreditation standards that govern ICUs. These standards will be imposed on all hospitals once they undertake the general responsibility of designing a unit that has been created to treat critically ill patients.

CONCLUSION

With the evolution of the medical profession and present-day health delivery systems, new subspecialties of critical care medicine have been established. Concurrently, specially designed hospital settings have developed to support the new practice. Critical care medicine and nursing have provided their own internal standards that courts will be able to use when developing legal standards of care to apply to maloccurrences in the critical care setting. The CCM profession should be aware that as it struggles to adopt a role that includes patient management as well as the provision of specialist physician services, its liability exposure will also change. It is a common legal maxim that for every duty assumed there is a corresponding potential for liability. This should not impede the progress of medicine, but rather should inform those who are establishing the role for critical care medicine.

Hospitals, too, are faced with a dilemma. It is well established that courts will look to such institutions as having a separate duty to provide quality patient care. As hospitals themselves establish specialized units and services, they should be aware that they will be held to the standard of having the appropriate resources: personnel and equipment to assure these services. Together, the hospital and the critical care profession should design a system for which they are willing to be held accountable.

NOTES

1. P. Safar, *The Critical Care Medical Continuum from Scene to Outcome,* in MAJOR ISSUES IN CRITICAL CARE MEDICINE 71-84 (J. Parrillo & S. Ayres 1984).

2. Weil, *The Society of Critical Care Medicine, Its History and Its Destiny,* 1 CRITICAL CARE MED. (1973).

3. Grenvik, Leonard, & Arens, et al., *Critical Care Medicine, Certification as a Multidisciplinary Subspecialty,* 9 CRITICAL CARE MED. 117-25 (1981) [hereinafter cited as *Critical Care Medicine*].

4. Grenvik, *Subspecialty Certification in Critical Care Medicine by American Specialty Boards,* CRITICAL CARE MED. (in press).

5. Abramson, Levine & Safar, *Emergency and Critical Care Medicine Physician Education—A Continuum?,* 3 AM. J. EMERGENCY MED. 569-71 (1985).

6. Waltz, *The Rise and Gradual Fall of the Locality Rule in Medical Malpractice Litigation,* 18 DE PAUL L. REV. 408, 411-15 (1969).

7. Brune v. Belinkoff, 354 Mass. 102, 235 N.E.2d 793 (1968).

8. RESTATEMENT (SECOND) OF TORTS §299 A, comment (d) (1965).

9. Grewe v. Mt. Clemens Gen. Hosp., 404 Mich. 240, 273 N.W.2d 429 (1978).

10. *Id.* at 404 Mich. 250-251.

11. Bassow, *Medical Products and Services Liability: Public Policy Requires Legislative Innovation and Judicial Restraint,* 53 DEN. L.J. 387 (1976).

12. Pitler v. Michael Reese Hosp., 92 Ill. App.3d 739, 415 N.E.2d 1255 (1980).

13. Skelton v. Druid City Hosp. Bd., 39 U.C.C. Rep. Serv. 369 (Ala. Sup. Ct. 1984).

14. Abramson, Silvasy-Wald & Grenvik, et al., *Adverse Occurrences in Intensive Care,* 244 J. A.M.A. 1582-84 (1980).

15. Carbone v. Warburton, 11 N.J. 418, 426, 94 A.2d 680, 683 (1953), *cited in* Brune v. Belinkoff, 354 Mass. 102, 235 N.E.2d at 797-798.

16. Darling v. Charleston Community Memorial Hosp., 33 Ill.2d 376, 211 N.E.2d 253 (1965), *cert. denied,* 383 U.S. 946 (1966).

17. South Highlands Infirmary v. Camp, 279 Ala. 1, 180 So.2d 904 (1965).

18. Skelton v. Druid City Hosp. Bd., 39 U.C.C. Rep. Serv. 369 (Ala. Sup. Ct. 1984).

19. *Id.*

20. A. Grenvik, Training and Certification in Critical Care Medicine 6 (Aug. 1982) (unpublished manuscript). Summarized in 4:6 National Institute of Health Consumers Development Conference Summary, Washington, D.C., Government Printing Office (1983).

21. *Critical Care Medicine, supra* note 3.

22. *Id.*

23. Grenvik, *supra* note 4.

24. B. JOHANSON, C. DUNGAN, D. HOFFMEISTER, & S. WELLS, Preface to STANDARDS FOR CRITICAL CARE (1981) [hereinafter cited as STANDARDS].

25. Glenin, *Formulation of Standards of Nursing Practice Using a Nursing Model,* in IMPLEMENTING THEORY INTO PRACTICE (1974).

26. STANDARDS, *supra* note 24.

Chapter 2

Risk Management in the Intensive Care Unit

Edward P. Richards III and Katharine C. Rathbun

Health care providers tend to resent the "intrusion," as they see it, of law into medicine. This is an unreasonable position, since legal rules, however imperfectly constructed, reflect societal values which must be (and should be) considered in medical decision making. This chapter discusses abstract legal notions and explores how to apply them to real-life Intensive Care Unit (ICU) activities in order to prevent litigation. The material in this chapter is drawn from the experience of the authors, which includes both risk management counseling and medical malpractice litigation. In many cases this practical experience has led to observations about medical practice that are contrary to "conventional" wisdom. The first part of the chapter reviews the basic principles of risk management. The second part applies these principles to personnel management, medical records, medical device usage, and incident reporting in the ICU.

PRINCIPLES OF RISK MANAGEMENT

ICU risk management has three goals:

1) To reduce patient injuries by eliminating substandard care;
2) To properly document the care that is delivered; and
3) To ensure that third parties causing patient injuries, such as medical device manufacturers, assume the responsibilities and costs of their actions.[1]

The fundamental goal of risk management is to reduce patient injuries. The risk manager must give new life to the term "quality medical care." To some people, quality care means doing every possible test and procedure.[2]

However, even if financial considerations are ignored, the complexity of "high-tech" medicine has created a therapeutic parallel to Heisenburg's uncertainty principle, i.e., the more you do to the patient, the greater the chance of iatrogenic injury.[3] All members of the medical care team, not just the risk manager, must differentiate aggressive treatment from overtreatment, and they must do this under the conflicting financial incentives of contemporary medical practice.

Ideally, a risk management program would prevent all injuries. This is clearly impossible. Medical care is unavoidably accompanied by risks to the patient and to the provider. More important, many risks that could be eliminated in theory are too expensive to prevent in practice. Determining the potential cost of an event that causes a patient (or staff) injury requires consideration of the provider's legal and public relations posture. While the probability of winning a lawsuit may be predictable, it is patient expectations that determine whether a lawsuit is filed. As a rule, patients lack the technical sophistication to recognize whether a bad outcome is an unavoidable complication or an iatrogenic injury.[4] Lacking this knowledge, a patient judges his or her care on the basis of two criteria: Was the outcome consistent with the perceived seriousness of the original medical condition? and Was the care delivered in a professional manner? (i.e., Did the ICU appear competent and were the providers responsive to the patient's needs?)

For example, obstetrics patients view pregnancy as a nonhazardous condition. Since the perceived risk associated with this condition is low, the patient is likely to sue if the outcome is bad. In the ICU, however, risk management is complicated by the potentially catastrophic results of deviations from accepted standards of patient care (incidents). Nonetheless, ICUs account for little malpractice litigation. The very factors that increase the severity of ICU incidents reduce the probability that these incidents will result in litigation. In most cases, ICU patients and their families perceive their condition to be serious. Therefore, they are usually more prepared for a bad outcome.

Economics of Risk Management

You cannot get something for nothing. The risk manager must balance potential losses against the cost of prevention. Losses are of three types:

1) The direct costs of legal claims. These include not only the compensation to the injured patient and all of the costs associated with processing and defending a claim, but also the loss of skilled personnel time through depositions and other litigation-related activities;

2) The cost of the risk management program itself: increased staff, overhead costs for incident reporting and analysis and the costs of changing patient care patterns; and

3) The cost of iatrogenic injuries that arise from the risk management efforts: for example, complications from tests that are ordered out of fear of malpractice suits rather than medical necessity.[5]

The basic economics of risk management are simple. The first dollars spent on risk management have the highest return in reduced financial losses from malpractice litigation. As more resources are devoted to risk management, the reduction in loss per dollar spent diminishes. The optimal operating point for a risk management program is where the cost of the program equals the reduction in litigation losses.[6]

The Duty To Act

When a risk management program is implemented, the hospital assumes the duty to manage the risks it discovers. This includes the prevention of some risks and the mitigation of the potential harm of others. This raises the question, Are we better off not knowing, for example, that a powerful member of the medical staff, because of illness or infirmity, is no longer able to manage the complexities of ICU care?[7] While the hospital has the legal responsibility for removing staff members it finds to be incompetent, this decision may be left to a medical staff committee and ultimately to the hospital board. If the hospital does not act, it could be liable for the damages caused by the incompetent staff member, and it may also be liable for punitive damages for allowing the danger to continue.[8] How should this problem be handled?

Historically, hospitals solved this problem by not inquiring into the actions of physicians. This is no longer a viable alternative. Courts are increasingly unwilling to accept ignorance as a defense. In addition, the potential losses for ignoring a risk increase as patients become more willing to sue.[9] Allowing a known risk to continue leads to positive feedback and the pipelining of claims. *Positive feedback* is a term for a process that is self-accelerating, i.e., where the occurrence of an event increases the probability of that event occurring again.[10] In risk management, feedback is the tendency of poorly supervised hospitals to attract less-qualified personnel, who in turn further reduce the quality of supervision and patient care. The term *pipelining* refers to the amount of material that accumulates in a pipe before anything comes out the other end.[11] If a hospital relies on litigation to identify risk management problems, then many injuries, with their attendant liability, may accumulate during the long delay between a patient injury and the filing of a lawsuit.

A dramatic example of pipelining occurred at the University of California at Davis Medical School.[12] Over a 22-month period, the cardiac surgery and kidney transplant services experienced a dramatic rise in morbidity and mortality.[13] This was ignored (allowing more people to be injured) for a long period after other physicians at the University stopped referring patients to the affected services. Once the first lawsuit was brought, the publicity surrounding the incident caused other injured patients to come forward.[14] This type of loss is so catastrophic that its prevention must outweigh the traditional reluctance to discipline medical staff members.

ESTABLISHING AN ICU RISK MANAGEMENT PROGRAM

The first task in establishing a risk management program is to eliminate "easy" risks. These are risks that are either simple and inexpensive to correct or that are so blatant and dangerous that all members of the medical care team will readily cooperate in their correction. Examples of easy risks to eliminate are physicians with improper credentials, expired licenses, forged credentials, etc., or replacement of equipment that has been recalled by the manufacturer but is still in use. Easy risks are often best identified by an outside audit team, because if these risks were obvious to hospital personnel, they would already have been eliminated.[15] Once the "easy" risks have been eliminated, the risk manager must establish proper channels of authority before attempting more complex risk management strategies.

Authority

Effective supervision of the wide variety of personnel involved in ICU patient care is one of the primary risk management problems. ICU staffing may include:

1. Physician Staff
    - the admitting physician
    - consultants retained by the admitting physician
    - ICU specialist staff
    - medical staff committees with authority for ICU protocols
    - residents and fellows
2. Nursing Staff
    - staff nurses

- floor nurses covering ICU nurse shortages
- contract or registry nurses covering ICU nurse shortages
3. Other Medical Personnel
   - respiratory therapy personnel
   - physical therapy personnel
   - dialysis personnel, etc.
   - medical students
4. Nonmedical Personnel
   - clerks
   - orderlies
   - maintenance personnel
   - engineering personnel
   - research personnel

This diverse mix creates ambiguous lines of authority and communication. The admitting physician and consultant physicians make patient care decisions and write orders. Residents and fellows may be responsible for the patient's care between visits by the attending physician, and ICU nurses often carry out medical decisions using standing orders. Usually, no single person has the sole responsibility for the patient's care or the authority to coordinate all of the care rendered to the patient.

Legal Considerations

The basic premise of tort (personal injury) law is that legal liability is vested in individuals and institutions in relation to their duty to the patient. When a patient injury results in a medical malpractice lawsuit, the patient's attorney usually will sue the hospital and all of the persons involved in the patient's care. The attorney will then dissect the chain of command in the ICU to determine who had legal responsibility for the patient's care. The court will ultimately sort out the tangle of overlapping authority and hold one or more persons liable for the patient's injuries. The court may see responsibility for the patient's care in different terms than the ICU team does. This may result in individuals being held legally responsible for actions taken by persons they were not supervising. For example, under some states' medical practice acts, members of the medical staff committee who approve ICU "standing orders" could be found liable for patient injuries caused by inappropriate application of those protocols.[16]

Legally and medically, physician authority is the cornerstone of ICU management. Patient care depends on timely decision making. In the ICU, however, it is difficult to separate the duties of the many involved medical personnel with the same clarity that is possible in the operating room. The result has been the spreading of liability across the entire ICU team.

The lack of clearly delineated responsibilities also makes it difficult for ICU team members to assure that care is rendered in a coordinated manner. To the extent that physician responsibility can be clearly delineated, the law will accept shared patient care responsibility among several physicians.[17] In the general management of the patient's care, however, where responsibilities are usually not so well delineated, it is clearly advantageous, both medically and legally, for one physician to be in charge.[18]

Recommended ICU Organization

The responsible physician in the ICU must be competent in critical care medicine. While a specialization in critical care medicine would be desirable, at a minimum the physician should meet criteria agreed upon by the hospital ICU committee. Most important, the physician *must* be available (ideally, physically present) for patient care decisions. No matter how qualified, the physician cannot provide adequate patient care unless he or she is readily available. For instance, it is difficult, if not impossible, to properly care for ICU patients in more than one hospital at a time.

Many hospitals attempt to operate their ICUs without sufficient physician coverage. Since ICU decisions must be made quickly, this means that the nursing staff is sometimes forced to make medical decisions. This weakness is hidden by "standing orders," whereby the fiction may be created that the nurse is following a set medical protocol rather than making medical decisions. If a patient is injured, the jury may see the standing orders as a sham to allow nurses to substitute for physicians. Physician coverage must also be arranged to ensure that there is a smooth transition between the different physicians who assume responsibility for a patients's care. This shifting of authority must be done in a formal manner. As discussed later, the best vehicle for coordinating the shifting of physician authority is the medical record. If an institution cannot arrange for proper physician coverage in the ICU, it should reexamine whether it can justify the existence of an ICU.

ICU Nurses

There should be one specified nurse in charge of coordinating all nonphysician personnel involved in a patient's care. This nurse should ensure that the patient receives appropriate nursing care, that the patient is fed, that the correct medications are given, that ordered tests are done and results posted, and that ancillary personnel such as respiratory therapists are properly integrated into the ICU routine. While the clinical skills of the ICU nurse are important, they are not enough to qualify him or her for the role of supervising nurse. In addition, this nurse must be familiar with the ICU routine and know how to get things done. This also applies to "contract" or temporary nurses and nurses assigned to carry out administrative tasks.

While a supervisory system based on individual responsibility is critical to risk management, it is of little use without an effective mechanism for transferring responsibility to cover periods when the nurse goes to lunch or goes home sick. This requires that another nurse be assigned the duties of the responsible nurse whenever he or she is away from the unit, even for a short time. The nursing director must provide enough staff to distribute the work load to ensure not only that a patient with substantial nursing needs does not suffer, but also that other patients are not deprived of needed care.

The determination of proper nurse staffing levels in the ICU is becoming a major issue in hospital cost-containment efforts.[19] While it is tempting for administrators to save money by reducing nursing staff, this decision should not be made on financial considerations alone. A nursing staff shortage can, in itself, be determined to be a breach of proper care sufficient to create liability for patient injuries. Thus, determination of required nurse staffing levels must be done in consultation with both the nursing director and the physicians in charge of the ICU. More important, the staffing must be arranged in a flexible manner to accommodate the expected but unpredictable occurrence of surges in the number of patients requiring intensive care.

Administration of the ICU

There should be a single, high-level administrator or director (preferably a critical care physician) in charge of the ICU. This director must act as a buffer between the ICU and the hospital, protecting the ICU from policies that would jeopardize patient care and monitoring the ICU to prevent it from becoming a financial drain on the hospital. To carry out these duties effectively, the administrator must be familiar with ICU activities and be available at all times to manage emergent situations. Most important, the director should have enough authority to act unilaterally if an administrative crisis develops. This authority must include hiring temporary nonphysician personnel, calling in backup ICU specialists, and bringing in outside equipment and technicians. Furthermore, because the law provides especially harsh sanctions for injuries caused by personnel who are known to be a risk, the director must have the authority to suspend personnel, both physician and nonphysician, from duty in the ICU until the normal hospital grievance or disciplinary process can review any questionable conduct.

Medical Records

Complicated staffing patterns along with the complex medical problems of the patients demand keeping an accurate, effective, and up-to-the-minute medical record that coordinates and documents patient care activities. Ironically, the focus on the medical record as a "legal" document has reduced both its legal and medical effectiveness. Medical personnel, constantly told that "the good medical record is the best defense," miss the point that the good medical record is valuable only to the extent that it documents the actual rendering of medical care. In some cases, a "good" medical record is legally disastrous because it demonstrates the incompetence of the underlying medical care. A poor record may prevent the medical care providers from establishing the good care they gave the patient, but a good record is not a substitute for good care. This confusion between good medical records and good medical care has led to the inclusion of so much data in the record that it may be impossible to retrieve medically necessary information in a timely manner.

Medical record keeping evolved during the early part of the twentieth century, when hospitals were little more than glorified hotels and the patient was unlikely to be seen by more than one physician. Simple narrative reporting was used because there were few events to record and little need for retrieving information from the record. The modern ICU is far removed from its historical predecessor, but the medical record remains a prisoner of its historical antecedents. While a complete discussion of the restructuring of the medical record is beyond the scope of this chapter, it should be noted that certain simple changes would make the ICU record more useful medically, while creating a more protective legal record of patient care.

Why are records kept? In addition to their use in patient care, records are kept for accreditation, legal requirements, accounting demands, and other nonpatient care purposes. These demands have distracted providers from the three medical uses for a good record:

1. Ensuring continuity of care as the responsibility for patient care shifts between different providers
2. Providing rapid access to recent information about the patient's condition, lab tests, drug therapy, etc.
3. Serving as an audit tool for evaluation of medical care.

These three needs are usually not satisfied by most existing ICU record-keeping systems. The problem of continuity of care and rapid access to recent data is so acute that off-chart record-keeping systems have evolved to supplement the traditional record. These off-chart records can pose serious legal problems if the information they contain is not recorded in the patient's hospital record.

The Risks of "State of the Art" Medical Care

One of the most difficult tasks in ICU risk management is determining the risks and benefits of new therapies and equipment as well as the competence of the staff to use them. This problem can be most difficult with respect to new equipment. ICU managers must constantly balance the demand for "state of the art" equipment against the difficulty of integrating new equipment into the ICU.

When new equipment is ordered, the usual result is a mix of older equipment already in use with new, unfamiliar machinery. As a result, few personnel are skilled in using every piece of equipment. Insufficient emphasis has been placed on the importance of proper equipment use as compared with the advantages of incrementally improved equipment. It would appear that patients are seldom injured by the failure to have a new machine. The patient may be at a greater risk of harm from a poorly understood piece of "state of the art" equipment than from a device that is technologically limited, but whose limitations and operation are well understood. The risk manager's problem is determining which requests for equipment represent this type of incremental change and which reflect the absence of necessary equipment. For example, a properly maintained defibrillator that is five years old may not have all the features of the newest model, but with skilled use it may be just as effective. However, if a defibrillator is not properly maintained, or if the hospital provides only six units when it needs ten, then a patient may be harmed because of the lack of a working defibrillator.

New therapies, especially those involving invasive procedures, pose a risk management problem because of the difficulty in evaluating their risks and benefits. While there are federal regulations for drug testing, the ICU setting poses additional problems since most patients are on several medications creating the possibility of drug interaction problems. Unlike new equipment, about which the risk manager will be aware through the purchasing process, new treatments and procedures may be informally "tried out" by physicians. The hospital, of course, must have strict rules concerning experimentation.[20] Irrespective of the merits of the treatment or procedure, it will disrupt the ICU routine and increase the chance of patient injuries. If the medical care team believes that a new treatment or procedure will improve patient care, then the proposed modification in the ICU routine should be carefully documented, discussed with all affected staff members, and closely supervised.

The ICU must have a formal training program for all personnel in the use of new equipment or procedures. There must also be a recertification program to ensure that all personnel maintain proficiency in the tasks for which they are certified. Certification requirements for use of specific equipment must include knowing how to use all the offered features of the equipment and recognition of equipment malfunction as well as the physiologic and therapeutic events that the equipment monitors or supports. Similarly, certification in a new procedure must include demonstration of the ability to properly perform the procedure, recognition and treatment of possible complications, and knowledge of when to use the procedure.

Equipment Maintenance

Most equipment maintenance programs are oriented toward mechanical equipment, which simply wears out with time. However, ICU equipment usually combines mechanical and electronic components. Electronic equipment does not "wear out," it just breaks down, usually without warning. The conventional notion of "preventive maintenance" is useless for electronic failures. The only way to manage the risk of electronic equipment breakdown is by meticulous attention to equipment performance. Electrical problems tend to be intermittent, making it difficult to fix equipment on the spot. When an equipment problem is reported, that particular piece of equipment should immediately be replaced with a spare. This "maintenance by exception" requires more spare equipment than is traditionally provided by scheduled maintenance.

Maintenance by exception requires immediate response to calls from the ICU. Once a problem has been reported, the hospital has the legal duty to ensure that patient injury from the equipment does not occur.[21] For life support equipment such as respirators and external pacemakers this means replacing the equipment at once, without waiting for maintenance personnel.

An exception-oriented maintenance program also requires around-the-clock availability of a maintenance coordinator. This person is responsible for the ICU equipment in the same way as the supervising physician and nurse are responsible for the patient's medical care. The maintenance coordinator must be familiar with ICU equipment and must have the authority to substitute defective equipment and requisition new equipment as necessary. He or she should also work with the medical team to develop protocols for equipment use and incident reporting. The supervising physician determines the medical indications for equipment use, but the maintenance coordinator must be involved in any decisions to modify equipment, change alarm systems, or use equipment for other than the manufacturer's recommended purposes.

Equipment Modification

Technical and medical personnel must appreciate the magnitude of the legal risks involved when modifications are made to correct equipment defects or to change equipment capabilities. If a patient is injured, the manufacturer will claim that the injury was due to the modifications rather than an intrinsic defect. Despite this legal risk, there are many situations when equipment modification is necessary for quality patient care. In such situations the maintenance coordinator should assess the bioengineering hazards associated with the proposed modification. If the benefit of the modification does not clearly outweigh the risks, then the proposed modification should not be approved. A discussion of the legal consequences of equipment modification is beyond the scope of this chapter, but it should be noted that the modification of equipment is a risky undertaking, which should be considered only with great caution.

Equipment Records

Events occur quickly in the ICU and patient care often involves several pieces of equipment. The medical record is, at best, a retrospective view of events that transpired. Usually, equipment in use is not logged and it is very difficult to determine whether a medical device contributed to patient injury. The problem of electrical shock hazards provides a good example. While undue emphasis appears to have been placed on electrical safety as opposed to mechanical and ergonometric safety factors (human factors such as the ease of calibration, clearly labeled controls, etc.), accurate assessment of electrical shock hazards is certainly crucial. However, often it is impossible. For example, unless all of the electrical equipment attached to a patient is tested after the occurrence of every dysrhythmia and unless the equipment fails consistently so that testing repeatedly demonstrates the failure, there is no way to know whether the dysrhythmia is endogenous to the patient or caused by an electrical problem. Thus, we cannot be certain whether electrical safety is an overrated problem or a major undetected risk.

The preceding example is a specific case of a general problem. When a serious incident occurs, patient safety is the first priority. The personnel do not have time to record machine settings and other details of equipment usage. Unfortunately, when the patient is stabilized and it is time to fill out the incident report, it is often impossible to determine the status of the machine(s) when the incident occurred. Moreover, small pieces of equipment (such as electrode cups and endotracheal tubes) tend to disappear, drug containers are discarded, etc. This makes it all but impossible to recreate the conditions existing just prior to the incident so that what actually happened to the patient may be exactly determined.

To solve this problem, the maintenance coordinator must help develop protocols for preserving equipment information in the medical record. This is important for both patient care and incident reporting. Since many problems, such as respirator-related infections, occur spontaneously as well as because of human error or equipment malfunction,[22] the only way to differentiate such problems is with trend analysis. This analytical technique requires record determinations with all of the specific pieces of equipment used in caring for each patient. Each piece of equipment should have an easy-to-use identification number (such as "RESP-1A" rather than a multidigit serial number) and a standardized procedure for recording changes in instrument setting. There should be a section of the medical record reserved for identifying each machine and its settings.

Analyzing Equipment Involved in Incidents

The final role of the maintenance coordinator is to analyze equipment involved in incidents. The conventional wisdom is to preserve all equipment involved in patient injury incidents until after the legal claim, if any, is settled. This can tie up equipment for many years, wreaking havoc with patient care resources, maintenance schedules, and budgeting for acquisitions. The legal reasoning for preserving equipment is threefold: first, the hospital could be seen as "covering up" if it does not preserve the equipment; second, once the equipment is suspected of harming a patient, it is unwise and possibly negligent to continue using it; third, if the equipment is not preserved, it will be difficult to sue the equipment manufacturer for indemnification, i.e., reimbursement from a party that caused an injury but is not sued by the patient.[23] For example, a patient may be injured by a hospital gown that catches fire in an oxygen tent. The patient sues the hospital but not the manufacturer of the gown. The hospital may sue the manufacturer of the gown for providing goods that produced a situation leading to the patient's injury. More important, if the hospital has carefully preserved the evidence against the manufacturer, the plaintiff may cooperate in suing the manufacturer directly, reducing the litigation costs for the hospital.

Since the issue of whether the product led to the patient's injury will be decided on the basis of expert testimony by engineering and medical personnel, the question becomes, Must all parties to the lawsuit have access to the equipment? The answer may be no if the following conditions are met: (1) the equipment has been evaluated by an independent engineer; (2) there is sufficient documentation on the equipment (blueprints, etc.) to evaluate the independent engineer's report; and (3) all parties have the same access to any information that is available about the equipment. If the hospital can obtain working drawings of the equipment and have an engineering analysis performed by an independent engineering group, there will be no need to preserve the equipment.

Situations that do not involve a serious patient injury usually do not require a full engineering analysis. Whether an injury is serious from this perspective is an economic decision. Is the potential recovery for the patient's injury small enough not to justify the cost of a full engineering analysis? An incident that leaves a patient brain damaged is certainly serious, whereas one that results in a superficial burn from a misapplied electrode would not be considered serious. The purpose of equipment analysis following nonserious patient injuries is to prevent further injuries, not to establish legal evidence. The hospital need only determine what led to the problem and how to prevent it in the future.

Those rare cases that involve very serious injury, such as brain damage in a young person, require special consideration. A full engineering evaluation should be initiated immediately to determine if equipment failure was involved. If so, the equipment must be preserved and the manufacturer should be asked to provide a replacement. If the manufacturer refuses to supply replacement equipment, it may be necessary to sue for a breach of the contract to supply the equipment, as well as for indemnification, if the patient recovers any damages. Since such actions would greatly strengthen the patient's case against the manufacturer, the mere suggestion of a suit by the hospital may produce a replacement. On the other hand, if the engineering analysis does not demonstrate a defect in the equipment, then preserving the equipment will only help vindicate the manufacturer. If the manufacturer is unwilling to provide replacement equipment to preserve evidence that is beneficial to the manufacturer, the hospital need feel no obligation to preserve the equipment.

Incident Reporting

The primary purpose of an incident reporting system is to improve patient care, both by preventing patient injuries and by mitigating the damages when a patient injury occurs. It is very important to understand that "incident" is not a pejorative term. Classifying an event as an incident does not imply that someone made a mistake; it means only that something unusual has happened. In the absence of an effective incident reporting system, the only indication of patient care problems may be medical malpractice litigation. While this is a dramatic measure of patients' perceptions of their well-being, it is a measure that is medically and legally dangerous because the long lag between a patient injury and the filing of a lawsuit leads to positive feedback and pipelining (see above). This is of particular importance to ICUs. Changing trends in high-technology litigation are making historical information about litigation losses immaterial. These changing trends as well as the risk of positive feedback and pipelining of claims strongly indicate that the incident reporting system should be used both as an early warning system and as an audit tool to measure the effectiveness of risk management strategies.

The use of incident reports to determine the effectiveness of risk management strategies demands a system that generates a substantial flow of information which, in turn, can be analyzed for trends in frequency and severity of adverse events. While the volume of reports is critical to data analysis, the reports will be useless unless there is a standard system for defining an incident. Without this uniform reference point, the scientific study of incidents is impossible. Although it is difficult to establish a rigorous definition, a working understanding of an incident is an adverse event that is defined by reference to accepted norms for patient care. Incidents are *outliers*, the mathematical term for an event outside the expected range of the data being monitored.[24] Outliers are important because they can have a disproportionate effect on the process being monitored. (The occurrence of a medical malpractice lawsuit is an example of an outlier.) While individual incidents are frequently impossible to predict, it is possible to anticipate the types of incidents that may occur. Through this prospective identification of incident types, it is possible to formalize the incident reporting system to an extent that will allow meaningful analysis of the data.

There are two basic classes of ICU risks: those that involve human factors and those that are related to equipment malfunction.[25] As these incident reports are analyzed, however, it becomes difficult to separate the causative factors into neat classes with well-defined boundaries. For example, the failure of an endotracheal tube would be an equipment failure. But a patient injury from that equipment problem might also involve a human failure to monitor the patient. Thus, it might be difficult to classify the cause of injury as solely due to equipment failure. Nonetheless, because of differing legal consequences, the incident reporting system should separate human factors from equipment problems to whatever extent possible.

Human factors may be further divided into failures to act and improper actions. Failure to act may include failure to monitor a patient, failure to render treatment when a problem is detected, or failure to render appropriate care in a timely fashion because of inadequate staffing. Improper actions may include medication errors, incorrect diagnosis, improperly performed procedures, or, at the extreme, intentional actions such as poisoning a patient. These should be distinguished in incident reports because a consistent pattern of problems due to failures to act will raise the question of adequate staffing levels, while problems due to improper action will pose the question of whether the personnel are properly trained or supervised.

Finally, a carefully designed incident reporting system must be effectively implemented. Five types of problems may interfere with effective implementation:

1. Incident reports are perceived as "nurse's work."

2. Incidents are underreported because of the fear of disciplinary action against the people involved in the incident.

3. Incident reports are filed only on incidents that are so obvious that they would be detected without an incident report. The classic example is a patient falling out of bed.

4. Incident reports are analyzed too slowly to allow the mitigation of patient injuries.

5. Incident report forms are poorly designed, thereby causing legal problems by identifying problem areas without providing enough information to determine how to solve the problem.

Incident reports are usually filled out by nurses and managed within the nursing chain of authority. This discourages other members of the ICU team, particularly physicians, from filing incident reports. Rather than being integrated into the incident reporting system, physician complaints are usually handled in an ad hoc manner by nursing directors or medical staff committees. The solution to this is to have a single system administered by a high-level administrative officer, preferably the legal counsel. Furthermore, all members of the ICU team should have equal responsibility for filing reports.

A shift in perception of the report as being a tool for disciplinary action to being a neutral information resource is critical to overcoming the reluctance of staff members to file incident reports. Achieving this requires a broadening of the definition of reportable incidents sufficiently to remove the stigma of being involved in a report. It must be stressed to all ICU personnel that the incident report is not an investigation form. If the hospital risk manager decides to conduct an investigation, this should be done independently of the incident reporting system. In the same way, personnel should not be disciplined or "counselled" because of incident reports. If the incident reports indicate a personnel problem, this should be investigated through the usual personnel department channels. This approach will work only if the incident report forms themselves are "fair," i.e., short, factual, and objective. This type of report is less threatening to the personnel involved, and it is more useful in risk management because it provides quickly reported objective information that can be "triaged" rapidly for further action.

An incident report should contain the following information:

1. The name of the patient
2. The name of the patient's admitting physician
3. The date and time of the incident
4. The names of all persons responsible for the patient's care, and their responsibilities (not just the persons involved in the incident)
5. The nature of the incident (equipment failure, drug allergy, medication error, etc.)
6. The persons involved in the incident
7. The nature of the patient's injuries, if any
8. The physician who evaluated the patient after the incident
9. The physical location of the patient at the time of the incident
10. The patient's condition before the incident
11. The patient's condition after the incident
12. The equipment or drugs involved in the incident

To facilitate analysis, as much of the incident report form as possible should consist of lists of items that can be checked off. For example, a list of incident types could include medication dosage errors, allergic reactions to drugs, incorrect route of administration, incorrect frequency of administration, etc. Use of predetermined lists will ensure that reports are comparable. When this is not possible, the instructions on each section of the form should state exactly what information is sought.

As with all other aspects of ICU care, the basic requirement for an effective system of incident reporting is that a single, identifiable person must be responsible for reviewing the reports and must have the authority to act on them. This person's duty will be to decide which reports require immediate action, which require further investigation, and which may be simply filed for future reference. If a report requires immediate action, either to mitigate the extent of an injury or to prevent other injuries, ICU personnel (medical, nursing, and engineering) and legal counsel must be notified. If the incident requires further investigation but no immediate action, it should be forwarded to the hospital's counsel for review and disposition.

Analyzing Trends

In addition to identifying reports that require immediate action or investigation, patterns in the seemingly random incident reporting data must be recognized. All incident reports should be entered into a computerized database to allow trend and cluster analysis to be performed. Trends are systematic changes in the distribution of data that will indicate anticipated future problems.[26] Clusters are unexpected groups of events that correlate with a given variable.[27] Using the example of pneumonia caused by an improperly sterilized respirator, the goal of cluster analysis might be to realize that the pneumonia cases correlated with use of a particular piece of equipment.

Incidents may cluster:

1. in space (a certain area of the ICU)
2. around personnel (such as a nurse who poisoned babies)[28]
3. around diagnoses (such as a problem handling AIDS cases)
4. around certain combinations of personnel and equipment (indicating a need for additional training)
5. in time (on certain shifts or certain times of the year, such as when the residents change assignment)[29]

If incidents become less frequent and more random, the risk management system is working effectively. If they become more frequent or there is pronounced clustering, they require investigation beyond the incident analysis system. The need for in-depth investigation makes it important that the incident reporting system be monitored by the hospital legal counsel. This can be done by the risk manager working closely with the counsel. However, it is more effective for the counsel to analyze the incident database directly.

CONCLUSION

The treatment of critically ill patients presents unique risk management problems. These problems require coordinated efforts from all members of the medical team. They cannot be solved by unilateral action or by administrative fiat. Fundamental to this cooperative effort is effective communication among team members and clear delineation of responsibility for each aspect of patient care. If these goals are accomplished, it then becomes possible to deliver high-quality care with a minimum of legal risk.

The overall reaction of most hospitals to a full-fledged ICU risk management program may be negative. But initiation of such a program combined with the other reforms discussed, although expensive, can lead to more economical ICU care.[30] The best, and perhaps only, effective way to control costs in the ICU without risking added patient injuries is to risk manage the care individual patients receive. As a byproduct of such a program, unnecessary care can be eliminated, while ensuring that necessary patient care is provided. Most important, effective risk management will provide the framework to study and improve ICU care in a controlled manner without undue patient risk. Ultimately, such control of ICU care will be essential to financial success under prospective reimbursement.[31]

NOTES

1. Airshields and Southmore Hosp. v. Spears, 590 S.W.2d 574 (Tex. Civ. App. 1979).

2. McAuliffe, *Measuring the Quality of Medical Care: Process versus Outcome*, 57 THE MILBANK MEMORIAL FUND Q. 118-52 (1979); Birnbaum, *Hightech/Low Touch?* 12 CRITICAL CARE MED. 1006-08 (1984); Preston, *Who Benefits from the Artificial Heart?* HASTINGS CTR. REP. 5-7 (Feb. 1985).

3. Berenson, Intensive Care Units (ICUs): Clinical Outcomes, Costs and Decisionmaking, Health Technology Case Study 28, Office of Technology Assessment, U.S. Congress, OTA-HCS-28, Nov. 1984, p 12.

4. Press, *The Predisposition to File Claims: The Patient's Perspective*, 12 L.M.H.C. 53-62 (1984).

5. E. RICHARDS & K. RATHBUN, MEDICAL RISK MANAGEMENT: PREVENTIVE LEGAL STRATEGIES FOR HEALTH CARE PROVIDERS (1983, p 22).

6. *Id.* at 24.

7. Crompton, *Medical Ethics and Hospital-Acquired Disease*, LANCET 146 (July 15, 1978).

8. Peters & Peraino, *Malpractice in Hospitals: Ten Theories for Direct Liability*, 12 L.M.H.C. 254-259 (1984).

9. Richards, *Malpractice Losses Are Building Again*, HOSPITALS 108-15 (Sept. 16, 1984).

10. Richards & Silvers, *Risk Management Theory: Reducing Liability in the Corporate and Medical Environments*, 19 HOUS. L. REV. 251-273, 252 (1982).

11. *Id.*

12. *Surgical Trauma in California*, TIME 72 (July 20, 1981).

13. *Id.*

14. *Id.*

15. *Repeated Questions*, LANCET 21-22 (Jan. 3, 1981).

16. 22 TEX. ADMIN. CODE §221.6(c).

17. W. PROSSER, THE LAW OF TORTS (1971) at 291.

18. *Supra* note 3, at 59.

19. Johnson v. Hermann Hosp., 659 S.W.2d 124 (Tex. Civ. App. 1983).

20. 45 C.F.R. §46 (1983).

21. Robinson, Abramson, Grenvik, & Meisel, *Medicolegal Standards for Critical Care Medicine*, 8 CRITICAL CARE MED. 524-26 (1980).

22. O'Connor, Bennett, & Alexander, et al., *Salmonellosis Infection Transmitted by Fiberoptic Endoscopes*, LANCET 864-66 (Oct. 16, 1982); Jarvis, White, & Munn, et al., *Nosocomial Infection*

Surveillance, 1983, 33/2SS M.M.W.R. 9-21 (1984); Brown, Hosmer & Chen, et al., *A Comparison of Infections in Different ICUs within the Same Hospital*, 13 CRITICAL CARE MED. 472-76 (1985).

23. Airshields and Southmore Hosp. v. Spears, *supra* note 1.

24. *Supra* note 10, at 267.

25. Abramson & Grenvik, *Equipment Problems in Intensive Care*, HEALTH DEVICES 285-87 (Aug.-Sept. 1980); Cooper, Newbower, Long & McPeek, *Preventable Anesthesia Mishaps: A Study of Human Factors*, 49 ANESTHESIOLOGY 399-406 (1978); Abramson, Wald, & Grenvik et al., *Adverse Occurrences in Intensive Care Units*, 244 J. A.M.A. 1582-84 (1980).

26. *Supra* note 10, at 267.

27. *Id.*

28. Elkind, P., *The Death Shift*, TEX. MONTHLY 106-13, 180-97 (Aug. 1983).

29. *Death at the Ann Arbor VA*, NEWSWEEK 19 (Sept. 1, 1975).

30. Young & Saltman, *Preventive Medicine for Hospital Costs*, HARV. BUS. REV. 126-33 (Jan.-Feb. 1983); Zawacki, *ICU Physician's Ethical Role in Distributing Scarce Resources*, 13 CRITICAL CARE MED. 57-60 (1985).

31. Chapman, *Deciding Who Pays to Save Lives*, FORTUNE 59-70 (May 27, 1985); Morreim, *The MD and the DRG*, HASTING CTR. REP. 30-38 (June 1985); Dolenc & Dougherty, *DRGs: The Counterrevolution in Financing Health Care*, HASTING CTR. REP. 19-29 (June 1985).

Chapter 3

Deciding about Treatment in the ICU

Nancy K. Rhoden

Today, more and more, critical care medicine is the subject of litigation and legal debate. Although patients are increasingly claiming the right to make their own medical decisions, the nature of treatment decisions in the intensive care unit sometimes makes implementation of this right problematic. Patients may be in shock, in severe pain, or overwhelmed by the suddenness or severity of their illness or injury. These physical and emotional factors can compromise their ability to fully comprehend their plight or rationally decide about treatment.

In addition, patients who appear competent to give informed consent to treatment may on occasion refuse recommended therapy for religious reasons, or because of anticipated disabilities, or for other, sometimes less rational, reasons. Refusal of treatment, especially since it occurs within the hospital context, creates great consternation for physicians and hospital personnel, who sometimes seek legal authorization to treat the patient despite his or her objections, especially if the patient's competency is questionable. Perhaps most difficult of all are cases where the patient is arguably or clearly incompetent, and others must make decisions about his or her care. This chapter will analyze the legal issues that arise in making treatment decisions in the ICU, first considering competent patients and then incompetent ones.

DECISIONS FOR COMPETENT PATIENTS

Informed Consent to Treatment

Treatment provided in the ICU, like medical treatment in general, requires the patient's consent. It has long been a fundamental precept of American law that "[e]very human being of adult years and sound mind has a right to determine what shall be done with his own body."[1] Early cases in this area concerned unauthorized procedures, in which the physician failed to obtain consent or exceeded the agreed upon scope of the operation.[2] In the absence of consent, a medical procedure, even though properly performed, is, in legal terms, the intentional tort of battery.[3] In recent years, it is more common for a patient to claim that while he or she consented to the procedure, the consent was not valid because it was not fully informed. A physician who fails to obtain informed consent—i.e., who fails to provide the patient with information sufficient to allow him or her to make a free and fully informed choice—may be found liable in negligence for falling below the professional standard of care.[4]

Since few, if any, medical procedures are without attendant risks, a crucial element of informed consent is telling the patient about the possible risks stemming from treatment. Such information is clearly necessary if the patient is to make a rational decision about accepting or foregoing the proposed therapy. Of course, physicians cannot discuss *all* possible risks with the patient: medicine is simply too complex for this to be feasible, and the disadvantages of "information overload" probably make it undesirable. Rather, courts have held that a doctor must disclose that information that is "material" to the patient's decision. Jurisdictions have differed, however, as to the applicable legal standard for deciding what information is material.

The majority of jurisdictions take the physician's perspective, asking what information a reasonable practitioner would disclose under the circumstances.[5] Other states, however, have rejected this standard and instead require that the physician provide all information that a reasonable person in the patient's position would find significant in reaching a decision.[6] This patient-oriented standard clearly places a heavier burden of disclosure upon the physician, and incorporates the inherent difficulty that physicians may not know what a reasonable patient would find material.[7] Nevertheless, many commentators believe that this standard more faithfully promotes the values of individual privacy, autonomy, and rational decision making that underlie the informed consent doctrine.[8]

Even if a doctor failed adequately to disclose the risks of treatment, a patient who sues for lack of informed consent must show that had crucial information been disclosed, he or she would have refused the treatment. In other words, as well as proving breach of duty (nondisclosure), a patient must also prove that but for that breach, he or she would have foregone the treatment and thus would not have been injured by it. Most courts require the plaintiff to prove that adequate disclosure would likely have caused the hypothetical "reasonable person" in the plaintiff's position to forego the treatment.[9] Recently, however, a few courts have held that this objective, "reasonable person" standard allows too little room for the individual patient's values and beliefs. These courts have instead simply required the plaintiff to prove that he himself or she herself would have foregone the therapy had all the facts been disclosed.[10]

As well as revealing the material risks of the proposed treatment, a physician should also disclose the hazards involved in foregoing treatment. Although there are very few cases involving this notion of "informed refusal," the California Supreme Court has recently held that a physician could be found negligent for failing to inform his or her patient of the risks of failing to have a "Pap smear" to test for cervical cancer.[11]

The doctor in the ICU must thoroughly inform the patient of the risks of either undertaking or refusing treatment. However, the nature of critical care medicine is such that informed consent is not always possible. A patient may arrive in the ICU unconscious and in need of immediate treatment. Although proxy consent is ordinarily required for the treatment of incompetent patients, in a medical emergency, where consent cannot be obtained but failure to treat will result in imminent harm, the law makes an exception to the informed consent doctrine and considers consent to be implied from the circumstances.[12]

Definitions of "emergency" may vary—it may be defined narrowly, encompassing only situations where medical care is needed to preserve life or limb, or broadly, to include cases where care is needed simply to alleviate pain or suffering.[13] As one group of writers has wisely recommended: "The definition of an emergency used in determining when the requirements of informed consent should be suspended must consider the extent to which their abandonment or relaxation undermines the values that the doctrine promotes."[14] Courts have occasionally suggested that in an emergency physicians should seek proxy consent from a relative.[15] Although as a practical matter this may be desirable, it is not legally necessary in emergency situations, since consent is considered to be implied from the circumstances (or, perhaps more accurately, the consent requirement is simply suspended).[16]

Other exceptions to the informed consent requirement include waiver, where the patient explicitly states that he or she does not want to receive information about the procedure,[17] and the so-called "therapeutic privilege," in which the physician can withhold information that would so upset the patient that it would impair his or her ability to make a rational decision.[18] The parameters of this latter exception are not yet clearly defined, and few cases have turned on its application.[19]

Unless one of these exceptions clearly applies, a physician in the ICU should disclose pertinent information to the patient and obtain his or her consent for treatment. Alternatively, if the patient is incompetent to decide (and it is not an emergency), consent should be obtained from an appropriate proxy decision maker, which will usually be a close relative or intimate friend.[20]

This brief synopsis of the legal requirements regarding informed consent should not be taken to mean that the doctrine is a simple one to implement or one that is susceptible to cut-and-dried legal standards. The legal mandate to "obtain informed consent" and the legal standards for disclosure, etc., while important, cannot themselves create a climate that fosters the genuine dialogue and shared decision making that are the ultimate goals of informed consent.[21] The doctor must not only provide the patient with information, but must be sensitive to the impact of different methods of conveying information, to the patient's capacity to understand and assimilate the information, to the emotional or contextual factors that may impair this capacity, and to any emotional or familial features of the situation that may affect the voluntariness of the patient's decision.[22] In the ICU, where the situation is, by definition, critical, achieving the ultimate goal of shared decision making may be even more difficult than in many other medical settings and situations. But it must be remembered that the legal requirements simply establish a minimum standard and hence are only a first step toward reaching that goal.

Refusal of Treatment

Inherent in the requirement of informed consent for treatment is the recognition that a competent patient has a right to choose to forego treatment. Legal recognition of this right to refuse is often based on the common law right to bodily integrity, which underlies the informed consent doctrine. It may also be based on the constitutional right to privacy, which protects an individual's right to make his or her own decisions about fundamental personal matters.[23] This right to privacy has been held to extend to a patient's decisions about medical treatment.[24]

Assuming a patient's treatment refusal is competent (the difficulties in defining and ascertaining competency are discussed below), it will be given great weight. However, in these cases a person's life is at stake. The state thus may have interests here as well, especially if the patient could be returned to a lengthy and healthy life and/or there are third parties heavily dependent upon the patient. Courts have frequently listed the potential state interests involved as (1) the preservation of life, (2) the protection of dependent third parties, (3) the prevention of suicide, and (4) the preservation of the ethical integrity of the medical profession.[25] The competent patient's rights of privacy and bodily integrity will be weighed against these various interests of the state.

The state's interest in preservation of life is strongest in those cases where, with treatment, the patient could fully recover and lead a lengthy and healthy life. Such cases are rare, and most commonly arise when a critically ill or injured patient has religious objections to treatment or to certain types of treatment—e.g., the objections of Jehovah's Witnesses to blood transfusions. In a number of early cases of this type, courts overrode the patient's refusal and ordered that the transfusion be performed. For example, in *United States v. George*,[26] a 39-year-old Jehovah's Witness voluntarily entered the hospital for treatment of a bleeding ulcer but refused consent to a blood transfusion. The court granted the hospital's request that the transfusion be ordered, holding that life was at stake and that it was unfair to ask a surgeon to operate but not to replace lost blood if necessary. Also, in *Application of President and Directors of Georgetown College, Inc.*,[27] a critically injured young mother refused consent to a transfusion. The court, while not making an explicit finding of incompetency, stated that the patient was "not in a mental condition to make a decision."[28] Based on the questions about her competency, plus the fact that her child was only seven months old and would effectively be abandoned if she died, the court ordered treatment.

These cases share the distinct features that the patients were young, could be returned to their normal, vibrant state of health, and were parents of dependent children. They are thus in sharp contrast to situations such as that in *In re Quackenbush*, where a 72-year-old man with gangrene of both feet and legs refused amputation.[29] In that case, though treatment, if successful, would save the patient's life, the treatment would be highly invasive and would leave this elderly man severely disabled. The court in *Quackenbush* relied on a balancing test previously set forth in the *Quinlan* case:

> [T]he State's interest *contra* weakens and the individual's right of privacy grows as the degree of bodily invasion increases and the prognosis dims. Ultimately there comes a point at which the individual's rights overcome the State interest.[30]

Since Mr. Quackenbush's anticipated quality of life after treatment would inevitably be poor, the court upheld his refusal, explicitly noting the contrast with the young patient who could be returned to excellent health by a minimally invasive procedure such as a blood transfusion.

Although the *Quackenbush* case did not present the issue of whether forcible treatment would be ordered were the patient young and capable of a complete recovery, this case, along with the *George* and *Georgetown* cases, could be read to suggest that such a patient can be forcibly treated over a competent refusal. Other cases, however, suggest otherwise. In *In re Osborne*,[31] a 34-year-old Jehovah's Witness, who was the father of two children, firmly refused a transfusion. The court upheld the refusal, as did a New York court in *In re Melideo*,[32] in which a childless 23-year-old Jehovah's Witness likewise refused a transfusion.

One expert in this area, Leonard Glantz, suggests that the Jehovah's Witnesses cases ordering treatment (e.g., *George* and *Georgetown*) do not really stand for the proposition that treatment of a young, otherwise healthy patient can be ordered over a competent refusal, but rather turn on the fact that while the patients in those cases would not *consent* to a transfusion, they had both indicated that if the judge ordered one, he, and not they, would be responsible.[33] Glantz argues that since the judges in these cases were informed, subtly or otherwise, that the patient would not oppose (and perhaps would welcome) a court order requiring a transfusion, this crucial feature distinguishes these cases from ones such as *In re Osborne*, in which Mr. Osborne stated that even a court-ordered transfusion would deprive him of everlasting life.

There are simply too few cases involving fully competent young patients with the potential for full recovery to make a definitive statement about whether, and when, their refusals will be upheld. However, there is a trend away from the approach taken in earlier cases such as *Georgetown* (which had analogized foregoing treatment to committing suicide)[34] and toward respecting competent refusals of medical treatment. The President's Commission for the Study of Ethical Problems in Medicine, which is highly influential in this area, states that:

> a competent patient's self-determination is and usually should be given greater weight than other people's views on that individual's well-being.[35]

While most cases respecting competent refusals have involved patients who either would die quite soon even with treatment or who would suffer pain and disability from the treatment, the *Melideo* case upholds the refusal of a blood transfusion by an otherwise healthy 23-year-old woman. The court emphatically stated that to order a transfusion over a competent adult patient's objection would violate her First Amendment right to freedom of religion. This holding is especially significant in light of the fact that this case possibly shared the peculiarity of the *George* and *Georgetown* cases, where the patient would not consent to a transfusion but might not mind a court-ordered one—neither Mrs. Melideo nor her husband appeared at the hearing, and her husband called the judge and stated that they were leaving the matter in his hands. *Melideo* thus illustrates the trend toward respecting a competent patient's articulated wishes, although a few courts may continue to paternalistically override the refusal of a young patient who could be returned to good health based on the state's interest in preservation of life.[36]

Along with preservation of life, another strong state interest is that of protecting dependent third parties, primarily children. As noted previously, the *Georgetown* court considered refusal of treatment to be tantamount to child abandonment. Even cases upholding refusals have carefully considered the interests of dependent children and the potential impact of the death of one of their parents. For example, in *In re Osborne,* the court emphasized that the patient's children would be cared for by his wife and other close relatives, and that the family business would continue to provide for their material needs. When present, this state interest is a powerful one. One expert has suggested:

> It is likely to be found superior to adult rights of privacy or self-determination in all but the clearest cases of viable and alternative sources of support and care for the dependents.[37]

Although this interest will be of less import when the adult is terminally ill, so that treatment can yield only a brief prolongation of life, some writers argue that it should prevail if treatment can give the parent as much as a few more years of life.[38]

Some commentators have argued, however, that potential benefit to third parties, even dependent children, should never override a patient's right to refuse treatment. Leonard Glantz points out that weighing the children's interests against the parent's raises a number of problems:

> One is the specter of being too poor to refuse treatment; that is, an individual can refuse treatment if the family is well taken care of but must undergo treatment if the children are dependent on the refusing party's salary. I suppose someone could get life insurance to insure the right to refuse treatment, but that seems an odd way to solve the problem.[39]

It does seem unfair to consider an individual's financial status in deciding whether he or she can effectively exercise his or her constitutional right to privacy. Another problem is that assessing harm to the children may involve courts in additional inquiries such as whether there has been child abuse, whether the parent and child get along, etc.[40] Moreover, mandating treatment in this context may have much broader implications. Would we subsequently have to consider forcing a parent to donate a kidney to a child who needs one? Although we cannot tell how heavily courts in future cases will weigh this interest, Glantz has presented a compelling case for refusing to let it override a competent patient's right to self-determination.

Possibly the hardest situation involving competent patients and dependent "third parties" is that of the patient who is pregnant. Here the third party's very life is threatened by the treatment refusal. In one case, *Raleigh Fitkin-*

Paul Morgan Memorial Hospital v. Anderson,[41] a Jehovah's Witness who was eight months pregnant was ordered to submit to a blood transfusion to save the life of her fetus. Since this case was decided before *Roe v. Wade* upheld a woman's right to choose to abort, various writers argue that it is no longer good law.[42] However, after viability, states can prohibit abortion unless the women's health is endangered by the pregnancy. Since in most states today the woman in *Raleigh-Fitkin* could not obtain an abortion, it is by no means clear that *Roe v. Wade* would undermine the holding in that case. Moreover, several recent cases have ordered pregnant women to have Cesarean sections in situations where vaginal delivery was likely to seriously endanger both the mother and the fetus.[43] There is far too little authority in this area to be able to draw even tentative conclusions. But we cannot rule out the possibility that a competent pregnant woman's refusal of treatment might be overridden if she were in the last months of pregnancy. At any rate, in these cases the state's interest in the dependent third party will surely warrant consideration.

The final two state interests—the prevention of suicide and the preservation of the ethical integrity of the medical profession—will seldom be implicated in the typical case of the competent treatment refusal. The state interest in the medical profession's integrity is not strong here, because physicians' ethics do not require them to treat competent patients against their will. (Of course, courts will not order doctors to practice bad medicine; i.e., if a transfusion is necessary for an operation, the physician will not be required to operate without one.) Nor do medical ethics demand that all efforts toward prolongation of life be made in all circumstances.[44] Likewise, the prevention of suicide is seldom truly at stake. Although the *Georgetown* court said that refusing life-saving treatment was tantamount to suicide, most other courts and commentators have recognized that such patients do not desire to die but are simply rejecting a type of treatment that they find unacceptable.[45]

Of course, in certain highly unusual cases, these state interests may be implicated. For example, in the case of Mrs. Bouvia, a competent adult with cerebral palsy who voluntarily entered the psychiatric unit of a California hospital and then sought to refuse ordinary food and water, these interests appeared paramount.[46] In that case, the court held that medical personnel were not obligated to assist a patient who was not dying but whose goal was to starve herself to death. But as the facts indicate, the *Bouvia* case is a highly unusual one, and one that few hospitals (it is hoped) will have to face.[47]

In sum, the law recognizes a competent patient's right to refuse life-saving or life-prolonging treatment. There is a very strong argument that whenever the patient is competent, this right should prevail. However, courts do consider the state's interests here, and the greater the chance of complete recovery with treatment and significant hardship upon dependents without it, the more likely a court will be to override this right.

DECISIONS FOR INCOMPETENT PATIENTS

When a competent patient refuses treatment, physicians must either abide by the refusal or seek a court order authorizing treatment. Courts in these cases will ask whether any of the state interests involved are strong enough to override the patient's fundamental rights of self-determination and privacy. A much harder situation is presented when a patient who is not competent either refuses or is incapable of consenting. Decisions for infants create particularly great difficulties. This matter is dealt with in Chapter 4. The problem to be considered here is how to make treatment decisions for adult, but incompetent, patients.

Ascertaining Incompetency

Some patients, such as those in comas, are manifestly incompetent, and in nonemergency situations doctors must seek consent from a family member or other valid proxy. Patients who are awake but confused or disoriented, however, present the preliminary problem of assessing their competence to consent to or refuse treatment. Logically, the same degree of mental capacity is required to consent to treatment as to refuse. However, questions about a patient's competence typically are raised only when the patient's expressed choice is not in agreement with the doctor's recommendation.[48] In these cases the patient's competence must be assessed, a task that is complicated by the fact that we lack a uniform, accepted definition of competency and that several tests, ranging from the most stringent to the most liberal, have been proposed.[49] A full exploration of the assessment of competence is not possible here. Rather, certain important aspects of defining and ascertaining competence or incompetence will be discussed.

First, the legal presumption is that a patient is competent to make treatment decisions until shown to be otherwise.[50] The fact that a patient is mentally ill, or unable to perform some other functions competently, while higher relevant, is not determinative. For example, in *In re Yetter*,[51] a 60-year-old patient in a mental hospital refused consent for a recommended breast biopsy, believing (wrongly) that her aunt had died from similar surgery and that it would impair her childbearing capacity. The patient's refusal was upheld. Although she was schizophrenic and the court believed her decision was unreasonable, it refused to find her incompetent, because she understood the general nature and effects of the proposed treatment.[52]

As the *Yetter* case illustrates, competency determinations must be directed at the specific decision at hand. It is often said that competency to consent to or refuse a medical procedure is the same mental capacity as that required to enter a contract. The question is, "Does the patient have sufficient mind to reasonably understand the condition, the nature and effect of the proposed treatment, attendant risks in pursuing the treatment, and not pursuing the treatment?"[53] The President's Commission articulates the following considerations relevant to assessments of capacity:

> Does the patient possess the ability to understand the relevant facts and alternatives? Is the patient weighing the decision within a framework of values and goals? Is the patient able to reason and deliberate about this information? Can the patient give reasons for the decision in light of the facts, the alternatives, and the impact of the decision on the patient's own goals and values?[54]

These factors, though they focus to some extent upon the patient's general framework of values and goals, clearly are situation-specific; i.e., it is the patient's competence to make this particular medical decision that is being assessed.

A corollary of this situation-specific focus is that a patient who is in general competent may display such an irrational response to his or her medical problem that he or she is incompetent to make a treatment decision. For example, in *State Department of Human Services v. Northern*,[55] a 72-year-old woman with gangrene of both feet refused amputation, even though it was necessary to save her life. While lucid and of sound mind generally, Miss Northern tended to believe that her feet were black because of dirt or soot, and refused to recognize her condition: "In the presence of this court, the patient looked at her feet and refused to recognize the obvious fact that the flesh was dead, black, shriveled, rotting and stinking."[56] Miss Northern believed her feet would heal on their own, and would not recognize that without their amputation, she would die. Thus she desired the impossible—to both live and keep her dead feet. The court found her "incapable of making a rational decision as to whether to undergo surgery to save her life or to forego surgery and forfeit her life."[57] Similarly, in *In re Schiller*,[58] the court determined that although Mr. Schiller had been living on his own prior to developing gangrene of his feet, he was unable, due to organic brain damage, to fully comprehend his situation and realize that amputation was needed to save his life.

Although to be found competent to decide a patient must be able rationally to reach a decision that is informed by recognition and acceptance of his or her condition, the decision need not be an objectively "reasonable" one.

Courts have criticized physicians for imputing incompetence simply because a patient's decision is not medically reasonable.[59] Emphasis on the rationality of the decision-making process, rather than the medical "reasonableness" of the outcome, is particularly important, because so many of these decisions are made informally by physicians and/or family members, without judicial review. Although some noted commentators have criticized these informal competency determinations and treatment decisions,[60] and although their legal status is somewhat uncertain, the President's Commission for the Study of Ethical Problems in Medicine adheres to the position that determinations of incapacity are best made without routine recourse to the courts.[61] Assuming that many such decisions continue to be made informally, physicians should strive to avoid confusing disagreement with incompetence and should seek input from colleagues or ethics committees (if available). Hospitals should likewise set up procedures for reaching and evaluating such decisions.[62]

Deciding for Incompetent Patients

Perhaps the most difficult problem in this area is deciding for patients who either obviously are, or who have been determined to be, incompetent to decide for themselves. A host of troubling issues arise, including who should decide for such patients, how these decisions should be made, whether withholding or withdrawing treatment from a patient who cannot consent to such an action constitutes homicide or medical neglect, and whether, even if nontreatment is proper, decisions not to treat should always be made or reviewed by the courts.

To begin with, we should note that while courts have disagreed about most of these questions, no court has held that withholding or withdrawing treatment from an incompetent patient is always inappropriate or unlawful. Courts have authorized nontreatment when the patient clearly indicated, while competent, that she opposed the specific type of treatment,[63] or when previously expressed beliefs strongly suggested opposition and the prognosis was hopeless anyway.[64] They have likewise upheld nontreatment when previously expressed beliefs were not conclusive but the patient's prognosis was completely hopeless,[65] and they have even done so in the absence of any prior beliefs and when some benefit from the treatment was possible but it would cause great pain and suffering for the incompetent patient.[66] Courts have repeatedly held that incompetent patients, like competent ones, have a common-law and/or constitutional right to refuse treatment, and that allowing proxy or court refusal in appropriate cases is the only way to protect that right.[67] Thus it is clear that withholding treatment need not violate existing law. The difficult questions are when such action is appropriate and how these decisions are to be made.

Substantive Standards for Treatment Decisions

Assuming a patient did not clearly refuse treatment while competent, courts will presume that he or she will want life-saving treatment, i.e., treatment that can cure or substantially ameliorate a life-threatening condition. This principle is illustrated in several cases where courts ordered limb amputation for elderly patients who had expressed some reluctance but had never clearly and rationally refused consent to surgery.[68] Surgery has been ordered even when the patient was lucid and rational in other respects.[69] Thus, without a firm, competent refusal, the state interest in preserving life will prevail and courts will order treatment, even when it is as invasive and debilitating as amputation.

On the other extreme are patients who even with treatment either will live only a very brief time or will never regain consciousness. The vast majority of courts have authorized withholding or withdrawing treatment from terminally ill or permanently comatose patients, although their standards and procedures for doing so have varied. There are by now too many cases in this area to examine them all specifically. Rather, we will briefly describe certain of the most important cases, the factors upon which they relied, and the tests they adopted.

The seminal case in this area is *In re Quinlan.*[70] Karen Ann Quinlan, a 22-year-old woman, was in a persistent vegetative state with no hope of recovery. Her father petitioned to be appointed her guardian, with express authority to authorize the removal of the respirator that was (he and the physicians believed) sustaining Karen's life. The court held that Karen's constitutional right of privacy was broad enough to encompass the right to decline medical treatment. Given her grim prognosis and the invasiveness of artificial ventilation, it found the state interests of preservation of life and promotion of the physician's right to treat in accordance with his best medical judgment insufficient to outweigh this interest. The court enunciated the standard, discussed previously in regard to competent patients, that "the state's interest *contra* weakens and the individual's right to privacy grows as the degree of bodily invasion increases and the prognosis dims."[71] Although Karen had allegedly once said that she would not want to be kept alive in a vegetative state, the court found her remarks too "remote and speculative" to be given significant probative weight.[72] However, it attempted a "substituted judgment" test, holding that protection of Karen's right to refuse treatment required that her guardian and family "render their best judgment . . . as to whether she would exercise it in these circumstances."[73]

With incompetent patients, most courts have followed the *Quinlan* court's lead in stressing the invasiveness of the treatment and the chances of a cure or a return to a cognitive existence.[74] Although not all courts have relied on constitutional theory,[75] all courts thus far have agreed with the substantive principle of *Quinlan* that if the patient has no reasonable possibility of returning to a cognitive or sapient state, withdrawal of treatment will be warranted, as will a "no-code" order, i.e., an order not to resuscitate if the patient suffers cardiac or respiratory arrest.[76]

The *Quinlan* court's notion that a decision maker should try to decide the way the patient most likely would have decided has likewise been influential. This substituted judgment standard has not only been used in other cases involving formerly competent patients whose previous opinions could be ascertained and analyzed,[77] but it has also been invoked in cases where the patient was never competent and thus had no established beliefs or values upon which the court could rely. One such case was *Superintendent of Belchertown State School v. Saikewicz*.[78] Mr. Saikewicz was a profoundly retarded, nonverbal 67-year-old man with a type of leukemia for which chemotherapy offered a 30 to 50 percent chance of a 2- to 13-month remission.[79] Along with the usual painful side effects of chemotherapy would be the additional problem that Mr. Saikewicz would be unable to understand the reason for the pain and would probably have to be restrained in order to be treated. Given the ratio of harm to benefit from chemotherapy in this case, the court could easily have held that a painless death, rather than painful and invasive treatment, was in Mr. Saikewicz's best interest. The Saikewicz court, however, eschewed the relatively objective "best interests" standard in favor of the substituted judgment test.

The substituted judgment standard can be difficult to apply even with formerly competent patients: how do we really know that a patient in Karen Quinlan's position, who feels no pain, might not wish to be kept alive on the off-chance that techniques of repairing brain injuries would be developed? But with patients who have never been competent, the substituted judgment standard is, as illustrated by the Saikewicz court's language, a thoroughly impossible directive:

> [T]he decision in cases such as this should be that which would be made by the incompetent person, if that person were competent, but taking into account the present and future incompetency of the individual as one of the factors which would necessarily enter into the decision-making process of the competent person.[80]

This fictitious test of "what would the incompetent patient decide if granted one miraculous moment of lucidity" will not work because during that moment of lucidity, he would be a competent person, and not the profoundly retarded Mr. Saikewicz. Since (1) such a patient could not have a reasoned preference for us to discover and (2) even if he did we could not discover it, adherence to this test constitutes a judicial descent into the absurd.

It has been suggested, in reference to both the Saikewicz case and the case of Earle Spring, where a Massachusetts court decided that a senile, incompetent patient would himself not want his dialysis treatments continued, that courts compose this fantasy on a theme of incompetence to avoid admitting that they are making quality of life judgments.[81] Some courts may also believe that without such a fiction, they will always have to require treatment if a life of any sentience at all can be even briefly prolonged.

This latter possibility is suggested by the consolidated cases of *Eichner* and *Storar* in New York. In *Eichner*, the court authorized withdrawal of artificial ventilation from a comatose, elderly cleric on the grounds that his prior statements constituted clear and convincing proof that he would not want treatment under the circumstances.[82] With regard to John Storar, a profoundly retarded man having transfusions to stem blood loss caused by terminal bladder cancer, the court quite reasonably rejected the substituted judgment test since, given Mr. Storar's mental capacity, it was equivalent to asking "if it snowed all summer would it then be winter?"[83] But the court then held that the transfusions could not be discontinued, on the grounds that they did not involve "excessive pain" and gave Mr. Storar increased energy. The dissent argued that the opinion of his mother, who visited him every day, should have prevailed, because the transfusions were painful and disruptive, because Mr. Storar could live only a few months more even with them, and because his mother had loved and cared for him all his life and was acutely sensitive to his best interests.[84] (Mr. Storar died before this decision was issued, and while still receiving transfusions.)

The *Storar* decision thus implies that if courts reject the substituted judgment fiction, they may feel constrained to order treatment unless there is clear and convincing evidence of the patient's prior beliefs or unless treatment is both completely futile and excessively painful. But this implication is wrong. Courts can both discard this fiction and authorize termination of treatment in appropriate circumstances. The dilemma in the *Saikewicz*, *Spring*, and *Storar* cases was that the patients were conscious and active and the proposed treatments—chemotherapy, dialysis, and blood transfusions—could prolong their lives for at least a few months. Moreover, competent patients would probably want treatment, despite the pain and discomfort involved.[85] Thus, withholding treatment from these incompetent patients would be treating them differently from competent ones. As George Annas points out, courts certainly do not want to imply that senile or mentally retarded persons can be treated differently from others, or that their lives have less value, and they use the substituted judgment fiction to justify nontreatment while avoiding this implication.[86]

Incompetent patients *are*, however, different from normal patients. Although their lives are no less valuable, the subjective experience of a painful, invasive treatment undoubtedly differs markedly depending on whether it is understood as necessary to cure or prolong life or is experienced simply as inexplicable pain inflicted by others. An incompetent patient may perceive treatment as torture, and when the treatment can only yield a relatively brief and painful prolongation of life, this seems a very good (and straightforward) reason to forego it. Courts need not obscure what they are doing. They need only recognize, rather than try to deny, that incompetent patients are different in morally relevant respects from normal ones, and, unless there is good evidence of what the incompetent patient would have wanted, they need only evaluate his or her best interests objectively, since, realistically, this is the only way courts or any other third party can evaluate them.

A very recent New Jersey case has made a significant step toward taking this more realistic approach to decision making for incompetent patients. The case involved Claire Conroy, an 83-year-old nursing home patient with severe organic brain syndrome, who was not comatose but who was no longer able to speak, eat, or move from a semifetal position.[87] Her guardian had sought permission to remove her nasogastric feeding tube. It was granted by the trial court and reversed by the appellate court. The New Jersey Supreme Court, in reversing the Appellate Court's decision (for reasons which will be discussed *infra*) and holding that under appropriate conditions artificial feeding could be terminated, recognized that a subjective test was unworkable for patients who had not, when competent, clearly expressed their desires.[88] It authorized termination of treatment under either of two best interests tests: the limited-objective test, where there is some trustworthy evidence of what the patient would have wanted and the burdens of life with treatment outweigh its benefits, and the pure-objective test, where there is no such evidence but the burdens clearly and markedly outweigh the benefits.[89] The majority opinion listed a number of factors to be considered, including prognosis, level of functioning, and degree of dependency, but, especially with the pure-objective test, put the primary emphasis upon pain,[90] a limitation about which the dissent was highly critical.[91] Despite this limitation, the forthright acceptance of an objective test should help make *Conroy* a decision almost as seminal in this area as was *Quinlan*.

What Types of Treatment Can Be Omitted?

A particularly difficult issue that is beginning to arise is whether the types of treatment that can be terminated include artificial methods of feeding. This issue is relatively new, perhaps because termination of other treatments, such as artificial ventilation, often is sufficient to cause death, and perhaps because some families, such as Karen Quinlan's parents, do not want feeding tubes removed. Its difficulty inheres in the fact that while all other procedures clearly constitute medical treatment, feeding, even though by artificial means, is still *feeding.* Since it is murder to withhold food from a person one has an obligation to feed,[92] the question thus arises whether discontinuing artificial methods of feeding a comatose or dying patient is more akin to terminating other medical procedures, such as artificial ventilation, or to willful and unlawful starvation of the patient.

One of the few cases dealing with this issue was a criminal prosecution of two California physicians who terminated intravenous feeding of a comatose and severely brain-damaged patient.[93] The prosecution was dismissed, and the court held that cessation of life support measures "is not an affirmative act but rather a withdrawal or omission of further treatment." The court further concluded that:

> Medical procedures to provide nutrition and hydration are more similar to other medical procedures than to typical human ways of providing nutrition and hydration. Their benefits and burdens ought to be evaluated in the same manner as any other medical procedure.[94]

According to this ruling, when artificial feeding is burdensome or futile, it, like artificial ventilation, can be withdrawn. Another decision, *In re Severns,*[95] while not specifically discussing the artificial feeding issue, authorized a "no-code" order, no antibiotics for infection and no reimplantation of a feeding tube in the trachea of a comatose patient.[96]

The recent decision of the New Jersey Supreme Court in *In re Conroy,* however, is undoubtedly the most important decision in this area to date. The appellate court in *Conroy* had held that cessation of tube feeding differed significantly from removal of a respirator:

> The trial judge ... authorized euthanasia.... If the trial judge's order had been enforced, Conroy would not have died as the result of an existing medical condition, but rather she would have died, and painfully so, as the result of a new and independent condition: dehydration and starvation. Thus she would have been actively killed by independent means....[97]

It had further stated that artificial feeding was not a medical procedure like any other, but rather was simply "routine nursing care" which could not be foregone.[98] The New Jersey Supreme Court emphatically rejected this dichotomy between artificial ventilation and artificial feeding. While the appellate court had misleadingly failed to acknowledge that artificial feeding can cause harms of its own, the Supreme Court recognized that nasogastric and intravenous methods of feeding can have complications that are sometimes serious and distressing to the patient.[99] These can include discomfort from the tubing, vomiting, accumulation of fluid in the lungs, and even pneumonia. Taking note of these potential harms, the Supreme Court held that artificial feeding is subject to the same analysis of potential benefits and harms as any other medical treatment.

In seeking to exempt artificial feeding from this standard benefit/burden calculus, the appellate court in *Conroy* had held that artificial feeding was mere "routine nursing care." This description of artificial feeding was patently untenable, because with even the simplest method—nasogastric feeding—tubes must be carefully inserted into the body. Other methods, such as intravenous feeding and, particularly, total parenteral nutrition, are far more risky, complex, and invasive.[100] Although it recognized that feeding has special emotional and symbolic significance, the Supreme Court in *Conroy* appropriately held artificial feeding to be more like other medical procedures than like bottle or spoonfeeding.[101] This is likewise the conclusion of the President's Commission:

> Since permanently unconscious patients will never be aware of nutrition, the only benefit to the patient of providing such increasingly burdensome interventions is sustaining the body to allow for a remote possibility of recovery. The sensitivities of the family and of care-giving professionals ought to determine whether such interventions are made.[102]

Of course, providing food and water to a patient, even by artificial means, has immense psychological importance to staff and families. Physicians should comply with the wishes of relatives who want feeding continued even when the patient's condition is hopeless. However, although medical personnel should not be able to force families to continue artificial feeding for terminal patients, the emotional impact of discontinuing feeding should be taken very seriously. Not only does feeding have immense psychological and symbolic import, but as we ponder the discontinuance of even this most basic type of treatment, the question of active euthanasia seems to loom larger and larger.

Procedures for Decision Making

Whatever type of treatment is at issue, the procedure for making treatment decisions for incompetent patients is of crucial importance. Although the courts in *Quinlan* and *Saikewicz* basically agreed about substantive standards, their procedural holdings were strikingly different. The *Quinlan* court recognized that fear of liability could influence physicians to continue treatment after it no longer served the patient's interests, and noted the need for procedures that would minimize this influence.[103] The court held that routine adjudication of nontreatment decisions was neither necessary nor desirable:

> We consider that a practice of applying to a court to confirm such decisions would generally be inappropriate, not only because that would be a gratuitous encroachment on the medical profession's field of competence, but because it would be impossibly cumbersome.[104]

Instead, it suggested oversight by hospital ethics committees, which would both review the patient's prognosis, determining that it was truly hopeless, and ensure that neither family nor physician was influenced by any improper considerations. Of course, judicial review could be sought in unusual or exceptionally difficult cases. But, in general, the court felt that concurrence of the patient's family and physician plus review by ethics committees would guard against abuses while avoiding the problems inherent in judicial decision making.

The *Saikewicz* court strongly disagreed, holding that courts are the appropriate institutions to make these life or death decisions:

> We take a dim view of any attempt to shift ultimate decision-making responsibility away from a duly established court of proper jurisdiction to any committee, panel or group, ad hoc or permanent. Thus, we reject the approach adopted by the New Jersey Supreme Court in the Quinlan case of entrusting the decision whether to continue artificial life support to the patient's guardian, family, attending doctors, and hospital "ethics committee" . . . . We do not view the judicial resolution of this most difficult and awesome question—whether potentially life prolonging treatment should be withheld from a person incapable of making his own decision—as constituting a "gratuitous encroachment" on the domain of medical expertise.[105]

The *Saikewicz* court unfortunately did not specify whether it simply meant that a court presented with such a question should not delegate its resolution to others or that *all* nontreatment decisions for incompetent patients must be made by the courts. Many hospital attorneys and commentators read the decision as requiring routine adjudication, even though families and physicians had traditionally made these sorts of decisions for terminally ill or permanently comatose patients.[106]

One subsequent opinion, *Matter of Dinnerstein*,[107] has partially clarified *Saikewicz* in this regard. The family and physician of Mrs. Dinnerstein, a 67-year-old woman in an essentially vegetative state with no hope of returning to a cognitive existence, agreed that a "no-code" order should be entered in her chart. They jointly sought a declaratory judgment that a doctor can enter such an order for this type patient without prior judicial authorization. (Alternatively, if court approval was required, they sought to obtain such approval.) The court agreed that prior approval was not necessary, interpreting *Saikewicz* as applying only to life-saving or life-prolonging treatments, i.e., treatments that could be "administered for the purpose and with some reasonable expectation of effecting a permanent or temporary cure of or relief from the illness or condition being treated."[108] According to the court:

> "Prolongation of life," as used in the *Saikewicz* case, does not mean a mere suspension of the act of dying, but contemplates, at the very least, a remission of symptoms enabling a return towards a normal, functioning, integrated existence.[109]

Since Mrs. Dinnerstein could never return to such an existence, the court held that concurrence of family and physician was all that was required for a "no-code" order.

The Massachusetts Supreme Court approved the *Dinnerstein* holding in a subsequent case, *In re Spring*.[110] However, it overruled the Appeals Court's ruling that judicial approval was likewise unnecessary before discontinuing dialysis treatments for a 78-year-old incompetent patient whose wife, son, and physician all favored discontinuation.[111] The Appeals Court had held that the *Saikewicz* requirement of judicial authorization applied only to difficult cases, such as ones involving life *saving* treatment or disagreement among the parties. The Supreme Court agreed that the termination of dialysis was appropriate (the patient had died of other causes before the final opinion was issued). But it disapproved of delegating decision-making power to the family and physician, holding: "when a court is properly presented with the legal question, whether treatment may be withheld, it must decide that question and not delegate it to some private person or group."[112] The court stated, however, that:

> Neither the present case nor the *Saikewicz* case involved the legality of action taken without judicial authorization, and our opinion should not be taken to establish any requirement of prior judicial approval *that would not otherwise exist.*

The Massachusetts Supreme Court listed various factors doctors should take into account in determining whether to apply for prior judicial approval, including:

> The extent of impairment of the patient's mental faculties, whether the patient is in the custody of a state institution, the prognosis without proposed treatment, the prognosis with the proposed treatment, the complexity, risk and novelty of the proposed treatment, its possible side effects, the patient's level of understanding and probable reaction, the urgency of decision, the consent of the patient, spouse, or guardian, the good faith of those who participate in the decision, the clarity of professional opinion as to what is good medical practice, the interest of third persons, and the administrative requirements of any institution involved.[113]

It did not, however, specify which sets of factors would be sufficient to make judicial approval necessary or unnecessary. Thus, Massachusetts physicians will still have to guess whether prior court approval is required, unless the situation clearly is governed by *Dinnerstein*. Although the Massachusetts Supreme Court pointed out that no prosecutor had thus far proceeded to trial against a physician who terminated or omitted life-preserving treatment in a hopeless case, the post-*Saikewicz* decisions, with the exception of *Dinnerstein*, will undoubtedly fail to either assuage physicians' fears that they risk liability or diminish their feeling that personal and medical decisions are being usurped by the judiciary.

Various other judicial decisions have been of equally little value in clarifying when, and whether, prior judicial approval is needed before treatment can be terminated. For example, in *Matter of Eichner*,[114] a New York intermediate court, in authorizing the removal of a respirator from a comatose patient, set forth elaborate procedures for resolving such cases in the future. (The procedures were so complex that one writer said they would require "a minimum of 4 to 6 physicians, 5 attorneys, and 1 judge ... to withdraw extraordinary life saving systems from a chronically ill, chronically vegetative patient."[115]) New York's highest court, the Court of Appeals, approved removal of the respirator (though, as usual, the patient was long since dead), but rejected the proposed procedures. However, it addressed the procedural issue only briefly, stating:

Neither the common law nor existing statutes require persons generally to seek prior Court assessment of conduct which may subject them to civil and criminal liability. If it is desirable to enlarge the role of the Courts in cases involving discontinuance of life sustaining treatment for incompetents by establishing, as the Appellate Division suggested in the *Eichner* case, a mandatory procedure of successive approval by physicians, hospital personnel, relatives, and the Courts, the change should come from the legislature.[116]

The opinion is encouraging in that it does not affirmatively require prior judicial approval. Nonetheless, since no procedure has been established, it is unclear when, if ever, family and physician can informally decide to terminate treatment without fearing, to at least some extent, civil or criminal liability. This uncertainty is exacerbated by the fact that in *Eichner*'s companion case, *Matter of Storar*, the Court of Appeals reversed the lower court's ruling that John Storar's blood transfusions could be discontinued.[117]

Given the disarray apparent in these state court opinions, as well as the fact that most of them were rendered long after the patient was dead, it is not surprising that the President's Commission recommends the approach suggested in *Quinlan*—decisions by family and physicians, with review by hospital ethics committees.[118] While court decisions may sometimes be necessary to establish guiding principles, surely litigation is not the procedure of choice in this area. As the Commission notes, litigation is costly, creates long delays, and can seriously strain the relationships between the parties by forcing them into adversarial roles. Moreover, it exposes these private matters to the scrutiny of the courtroom and often to the glare of the public media.[119] Ethics committees, however, can provide detached and objective review and can do so more efficiently and more sensitively than an adversarial procedure allows.[120] Whether state courts and legislatures will adopt the Commission's recommendations remains to be seen. But its approach is a wise and moderate one. Learned Hand is reported to have once said, "I dread litigation almost as much as disease and death."[121] In these tragic situations, where disease and death are unavoidable, surely patients and their families should, if at all possible, be spared the burdens of facing litigation as well.

Advance Directives

One way to avoid litigation and to allow an incompetent patient's interest in avoiding prolonged and futile treatment to be respected is to allow or encourage patients to state their wishes in advance. In 1976, California enacted the Natural Death Act,[122] the first statute to explicitly authorize an individual to direct, in advance, that life-saving treatment be withdrawn when death is imminent. A number of other states, now a majority, have passed similar statutes, which will be generically called "Natural Death Acts."[123] The intent of these acts is to validate "living wills," which were initially developed as documents indicating a person's beliefs about treatment but lacking binding legal effect. Although the legal impact of living wills is highly uncertain in the states without natural death legislation (though they constitute excellent evidence of the patient's desires while competent), they will have legal effect in states with such legislation, provided they comply with their state's statutory requirements.

The legal relevance of living wills has been recognized by the Supreme Court of Florida in a recent decision, *John F. Kennedy Memorial Hospital v. Bludworth*.[124] Although the lower court in this case had held that the living will made out by a previously competent, but now permanently vegetative, patient could be implemented only via a court order authorizing a court-appointed guardian to consent to nontreatment, the Supreme Court recognized that a major purpose of such documents is precisely to avoid litigation. Hence it held that in proper circumstances, i.e., when physicians certify that the patient is in a permanent vegetative state, family and physician can agree to discontinue life-sustaining treatments without a judicial procedure. The court held that in making such a decision, proxy decision makers should give great weight to the fact that the patient had previously executed a living will.[125]

Unfortunately, some Natural Death Acts are so narrowly drawn that they apply to only a very small group of patients. In California and a few other states, a directive is binding only if issued after the patient has been informed of a terminal condition.[126] Moreover, in the majority of states, directives to withdraw or withhold life-sustaining treatment come into effect only when the patient's death is imminent, such that treatment would merely prolong or interrupt the process of dying.[127] Such statutes do not, on their face, appear to apply to patients in chronic vegetative states, patients with end-stage renal disease whose life could be prolonged by dialysis, or other patients whose painful, burdensome, or extremely limited condition could be artificially prolonged long enough that death is not "imminent."[128] According to the President's Commission:

> The class of persons thus defined by many of the statutes, if it indeed contains any members, at most constitutes a small percentage of those incapacitated individuals for whom decisions about life sustaining treatment must be made.[129]

Many statutes have other limitations, such as the absence of penalties for physicians who refuse to follow valid and binding directives.[130] In addition, it has been noted that some health care providers may believe that treatment can be terminated *only* if the patient has drawn up a living will in accordance with the state statute, thereby unduly circumscribing the rights of patients who might want treatment discontinued but lack a living will.[131] Despite these drawbacks, the Commission is undoubtedly correct to endorse living wills and to recommend that they be expressly endowed with legal effect under state law.[132]

Natural Death Acts, with the exception of Delaware's,[133] authorize advance substantive instructions, but do not provide for appointment of a proxy decision maker if the patient becomes incapacitated. However, 42 states have statutes authorizing persons to create durable powers of attorney, i.e., powers of attorney that remain operative even if the person becomes incompetent, unlike common law powers of attorney.[134] Persons can, at least theoretically, use such statutes to appoint a trusted friend or relative to make proxy health care decisions if they become incompetent to decide for themselves. Such statutes were not expressly enacted for this purpose and, as the Commission and certain commentators point out, additional procedural safeguards may be necessary to use them in this context.[135] However, given the narrow application of Natural Death Acts, durable power of attorney statutes, appropriately modified, could provide a more flexible and generalized method of making health care decisions for incompetent patients. Thus, as the President's Commission concludes, we need legislation that is broader than most Natural Death Acts, which authorizes proxy decision making, and which balances the dual goals of avoiding abuse and allowing for flexibility in decision making by patients and proxies.[136]

CONCLUSION

Patients in the ICU must be informed of the risks and benefits of either accepting or rejecting treatment. Competent adult patients have a right to refuse treatment and, if challenged by the hospital, this right will generally be upheld, because state interests in forcibly treating a competent patient are unlikely to be strong enough to override the patient's rights. The state interests are particularly weak when the patient cannot live long anyway or the treatment would leave him or her extremely disabled. However, some courts may override the refusal of competent patients who could be restored to vibrant health and who have dependent children. Despite this, the trend in most jurisdictions is to accord increasing respect to individual patient autonomy, which suggests that even refusals in the latter type case may well be honored.

The situation is much more difficult when treatment decisions must be made for an incompetent patient. Assessing incompetency may, in certain cases, be a difficult matter, but it is clearly a prerequisite to proxy decision making in questionable cases. When an incompetent patient was previously competent, courts will ask what he or she would have wanted done. Although some courts will try to use this substituted judgment test even when the patient was never competent, in these cases it is unworkable and should be replaced by the more objective best-interests standard. This test can allow nontreatment in appropriate circumstances without resort to dubious legal fictions.

Whichever test is used, jurisdictions are in serious disagreement as to when and whether nontreatment decisions must be made or reviewed by courts. However the judicial role is ultimately defined, it seems far preferable to avoid routine recourse to the courts by respecting the decisions of valid proxies (usually close relatives) and/or by seeking objectivity through ethics committee review of questionable cases. Although it may remain necessary to have courts decide test cases, as a standard procedure, ethics committees have the distinct advantages of being less adversarial, less cumbersome, and more likely to reach a final decision before the patient is dead.

NOTES

1. Schloendorff v. Soc'y. of N. Y. Hosp., 211 N.Y. 125, 126, 105 N.E. 92, 93 (1914).

2. *See id. See generally* Annotation, 56 A.L.R.2d 695, 709-16 (1957).

3. Schloendorf, 105 N.E. at 95.

4. *See, e.g.*, Natanson v. Kline, 186 Kan. 393, 350 P.2d 1093 (1960), *clarified*, 354 P.2d 670; Cobbs v. Grant, 8 Cal.3d 229, 104 Cal. Rptr. 505, 502 P.2d 1 (1972).

5. *See, e.g.*, Marchlewicz v. Stanton, 50 Mich. App. 344, 213 N.W.2d 317 (1973); Buckner v. Allergan Pharmaceuticals Inc., 400 So.2d 820 (Fla. App. 1981), *petition denied*, 407 So.2d 1102; Karp v. Cooley, 493 F.2d 408 (5th Cir.), *cert. denied*, 419 U.S. 845 (1974).

6. Canterbury v. Spence, 150 App. D.C. 263, 464 F.2d 772, *cert. denied*, 409 U.S. 1064 (1972); Cobbs v. Grant, 8 Cal.3d 229, 104 Cal. Rptr. 505, 502 P.2d 1 (1972); Wilkinson v. Vesey, 110 R.I. 606, 295 A.2d 676 (1972).

7. C. LIDZ et al., INFORMED CONSENT: A STUDY OF PSYCHIATRIC DECISIONMAKING IN PSYCHIATRY (1984).

8. *See, e.g.*, D. MEYERS, MEDICO-LEGAL IMPLICATIONS OF DEATH AND DYING 81-82 (1981); LIDZ, *supra* note 7, at 14.

9. Canterbury v. Spence, 150 App. D.C. 263, 464 F.2d 772, *cert. denied*, 409 U.S. 1064 (1972); Wilkinson v. Vesey, 110 R.I. 606, 295 A.2d 676 (1972).

10. Scott v. Bradford, 606 P.2d 554 (Okla. 1979); McPherson v. Allis, 305 N.C. 266, 282 S.E.2d 892 (1982) (*superseded by statute*).

11. Truman v. Thomas, 27 Cal.3d 285, 165 Cal. Rptr. 308, 611 P.2d 902 (1980).

12. Canterbury v. Spence, 464 F.2d at 788; Gravis v. Physicians and Surgeons Hosp., 415 S.W.2d 674 (Tex. Civ. App. 1967), *rev'd on other grounds*, 427 S.W.2d 310.

13. LIDZ, *supra* note 7, at 16.
14. *Id.*
15. Canterbury v. Spence, 464 F.2d at 789.
16. MEYERS, *supra* note 8, at 100. One state statute, however, authorizes implied consent only when a person authorized to consent on behalf of the patient is "not readily available." NEV. REV. STAT. §41A.120(2) (1985).
17. Cobbs v. Grant, 8 Cal.3d at 244.
18. *Id.* at 246.
19. LIDZ, *supra* note 7, at 18.
20. PRESIDENT'S COMMISSION FOR THE STUDY OF ETHICAL PROBLEMS IN MEDICINE AND BIOMEDICAL AND BEHAVIORAL RESEARCH, MAKING HEALTH CARE DECISIONS 182 (1982).
21. *See id.* at 30-31.
22. *See generally id.* at 55-111.
23. Griswold v. Connecticut, 381 U.S. 479 (1965) (use of contraceptives).
24. Satz v. Perlmutter, 362 So.2d 160, 162 (Fla. Dist. Ct. App. 1978), *aff'd*, 379 So.2d 359 (1980); In re Quinlan, 70 N.J. 10, 355 A.2d 647 (1976), *cert. denied*, 429 U.S. 922.
25. Satz v. Perlmutter, 362 So.2d at 162; *see* Superintendent of Belchertown State School v. Saikewicz, 370 N.E.2d 417, 425 (Mass. 1977) (enunciating these state interests in the context of a treatment decision for an incompetent patient).
26. 239 F. Supp. 752, 753 (D. Conn. 1965).
27. 118 App. D.C. 80, 331 F.2d 1000, 1008 (1964).
28. 331 F.2d at 1007.
29. 383 A.2d 785, 789 (N.J. 1978).
30. In re Quinlan, 70 N.J. at 40, 355 A.2d at 663.
31. 294 A.2d 372 (Dist. Ct. App. 1972).
32. 88 Misc.2d 974, 390 N.Y.S.2d 523, 524 (1976).
33. Glantz, *Legal Limits on the Right to Refuse Treatment*, in DILEMMAS OF DYING: POLICIES AND PROCEDURES FOR DECISIONS NOT TO TREAT 53-54 (C. Wong & J. Swazey 1981). *See* United States v. George, 239 F. Supp. at 753; Application of President and Directors of Georgetown Hosp., 331 F.2d at 1008.
34. 331 F.2d at 1002.
35. PRESIDENT'S COMMISSION FOR THE STUDY OF ETHICAL PROBLEMS IN MEDICINE AND BIOMEDICAL AND BEHAVIORAL RESEARCH, DECIDING TO FOREGO LIFE-SUSTAINING TREATMENT 27 (1983).
36. *See* MEYERS, *supra* note 8, at 251-53.
37. *Id.* at 249.
38. Frey, *The Right to Treat a Competent Adult Who Refuses Treatment to Prolong Life*, MED. TR. TECH. Q. 432 (1981).
39. Glantz, *supra* note 33, at 58.
40. *Id.*
41. 42 N.J. 421, 201 A.2d 537 (1964).
42. Glantz, *supra* note 33, at 59; Annas, *Forced Cesareans: The Most Unkindest Cut of All*, 12 HASTINGS CTR. REP. 16, 17 (June 1982).

43. Jefferson v. Griffin Spalding Cy. Hosp. Auth., 247 Ga. 86, 274 S.E.2d 457 (1981); *see* Bowes & Selgestad, *Fetal vs. Maternal Rights: Medical and Legal Perspectives*, 58 AM. J. OB. & GYN. 209 (1981) (discussing a similar case in Colorado).

44. *See, e.g.*, Satz v. Perlmutter, 362 So.2d 160 (Fla. Dist. Ct. App. 1978), *aff'd*, 379 So.2d 359 (1980).

45. *See* In re Quinlan, 70 N.J. 10, 355 A.2d 647 (1976), *cert. denied*, 429 U.S. 922; Glantz, *supra* note 33, at 55; Byrn, *Compulsory Life-Saving Treatment for the Competent Adult*, 40 FORDHAM L. REV. 16 (1975).

46. *See* Bouvia v. County of Riverside, No. 159780 (Super. Ct., Riverside County, Dec. 16, 1983).

47. In another very recent case, an elderly nursing home patient refused to eat. Here the court did not order force-feeding or artificial forms of nutrition. Application of Plaza Health & Rehab. Center, Sup. Ct., Onondaga Cy., Feb. 2, 1984. But the patient, Mr. Henninger, had led a long and full life. Moreover, his case did not involve the complicating factors so readily apparent in the Bouvia case, such as that Ms. Bouvia had recently separated from her husband and suffered other setbacks that could readily make someone lose hope, but whose effect could possibly be only temporary.

48. PRESIDENT'S COMMISSION, MAKING HEALTH CARE DECISIONS, *supra* note 20, at 62.

49. *See* Roth, Meisel & Lidz, *Tests of Competency to Consent to Treatment*, 134 AM. J. PSYCHIATRY 279 (1977).

50. MEYERS, *supra* note 8, at 265; In re KKB, 609 P.2d 747 (Okla. 1980).

51. 62 D. & C.2d 619 (Pa. 1973).

52. On the right of mental patients to refuse treatment with psychotropic drugs, *see* Rogers v. commissioner, 458 N.E.2d 308 (Mass. 1983).

53. In re Schiller, 372 A.2d 360 (N.J. 1977).

54. PRESIDENT'S COMMISSION, MAKING HEALTH CARE DECISIONS, *supra* note 20, at 60.

55. 563 S.W.2d 197 (Tenn. App. 1978), *motion to expedite denied*, 435 U.S. 950, *appeal dismissed as moot*, 436 U.S. 923 (1978).

56. 563 S.W.2d at 210.

57. *Id.*

58. 372 A.2d 360, 368 (N.J. 1977).

59. Lane v. Candura, 376 N.E.2d 1232, 1235 (Mass. App. 1978).

60. *See, e.g.*, J. ROBERTSON, THE RIGHTS OF THE CRITICALLY ILL (1983); Baron, *Assuring 'Detached but Passionate Investigation and Decision': The Role of Guardians Ad Litem in Saikewicz Type Cases*, 4 AM. J. L. & MED. 111 (1978).

61. PRESIDENT'S COMMISSION, DECIDING TO FOREGO LIFE-SUSTAINING TREATMENT, *supra* note 35, at 125-26.

62. *Id.* at 126.

63. Guardianship of Dolores Phelps, No. 459-207 (Milwaukee County Court, Probate Decision, 1972) (41-year-old Jehovah's Witness whose refusal to consent to a blood transfusion prior to becoming unconscious was upheld over her nephew's attempt to compel a transfusion).

64. In re Eichner, 52 N.Y.2d 363, 438 N.Y.S.2d 266, 420 N.E.2d 64 (1981), *cert. denied*, 102 S. Ct. 309 (guardian allowed to authorize withdrawal of respirator from 83-year-old comatose cleric who had indicated he would not want heroic means used to prolong his life were he in a vegetative state).

65. In re Quinlan, 70 N.J. 10, 355 A.2d 647 (1976), *cert. denied*, 429 U.S. 922.

66. Superintendent of Belchertown State School v. Saikewicz, *supra* (withholding of chemotherapy from 67-year-old profoundly retarded man allowed in light of limited chance of benefit and the pain and side effects that would be caused by the treatment).

67. Saikewicz, *supra*, 370 N.E.2d at 424.

68. In re Schiller, 148 N.J. Super. 168, 372 A.2d 360 (1977); Application of Long Island Jewish-Hillside Medical Center, 342 N.Y.S.2d 356, 73 Misc.2d 395 (S. Ct., Special Term 1973).

69. State Department of Human Services v. Northern, *supra* note 55.

70. 70 N.J. 10, 355 A.2d 647, *cert. denied*, 429 U.S. 922 (1976).

71. 355 A.2d at 664.

72. *Id.* at 653.

73. *Id.* at 664.

74. *See, e.g.*, Superintendent of Belchertown State School v. Saikewicz, *supra*, at 425-26.

75. *See* In re Eichner, 52 N.Y.2d 363, 438 N.Y.S.2d 266, 420 N.E.2d 64, 70 (1981) (refusing to consider the constitutional issue).

76. In re Eichner, *supra* note 75; Matter of Dinnerstein, 380 N.E.2d 134 (Mass. App. 1978).

77. *See, e.g.*, In re Spring, 405 N.E.2d 115 (Mass. 1980) (authorizing the discontinuance of dialysis treatments on the grounds that a formerly competent patient would choose not to have a senile and incompetent, though not unconscious, existence prolonged via painful dialysis treatments).

78. 373 Mass. 728, 370 N.E.2d 417 (1977).

79. 370 N.E.2d at 420.

80. *Id.* at 431.

81. Annas, *Quality of Life in the Courts: Earle Spring in Fantasyland*, 13 HASTINGS CTR. REP. 9 (June 1983).

82. 420 N.E.2d at 72.

83. *Id.* at 72-73.

84. *Id.* at 78, Justice Jones, dissenting.

85. *See* Saikewicz, 370 N.E.2d at 428.

86. Annas, *supra* note 81, at 9-10.

87. In re Conroy, 98 N.J. 321, 486 A.2d 1209, 1217 (1985).

88. 486 A.2d at 1231.

89. *Id.* at 1231-32.

90. *Id.* at 1232.

91. *Id.* at 1247-49 (Handler, J., concurring in part and dissenting in part).

92. *See* People v. Burden, 72 Cal. App.3d 603, 140 Cal. Rptr. 282 (1977).

93. Barber v. Superior Court, 195 Cal. Rptr. 484, 147 Cal. App.3d 1006 (1983).

94. 195 Cal. Rptr. at 490.

95. 425 A.2d 156 (Del. Ch. 1980).

96. *Id.* at 156-60.

97. In re Conroy, 190 N.J. Super. 453, 464 A.2d 303, 315 (App. Div. 1983), *rev'd*, 486 A.2d 1209 (N.J. 1985).

98. 464 A.2d at 311.

99. 486 A.2d at 1236. *See* Zerwekh, *The Dehydration Question*, 83 NURSING 47 (1983); Micetich, et al., *Are Intravenous Fluids Morally Required for a Dying Patient?* 143 ARCH. INT. MED. 975 (1983).

100. Lynn & Childress, *Must Patients Always Be Given Food and Water?* 13 HASTINGS CTR. REP. 17, 18 (October 1983).

101. 486 A.2d at 1236. *See also* Lynn & Childress, *supra* note 100, at 20; MEYERS, *supra* note 8, Supp. 1983, at 56.

102. PRESIDENT'S COMMISSION, DECIDING TO FOREGO LIFE-SUSTAINING TREATMENT, *supra* note 35, at 190.

103. 355 A.2d 667-69.

104. *Id.* at 669.

105. 370 N.E.2d at 434-35.

106. *See* Relman, *The Saikewicz Decision: A Medical Viewpoint*, 4 AM. J. L. & MED. 233 (1978).

107. 380 N.E.2d 134 (Mass. App. 1978).

108. *Id.* at 137-38.

109. *Id.* at 138.

110. 405 N.E.2d 115 (Mass. 1980).

111. 399 N.E.2d 493 (Mass. App. 1979), *overruled*, 405 N.E.2d 115 (1980).

112. 405 N.E.2d at 122.

113. *Id.* at 120-21.

114. 73 App. Div. 2d 431, 426 N.Y. S.2d 517 (1980), *modified & restricted on appeal*, 52 N.Y.2d 363, 438 N.Y.S.2d 266, 420 N.E.2d 64 (1981).

115. Paris, *Court Intervention and the Diminution of Patients' Rights: The Case of Brother Joseph Fox*, 303 NEW ENGL. J. MED. 876-77 (1980).

116. 420 N.E.2d at 74.

117. *Id.* at 73.

118. PRESIDENT'S COMMISSION, DECIDING TO FOREGO LIFE-SUSTAINING TREATMENT, *supra* note 35, at 168-70.

119. *Id.* at 159.

120. *Id.* at 168-69.

121. Quoted in Gerety, *Conversations about Death and Power*, 10 HASTINGS CTR. REP. 19, 21 (August 1980).

122. CAL. HEALTH & SAFETY CODE §§7185-7195.

123. PRESIDENT'S COMMISSION, DECIDING TO FOREGO LIFE-SUSTAINING TREATMENT, *supra* note 35, at 137.

124. 452 So.2d 921 (Fla. 1984).

125. *Id.* at 926.

126. CAL. HEALTH & SAFETY CODE §7188; OR. REV. STAT. §97.050-090.

127. *See, e.g.*, CAL. HEALTH & SAFETY CODE §§7187(e), 7191(b); (Deering Supp. 1982); Ala. Natural Death Act, ALA. CODE §22-8A-3(3); OR. REV. STAT. §97.050(3).

128. MEYERS, *supra* note 8, at 494; PRESIDENT'S COMMISSION, DECIDING TO FOREGO LIFE-SUSTAINING TREATMENT, *supra* note 35, at 143.

129. *Id.* at 143.

130. *Id., App. D, at 310-11*, comparing state statutes.

131. *Id.* at 144.
132. *Id.* at 137-39.
133. DEL. CODE ANN. tit. 16, §2502(b) (1982).
134. PRESIDENT'S COMMISSION, DECIDING TO FOREGO LIFE-SUSTAINING TREATMENT, *supra* note 35, at 145-46.
135. *Id.* at 147; MEYERS, *supra* note 8, 1983 Supp. at 87.
136. PRESIDENT'S COMMISSION, DECIDING TO FOREGO LIFE-SUSTAINING TREATMENT, *supra* note 35, at 149-53.

Chapter 4

Critically Ill Infants

Robyn S. Shapiro and Joel E. Frader

Recent developments in medical technology such as artificial respirators, pharmacologic manipulation of the cardiovascular system, and dialysis for kidney failure have raised ethical and legal dilemmas in the neonatal intensive care unit. For instance, should life-sustaining systems be disconnected so that a child in an irreversible vegetative state may die? Should an operation be done on a mentally retarded newborn to cure a physical defect? May parents decline to authorize conventional but painful treatment for their child that provides only a slim chance of cure in favor of a new and unproven but painless method of treatment?

The impaired newborn, the competent adult patient, and the incompetent adult patient all have the same substantive right to refuse potentially life-prolonging treatment in appropriate circumstances. However, in the cases of incompetent adults and impaired newborns, it is difficult to ensure that the patient's right is protected and implemented. Further complexities arise in the situation of incompetents, because their interests may conflict with those of family members and/or the government. With newborns, even greater complexity results from the inherent difficulties in making accurate medical prognoses. There are still no clear-cut legal criteria to guide parents, doctors, and the courts in resolving dilemmas regarding medical treatment for impaired newborns.

This chapter analyzes the right of parents to refuse potentially life-saving medical treatment for their impaired infant, as that right follows from the right of the competent adult patient and the incompetent adult patient to refuse treatment. The potential conflicts of interests of the parties involved in pediatric treatment decisions and the manner in which courts have balanced them are also discussed. Finally, the chapter focuses on the additional complexities of medical decision making for newborns and alternative solutions to such decision-making dilemmas.

THE RIGHT TO REFUSE TREATMENT

The Competent Adult Patient

A competent adult has a right to refuse medical treatment, even if the ultimate result is death.[1] This right is grounded in the doctrine of informed consent and the constitutional right to privacy.[2] Under informed consent, medical treatment can be given only after the patient has been informed about the treatment and has validly consented to it.[3] The requirement of valid consent implies the patient's right to refuse the treatment.[4] In recent cases, courts have broadened the constitutional right to privacy to include explicitly the right to decline medical treatment.[5] As one court explained:

> The constitutional right to privacy, as we conceive it, is an expression of the sanctity of individual free choice and self-determination as fundamental constituents of life. The value of life as so perceived is lessened not by a decision to refuse treatment, but by the failure to allow a competent human being the right of choice.[6]

The following four state interests potentially conflict with the patient's right to refuse treatment: (1) preservation of life, (2) protection of the interests of third parties (usually minor children),[7] (3) prevention of suicide, and (4) preservation of the ethical integrity of the medical profession.[8] However, in situations involving terminally ill competent adults where no innocent third parties' rights are present and the sole state interest is preservation of life,[9] courts have held that the patient's decision to refuse treatment prevails.[10]

The Incompetent Adult Patient

It is well established that the incompetent adult has as much right as the competent adult to refuse medical treatment in appropriate circumstances.[11] However, since the incompetent adult cannot express his or her wishes, others must be entrusted with the responsibility for treatment decisions.

Who Decides?

The question of who should have responsibility for treatment decisions regarding incompetent adults has been answered differently by courts throughout the country. At this time it is not possible to discern a clear trend in judicial determinations. The case of *In re Quinlan*[12] involved a 20-year-old comatose woman who was placed on a respirator but who remained in a vegetative state. The patient's parents wanted her respirator removed, but the treating physician refused because she was not legally brain dead. The family commenced legal action, and the trial court upheld the physician's position. On appeal, the New Jersey Supreme Court reversed and gave Quinlan's father, as legal guardian, authority to remove the respirator. In addressing the question of *who* could terminate life support for the incompetent patient, *Quinlan* established a three-tier procedure:

> [U]pon the concurrence of the guardian and family of Karen, should the responsible attending physicians conclude that there is no reasonable possibility of Karen's ever emerging from her present comatose condition to a cognitive, sapient state and that the life-support apparatus now being administered to Karen should be discontinued, they shall consult with the hospital "Ethics Committee" or like body of the institution in which Karen is then hospitalized. If that consultative body agrees that there is no reasonable possibility of Karen's ever emerging from her present comatose condition to a cognitive, sapient state, the present life-support system may be withdrawn and said action shall be without any civil or criminal liability therefore on the part of any participant, whether guardian, physician, hospital or others.[13]

In *Superintendent of Belchertown State School v. Saikewicz*,[14] the Supreme Judicial Court of Massachusetts rejected *Quinlan's* three-tier approach and held that *the court* should decide whether potentially life-prolonging treatment should be withheld from the incompetent adult. In that case, the question was whether or not Saikewicz, an incompetent 67-year-old man, should receive chemotherapy for incurable acute monocytic leukemia. The chemotherapy treatments might have prolonged Saikewicz's life for several months, but they were likely to cause severe side effects. The court first addressed what it perceived to be Mr. Saikewicz's actual interests and preferences, and then, on that basis, decided that the chemotherapy could be withheld. The court stated:

> We take a dim view of any attempt to shift the ultimate decision-making responsibilities away from the duly established courts of proper jurisdiction to any committee, panel or group, ad hoc or permanent. Thus, we reject the approach adopted by the New Jersey Supreme Court in the *Quinlan* case of entrusting the decision whether to continue artificial life support to the patient's guardian, family, attending doctors, and hospital "ethics committee."[15]

In entrusting the medical decision making for Mr. Saikewicz to the court, the *Saikewicz* opinion reasoned that it is the role of the judiciary in our society to resolve difficult moral problems, and that no other person or group has the authority to decide questions of life and death. The opinion reads:

We do not view the judicial resolution of this most difficult and awesome question—whether potentially life-prolonging treatment should be withheld from a person incapable of making his own decision—as constituting "gratuitous encroachment" on the domain of medical expertise. Rather, such questions of life and death seem to us to require the process of detached but passionate investigation and decision that forms the ideal on which the judicial branch of government was created. Achieving this ideal is our responsibility and that of the lower court, and is not to be entrusted to any other group purporting to represent the "morality and conscience of our society" no matter how highly motivated or impressively constituted.[16]

In 1980, the procedural approach of *Saikewicz* was followed by the Massachusetts Supreme Judicial Court in *In re Spring*. In *Spring*, the family of a 78-year-old incompetent man suffering from kidney failure petitioned the court for permission to terminate his life-prolonging dialysis treatment. The Massachusetts Supreme Judicial Court, modifying the decision of a lower court,[17] concluded that it was an error to delegate the decision to the family and the doctor and reiterated its belief that *the court* must make such decisions.[18]

How Is the Decision Made?

Judicially decreed guidelines as to when medical treatment may be withheld from an incompetent adult also vary from jurisdiction to jurisdiction. In *In re Quinlan*,[19] the New Jersey Supreme Court held that "The focal point of decision [as to when treatment should be withheld] should be the prognosis as to the reasonable possibility of return to cognitive and sapient life, as distinguished from the forced continuance of that biological vegetative existence to which Karen seems to be doomed."[20] Since there was no hope that Karen would return to cognitive, sapient life, the court found that she did not have to suffer attachment to a respirator. In the court's words: "[N]o...compelling interest of the State could compel Karen to endure the unendurable, only to vegetate a few measurable months with no realistic possibility of returning to any semblance of cognitive or sapient life."[21] The best interests of the patient are the primary concern for decision makers.

The test used in Massachusetts and New York for determining when medical treatment should be withheld from an incompetent adult is more subjective. In *Saikewicz*, the Massachusetts Supreme Judicial Court adopted a "substituted judgment" standard: since an incompetent adult has the same right as a competent adult to decline treatment, the court must determine whether or not the incompetent patient would exercise that right under the circumstances, if he or she were competent. If the court determines that the incompetent patient himself or herself *would* choose to decline treatment, the treatment should be withheld—even if such a decision does not conform to what is thought wise or prudent by most people.[22] In recognition of the imprecision in any attempt to ascertain the interests and preferences of the incompetent patient, the *Saikewicz* court advanced certain guiding principles, which included the admonition that the court may not consider the patient's "quality of life" in applying the "substituted judgment" test. The possibility of a longer life carries the same weight for a mentally incompetent or retarded person as for anyone else, the court reasoned, because the value of life under the law has no relation to intelligence or social position.[23]

Following the *Saikewicz* test, the court in *In re Spring*[24] held that the court's decision to withdraw medical treatment for an incompetent patient should be a "substituted judgment" of what that patient would decide if he or she were competent. The *Spring* court ordered termination of the patient's treatment based, in part, on the facts that (1) the patient would die without the treatment; but (2) with the treatment he would probably survive for only a matter of months; (3) the treatment would not even temporarily restore the patient to a normal, cognitive, integrated, and functioning existence; (4) the treatment caused unpleasant side effects, some of which were controlled with heavy sedation; and (5) termination of the treatment would not cause discomfort.

PEDIATRIC MEDICAL TREATMENT DECISIONS

Withholding medical treatment from a child differs from withholding medical treatment from an incompetent adult because the rights of the child's parents are involved. In most cases, parents have a right to make fundamental decisions regarding the upbringing of their children.[25] The United States Supreme Court has said: "[I]t is cardinal with us that the custody, care and nurture of the child reside first with the parents, whose primary function and freedom include preparation for obligations that the state can neither supply nor hinder."[26]

If the parent fails to care for the child, however, the state will protect the child from the actions or inaction of the parent.[27] With respect to children, most scholars agree that the appropriate legal standard to be upheld is that of the best interests of the child.[28] As one court explained:

> While. . .[the child] "belongs" to his parents, he belongs also to his state. . . . [T]he fact [that] the child belongs to the state imposes upon the state many duties. Chief among them is the duty to protect

his right to live and grow up with a sound mind in a sound body and to brook no interference with that right by any person or organization.[29]

Thus, in many cases where it has been clear that a child would benefit from certain types of medical care and the parents have refused to provide it, the courts have ordered the needed treatment.[30] For example, in the Massachusetts Chad Green case,[31] Chad's parents stopped his chemotherapy treatments, which the hospital believed was necessary to fight the child's acute lymphocytic leukemia. The treating hospital sought a court order to resume the treatments. Evidence at the court hearing disclosed that without the treatments Chad would die within a few weeks, but with them he had a slightly better than 50 percent chance of complete recovery. Medical testimony at the trial was uncontradicted in favor of the chemotherapy, and the court ordered resumption of the treatments. Similarly, in *Jehovah's Witnesses v. King County Hospital Unit No. 2*,[32] *People ex. rel. Wallace v. Labrenz*,[33] and *John F. Kennedy Memorial Hospital v. Heston*,[34] the courts ordered life-saving blood transfusions where parents who were Jehovah's Witnesses refused to consent to such transfusions for their children. And more recently, in Tennessee, Pamela Hamilton's parents asked that the court *not* order radiation and chemotherapy treatments for their 13-year-old daughter's bone cancer. Doctors testified that without such treatments, Pamela would die. Pamela's father, a minister in the Church of God in the Union Assembly, testified that the family's Fundamentalist sect did not permit its members to seek medical treatment, but rather counseled them to rely on the power of prayer. The court declared Pamela a neglected child, gave the state temporary custody, and ordered the medical treatment.[35]

Courts have also overruled parents' medical treatment decisions in cases where the medical situation is not life threatening, but the child's failure to receive certain medical care would be significantly harmful to his or her health. In the second Chad Green case,[36] for instance, evidence revealed that the laetrile, the large doses of vitamins A and C, the enzyme enemas, and the folic acid treatments that Chad's parents had arranged for him to receive had caused chronic cyanide poisoning, hypervitaminosis A, which had damaged his central nervous system and liver, and possible colon damage. The court proscribed these treatments.[37] Similarly, on grounds that a child's medical situation need not be immediately life threatening for the court to intervene, the court overruled a father's refusal to authorize removal of his children's tonsils and adenoids in *In re Karwath*[38]; in *In re Gregory S.*,[39] the court overruled a mother's refusal to permit medical or dental care for her child suffering from umbilical hernia, cavities, and fractured teeth; and in *In re*

Rotkowitz,[40] the court overruled a father's objection to surgical correction of his child's leg deformity.

Parents' medical treatment decisions regarding their children that conflict with the doctors' advice have been upheld by the courts when it has not been clear that the parents' action would unduly harm the children. For instance, in *In re Hofbauer*,[41] parents did not want their eight-year-old, who was afflicted with Hodgkin's disease, to be treated with chemotherapy and radiation. Instead, the parents favored metabolic therapy. In neglect proceedings brought against the parents, they were found not liable and were allowed to retain custody of their child because (1) they justifiably feared the side effects of radiation and chemotherapy; (2) metabolic therapy was controlling the disease; (3) they were willing to have conventional therapy administered in the future, if necessary; and (4) they were loving parents and genuinely concerned about their child's welfare. Similarly, in *In re Seiferth*,[42] the court refused to overrule the parents and order surgery for a 15-year-old with a cleft plate and harelip, saying that the child's condition was not an emergent threat to his health or life. The court refused to order the surgery despite evidence that the operation would improve the child's speech, appearance, and psychological maturation.[43]

Parents' decisions not to treat their children have also been upheld in cases where no known treatment would substantially prolong the child's life. For instance, in *In re Green*,[44] the court refused to order a splenectomy over the objections of parents of a child who also had sickle-cell anemia. Since the child was certain to die of the sickle-cell disease, the court would not overrule the parents' decision to spare him the ordeal of the splenectomy. Similarly, in *Custody of A Minor*,[45] the court refused to order treatment for a 4½-month-old abandoned child (in the custody of the Social Services Department) who was suffering from pulmonary atresia, hypoplastic right ventricle, hypoplastic pulmonary artery, and small patent ductus arteriosus. The decision was based on the fact that death with such conditions normally occurs within a year with or without treatment. And more recently, in *In re Guardianship of Andrew Barry*,[46] the parents of a terminally ill 10-month-old successfully petitioned for approval to remove the child's life-support system. The court said that since the child was wholly lacking in cognitive brain function and completely unaware of his surroundings with no hope of developing any awareness, his privacy rights to refuse the life support outweighed the state's interests in preserving life.

In summary, courts have tended to overrule parental refusal of consent for medical treatment when the proposed therapy promised clear medical benefit. Parental refusal may be upheld when benefits are marginal or substantially controversial.

MEDICAL DECISION MAKING FOR THE IMPAIRED NEWBORN

Medical Background

Families and physicians face difficulties in deciding how much medical intervention to extend to critically ill newborns at all points along the spectrum of newborn medical disorders. Ironically, the cases that have attracted the greatest attention appear to be among the least frequent. The publicity surrounding dramatic cases, like the Down's syndrome Baby Doe of Bloomington, Indiana, in April 1982, has misled many who believe that babies born with such defects constitute the majority of legally or morally difficult cases. There is no doubt that congenital malformation syndromes (that is, complexes of observable defects) make up an important segment of patients where decision making is controversial. However, much of the lay and professional literature has overlooked the far larger group of premature and/or low-birth-weight infants who receive the bulk of neonatal intensive care.

It is important to note that there is no basic information about the frequency of the ethical controversies in neonatal care. We do not know how often families and/or physicians consider or act so as to withhold treatment from critically ill infants. Beyond quantitative data, there is scant information about the quality of such decision making. What follows is a discussion of some of the medical conditions where legal and ethical dilemmas arise in newborn care.

Prematurity/Low Birth Weight

Each year in the United States approximately 250,000 low-birth-weight (under 2500 grams or approximately 5¼ lbs.) infants are born. The majority of these babies are premature. According to one expert, a quarter of these infants are "at high risk for serious lifetime disability."[47] The medical problems these babies suffer include malnutrition, respiratory insufficiency, brain hemorrhage, life-threatening infection, and brain injury from various biochemical imbalances. All of these problems stem from the immaturity of body systems—these infants are born too soon and medical science cannot yet adequately mimic the intrauterine environment.

The consequences of these medical conditions, and at times the consequences of treatment no matter how skillfully applied, include severe brain injury with retardation, seizures, blindness, deafness, cerebral palsy, and other conditions; chronic lung disease (bronchopulmonary dysplasia) with limited exercise tolerance, a predisposition to respiratory infection, and asthma; gastrointestinal problems including, in some cases, the lifelong need for total intravenous nutrition; chronic liver disease; chronic kidney disease; and assorted other medical problems. In addition, among low-birth-weight infants, the incidence of congenital malformations (such as those discussed below) is substantially higher than in the population of infants born after a full term of gestation (38 weeks).[48]

Of disorders affecting premature infants, two deserve expanded comment: respiratory insufficiency and brain hemorrhage. Of these low-birth-weight infants 10 to 15 percent develop respiratory distress syndrome (RDS).[49] As a rule of thumb, the smaller and/or the more premature the infant, the more likely the baby will have RDS. Resulting from the immature lungs' inability to synthesize biochemicals needed for full lung expansion, the disorder impairs the body's capacity to take in adequate oxygen and breathe out carbon dioxide. If sufficient oxygen cannot be provided by various treatments, body tissues, especially in the brain, may be damaged. At the same time, treatment has substantial risks. Needed oxygen may damage the eyes and lungs. The force needed to mechanically inflate the lungs may also damage the lung tissue and contribute to brain hemorrhage by impeding blood flow out of the brain into the chest cavity.

Thus, the treatment of infants with severe RDS may create injury to vital tissue or perhaps only prolong dying. Once fatal damage has been done to the brain, lungs, or other organs, the remaining tissues may keep the body alive for untold hours, days, or weeks. Prior discussions of legal concerns in newborn medicine have not adequately emphasized the nature of the scientific difficulty in these cases, that of medical uncertainty. Doctors do not know enough about the nature of these diseases or the impact of the treatments to accurately assess or predict outcome in many individual cases. Neonatal experts cannot say at what point insufficient oxygen to the brain results in irrevocable injury. There is not sufficient information to decide how much, delivered with what force over what period of time, oxygen treatment may cause disabling lung or eye damage.

Similar difficulties exist with the entity called intraventricular hemorrhage (IVH). This condition involves bleeding in and around the fluid-filled cavities (ventricles) of the brain. IVH appears to be the result of multiple influences. Its cause not withstanding, IVH is "the most common and most serious neurologic disorder of preterm infants."[50] The damage and mortality depend on the location and extent of bleeding, among other factors.

Often sudden deterioration in the infant's overall condition accompanies IVH. The level of technologic effort required to save the baby's life may escalate substantially when bleeding occurs. Even when immediate measures are available to diagnose and assess the extent of hemorrhage, prediction of outcome is not accurate enough to allow most neonatologists to feel comfortable recommending withdrawal or limitation of treatment even with the severest bleeding. The uncertainty surrounding prognosis makes the job of obtaining fully informed consent for continued treatment problematic.

Fetal-Placental Disorders

Other problems associated with life-threatening illness where decision making may be difficult include abnormalities of the fetal-placental unit. For example, *placenta previa* involves the abnormal placement of the placenta in a location that may impede normal progress of the delivery for the baby but, more important, may cause sudden, serious bleeding. *Abruptio placenta* involves premature separation of the placenta from the wall of the uterus with possible severe hemorrhage and shock for mother and/or infant. In other circumstances, the umbilical cord connecting fetus and placenta may be prolapsed, i.e., enter the birth canal preceding the baby and become kinked, thus cutting off the infant's blood supply. The umbilical cord may also become wrapped and knotted around the infant's neck or limbs. In all of these situations, the common danger is disruption of adequate blood and, hence, oxygen to the baby, especially to the brain. All of these conditions may lead to considerable brain or other organ damage.

Birth Injury

Birth injuries also may result in critical illness. In infants weighing over 2500 grams at birth, injury incident to the birth process is the fourth most common cause of death. Counting for all births, birth injury is the eighth leading cause of death in the newborn period.[51] Short of death, severe injury to the brain or spinal cord may occur during delivery. Serious lifelong handicap may result. As with all the above conditions, even with careful assessment using the most sophisticated methods, accurate prognostication remains difficult much of the time.

Neural Tube Defects

Other medical conditions are the ones most people think of when considering neonatal moral dilemmas. These include the malformation and deformation syndromes. Malformations result from abnormal development inherent to the fetus; deformations come from physical restrictions external to the baby, as in abnormalities of the uterus.

Among the most frequent malformations are defects in the development of the central nervous system. These related disorders include anencephaly, where most or all of the head is absent; hydranencephaly, where the head may appear normal but most of the brain has not developed; and encephaloceles, where a portion of the skull has not closed normally and an outpouching of tissue is found with greater or lesser amounts of brain or other nervous tissue within. Anencephaly and hydranencephaly are defects incompatible with human life as we know it. Babies with encephaloceles may have normal or near normal lives or extensive mental and physical impairment, depending on the nature and location of the defect.

Also included in this spectrum of disorders is the relatively common defect *spina bifida cystica*. Here, a portion of the spinal cord and/or its coverings have failed to develop normally leaving a sac protruding from the back with varying amounts of nervous tissue enclosed. Depending on the type and location of the defect, disability may be trivial or severe. Of least clinical concern are meningoceles where no functioning nervous tissue is affected. Myelomeningoceles by definition include nerves. In these cases, the location of the defect is of greatest importance. The closer the opening to the head, the greater the disability. Myelomeningoceles involve handicaps of motor (muscular) function with permanent paralysis of the muscle groups, most commonly those used for walking and bowel and bladder control. When the bladder does not function adequately, recurrent infections of the urinary tract with eventual severe kidney damage or failure may result. In addition, sensation is usually impaired or absent below the level of the spinal defect.

The location of the defect is also related to the likelihood of hydrocephalus. The higher the spinal opening on the back, the more likely there will be impairment of the flow of fluid from within and around the brain to the canal surrounding the spinal cord. However, even 60 percent of those with a lower back defect develop hydrocephalus. When flow is blocked, placement of a shunt (plastic tubing from within the brain to the abdominal cavity) to divert the fluid is usually required to prevent excess head growth and damage to brain tissue from a buildup of pressure within the skull. Early shunting may prevent or minimize most intellectual impairment. In addition to actual nerve and muscle damage, the bony spine is abnormal. Again, depending on the location of the defect, the bony abnormality may lead to long-term difficulties with curvatures of the spine and progressive impairment of mobility, breathing, and/or cardiovascular function. The degree of eventual disability depends most on the location of the defect and then the effectiveness of treatment, including rehabilitation, available to the patient.

Surgical treatment of myelomeningocele involves closure of any open defects and covering of the area with skin or synthetic graft material. Surgery attempts to create a barrier to infection. Few argue that surgery has a role in restoring any neurologic function, though it may prevent deterioration of nerve tissue.[52] Immediate surgical repair may be medically indicated when the spinal tissue is exposed at birth. Other surgery, such as skin and bone grafting may be done electively, without urgency. But the controversy over the care of patients with myelomeningocele should not center on surgical considerations.

Those who argue for nontreatment of *spina bifida cystica* patients do so on grounds that the patient will suffer excessively because of the multiple handicaps mentioned above. Delay of surgery for babies with open wounds increases the likelihood of infection, which may in turn lead to death. Except when the spinal defect is so high on the back that nervous control of muscles involving breathing is affected, nothing about the disorder itself can be said to be immediately fatal. In the newborn period, if death does not result from nervous system infection, children provided fluids and nutrition rarely die of causes other than infection. Those children who receive no surgical treatment may have increasing head size over months and years, making good nursing care difficult. As stated above, in these cases of *spina bifida cystica*, life-threatening disorders requiring technologically sophisticated medical or surgical treatment are rare. Thus, allowing such patients to die involves the much more legally and psychologically problematic decision to withhold food and water.

Chromosomal Abnormalities

Another controversial group of patients are those born with defects in chromosomes, the microscopically visible genetic structures of cells. By far the most common and controversial of these disorders is Down's syndrome, or trisomy 21. The latter name refers to the presence of an extra or third chromosome known as chromosome 21. Down's syndrome occurs once in every 600-700 live births. The collected problems include decreased muscle tone, mental retardation, abnormalities of the eyelids, minor hand and foot malformations, reproductive disorders, congenital heart defects, increased risks of leukemia (approximately 1 percent of Down's syndrome patients), gastrointestinal anomalies, and defects of the thyroid gland.[53]

Of these problems, two may cause critical illness in the newborn period. In rare cases, the congenital heart disease will be life threatening in the first few days or weeks of life. The other condition that threatens life in the early days is the one that has received the greatest attention in the media. This defect consists of a blockage of the gastrointestinal tract, most commonly in the small intestine, but occurring elsewhere, especially in the esophagus with or without associated abnormalities of the airway. These obstructions require surgical correction for the baby to take nutrition by mouth. However, fluid and nutrition can be provided by vein prior to surgery and during the recovery phase for indefinite periods. Thus, surgery, while eventually life-enhancing or life-saving, is not urgent except under rare circumstances. Almost invariably there is time for physicians and parents to give careful consideration to the extent of medical and surgical intervention.

The controversy surrounding surgery for patients with Down's syndrome requires some clarification. Usually, the procedure to correct the obstruction carries little greater risk in Down's syndrome babies than in children with similar defects without the chromosomal abnormality. The decision to operate then turns, not on the gastrointestinal problem, but on the nature of the underlying chromosomal disorder. The question is whether the mental and other handicaps of the Down's syndrome patients justify a decision to withhold surgical repair. It should be noted that no methods now exist to accurately predict an individual baby's mental capacity. The intellectual development possible for Down's patients ranges from profound to mild retardation. Similarly, no means exist for predicting the risk of leukemia for individual patients. Thus, quality of life estimates cannot be made in the newborn period.

Trisomy 18 occurs once in 3000-3500 live births.[54] This disorder involves profound retardation, malformations of the ears, jaw, hands, and feet. More than half of the babies with this disorder have congenital heart defects. Many have cleft lips and/or palates. Life-threatening problems in these newborns may involve maldevelopment of the diaphragm (the muscle separating the chest and abdominal cavities) with associated lung defects. Abnormalities of the abdominal wall also occur, such that the abdominal contents remain partially or completely external to the cavity. Many infants with trisomy 18 have abnormal respiratory control and die with sudden cessation of breathing. Thirty percent of these patients die in the first month after birth, despite treatments provided; 50 percent die by two months. Only 10 percent survive more than a year and all survivors have severe mental impairment. The natural course of this disorder has led to little enthusiasm for correcting life-threatening problems discovered in the newborn period.

Trisomy 13 occurs approximately once in every 5000 live births.[55] Over half of the babies with this disorder have defects in the formation of the brain, skull, and face, including eyes. Neurologic problems include seizures, abnormal respiratory control, and severe mental retardation. Clefts of the palate and lip are common. Eighty percent have congenital heart disease. Similar to the trisomy 18 disorder, 45 percent of these patients die in the first month, nearly 70 percent in the first six months, and fewer than 20 percent survive a year. The survivors have severe retardation. There are few proponents of aggressive treatment of trisomy 13 newborns with life-threatening disorders.

Genetic Disorders

Other major diseases occur without chromosomal abnormalities, though some have clearly identified genetic defects. Some of these inherited disorders involve life-threatening or life-diminishing abnormalities of body chemistry and metabolism. A well-known and relatively common example is phenylketonuria (PKU). In this condition, occurring about once in every 15,000 live births, one of several enzymes needed for normal metabolism of protein constituents is abnormal.[56] As a result, one protein component, the amino acid phenylalanine, builds up to high levels in the blood. This excess phenylalanine exerts a toxic effect on the developing brain. Without restriction of foods (such as milk) rich in this amino acid, severe mental retardation results.

Simple and inexpensive blood testing of newborns for this disorder is mandatory in many states. Treatment involves major dietary restriction, which must be accomplished without excess deprivation of essential nutrients, including phenylalanine. The diets are expensive and psychologically difficult for child and parent, but effectively limit mental deficits if continued through the first six years of life. Diagnosis and treatment of this and similar disorders have not been legally or ethically controversial. However, other metabolic defects, like the self-mutilating Lesch-Nyhan syndrome, can be diagnosed early in life, but no effective therapy exists. Providing life-supportive therapy for patients with such inexorably progressive and lethal disorders may be seen as prolonging suffering and is more controversial in some medical circles.

Sporadic Malformations

Finally, another category of disorders occasions difficulties in decision making. These are the malformation syndromes without clear genetic bases, for example, children with some life-threatening congenital heart defects or those with multiple defects in many organ systems. Of those with heart disease, the most controversial group are patients with the hypoplastic left heart syndrome. In this group of heart defects, one or more of the parts of the heart necessary to pump oxygenated blood from the lungs to the rest of the body have not developed properly. Until very recently, no treatment provided even short-term prolongation of life. Children with this disorder died in days to weeks following birth.

Two surgical developments in the late 1970s and early 1980s were at the forefront of efforts at aggressive treatment. Dr. William Norwood, a pediatric cardiothoracic surgeon, developed a technique for using the normally developed right half of the heart to supply blood flow to the aorta and thus to the rest of the body. At the same time, oxygenated blood returning to the left heart is diverted to the right side. Thus far, few cardiothoracic surgeons other than the orginator have had much success with the Norwood procedure. In another direction, interest had been growing in the use of cardiac transplantation for infants with lethal heart defects. The refinement of techniques to suppress the rejection of "foreign" tissue led to major advances in organ transplantation by 1984, though there had been little experience with infants. However, confidence in immunosuppressive therapy convinced one surgical group, in late 1984, to attempt heart transplantation for hypoplastic left heart syndrome using a baboon heart. Clearly, changes in medical understanding and technology continue to raise questions about the limits of treatment for conditions only yesterday considered hopeless.

Similarly, children born with multiple, often very disfiguring, malformations of skull, facial structures, airways, etc., are now offered extensive treatment that has only recently been developed. This statement also holds true for conjoined twins, commonly called Siamese twins. Advances in life support for pre-, intra-, and postoperative care and developments in plastic and reconstructive surgery now make possible previously unthinkable treatment. Controversy surrounds such concerns as unavoidable "sacrifice" of one of the conjoined twins, the residual mental or other handicap following treatment, and the unknown, unforeseeable risks of medical innovation.

From a medical perspective, the decision to extend treatment to critically ill or severely impaired infants involves the same weighing of risks, harms, and benefits of treatment as with older children and adults. However, one factor renders the decision making uniquely difficult: the degree of medical uncertainty in newborn medicine. Physicians have not yet developed tools to adequately predict the effect of many neonatal disorders or their treatments. The difficulty in knowing outcome is particularly striking with regard to neurologic function. The adaptability of the newborn brain is only rudimentarily understood. The capacity of the newborn and developing infant to experience pain and suffering must also be better defined and considered. This great uncertainty makes it difficult for doctors to provide families, ethics committees, courts, or policy makers with adequate, prognostic information for informed decision making regarding critically ill newborns. Many of the legal and moral controversies may diminish if we can better define and subsequently balance the nature of the benefits and harms of medical intervention.

In the absence of clear-cut medical indications and contraindications to treatment, it is not surprising that clear guidelines for the treatment of critically ill or handicapped infants have not emerged and that pediatric euthanasia has been haphazard and perhaps arbitrary. The following cases illustrate the variety of court decisions when medical benefits are marginal or controversial. In 1972, a Maryland Down's syndrome infant with duodenal atresia died of starvation over a 15-day period after his parents refused consent for corrective surgery.[57] And in the April 1982 Bloomington, Indiana, Baby Doe case, the court refused to order life-saving surgery over parental objections for Infant Doe, who was born with Down's syndrome and tracheoesophageal fistula.[58] Yet, in *Maine Medical Center v. Houle*,[59] the court ordered treatment, over parental objections, for a brain-damaged infant born with no left eye, a rudimentary left ear with no ear canal, a malformed thumb, several fused vertebrae, and tracheoesophageal fistula that prevented his ingestion of food. In this same vein, the court overruled the parents and ordered surgery for a child born with spina bifida in *In re Cicero*.[60] Evidence in that case showed that with the surgery, the child could walk with braces but would have no bladder or bowel control and would be mentally retarded; without the surgery, she would not live beyond six months. In ordering the surgery, the court said that where there is a chance to live a useful, fulfilled life, parental inaction may not deny that chance. And the court also ordered treatment, over parental objection, in the case of Karen Ann McNulty,[61] who was born with congenital rubella. Karen had cataracts on both eyes, congenital heart failure, coarctation of the aorta, and respiratory problems. She was also mentally retarded and apparently deaf. In ordering the cardiac surgery, which has a 50-60 percent mortality rate, the court said: "If there is any life-saving treatment available it must be given regardless of quality of life that will result."

PROPOSED SOLUTIONS FOR THE IMPAIRED NEWBORN

Federal Legislation and Regulation

In response to the Bloomington Baby Doe case,[62] President Reagan sent a memorandum to Richard Schweiker, then Secretary of the Department of Health and Human Services (DHHS), instructing him to notify health care providers that Section 504 of the 1973 Rehabilitation Act[63] "forbids recipients of Federal funds from withholding from handicapped citizens, simply because they are handicapped, any benefit or services that would ordinarily be provided to persons without handicaps."[64] On May 18, 1982, the DHHS Office for Civil Rights issued a "Notice to Health Care Providers," which informed administrators of the nations' 6,800 hospitals that under Section 504 of the Rehabilitation Act, they risked losing federal funds if they withheld treatment or nourishment from handicapped infants. The Notice stated:

> "[I]t is unlawful ... to withhold from a handicapped infant nutritional sustenance or medical or surgical treatment required to correct a life-threatening condition if: 1) the withholding is based on the fact that the infant is handicapped; and 2) the handicap does not render the treatment or nutritional sustenance medically contraindicated.[65]

Several professional and medical organizations found the DHHS notice unnecessary and troublesome and took public stands against it. On May 18, 1982, for instance, the American Hospital Association issued a formal statement denying that "hospitals have in any way been guilty of discrimination" and promising to make every effort "to assure that such simplistic solutions to complex situations involving health care delivery are avoided."[66] And on June 21, the American Academy of Pediatrics released its position, saying that DHHS' effort "to solve this complex problem through strict interpretation and enforcement of the letter of Section 504 may have the unintended effect of requiring treatment that is *not* in the best interest of handicapped children."[67]

On March 2, 1983, DHHS issued an interim final rule requiring hospitals receiving federal funds to post in pediatric wards, nurseries, delivery rooms, and neonatal intensive care units warning signs saying "Discriminatory failure to feed and care for handicapped infants in this facility is prohibited by federal law. Failure to feed and care for infants may also violate the criminal and civil laws of your state."[68] The rule also established a 24-hour toll-free hotline to DHHS for the reporting of parents, physicians, and hospitals not in compliance with the regulations. The rule became effective on March 22, 1983, and anonymous calls to the DHHS hotline thereafter triggered the descent of DHHS nonmedical investigative teams upon numbers of hospitals. Soon after the proposal of this interim final rule, however, the American Academy of Pediatrics, the National Association of Children's Hospitals and Related Institutions, and Children's Hospital National Medical Center brought suit against DHHS and its Secretary, Margaret Heckler, challenging the rule. On April 14, 1983, Judge Gerhard Gesell of the United States District Court for the District of Columbia ruled that the interim final rule was invalid because, *inter alia*, (1) DHHS had failed to follow mandatory procedures for advance notice of and public comment on the rule; (2) the rule did not adequately define "customary medical care" vis-a-vis seriously handicapped infants; (3) the hotline was "ill considered" and could be seriously misused; (4) the DHHS investigators might jeopardize the quality of care in neonatal intensive care units; and (5) the rule was "arbitrary and capricious" and "virtually without meaning beyond its intrinsic in terrorem effect."[69]

In July 1983, the DHHS issued a virtually identical "revised" set of regulations, intended to become effective after the mandated 60-day comment period.[70] The final DHHS rule that emerged from the comment process continued the use of the hotline and the posted notices in hospitals, but the required notices were smaller and only needed to be posted so as to be visible to those directly affected (i.e., medical and nursing staff). The new rule stressed that Section 504 comes into effect "when non-medical considerations, such as subjective judgments that an unrelated handicap makes a person's life not worth living, are interjected in the decision-making process" and that the care of infants for whom treatment would be futile was exempt from the regulations. In addition, the new rule focused on the use of individual Infant Care Review Committees (ICRCs). Under the new rule, if a hospital had an ICRC, the first telephone number listed on the sign for reporting violations of Section 504 was the ICRC, followed by the state child protective services agency phone number and then the DHHS hotline. Upon receipt of a complaint, DHHS was to first contact the ICRC of the hospital in question, if one existed; and if DHHS desired an on-site investigation, such investigation would begin with a meeting between the ICRC (if one existed) and the DHHS official. Finally, under the new rule, state child protective services agencies were encouraged to consult with a hospital's ICRC whenever a report of suspected medical neglect was made pertaining to a hospital.[71]

While DHHS was preparing the final Baby Doe rule, Baby Jane Doe became the focus of controversy in the New York state and federal courts, testing the scope of DHHS's regulatory authority. Baby Jane Doe was born with multiple birth defects, including spina bifida, microcephaly (an abnormally small head), and hydrocephalus. Immediately after birth, the baby was transferred to Stony Brook University Hospital for surgery to correct her spina bifida and hydrocephalus. The surgery was likely to prolong her life, but it could not improve many of her disabling conditions, including severe mental retardation. After consulting with health care personnel, clergy, and others, the parents decided against the surgery in favor of "conservative" medical treatment—i.e., good nutrition, antibiotics, and dressing the exposed spinal sac. On October 16, 1983, an attorney brought suit in New York state court seeking the appointment of a guardian ad litem for Baby Jane Doe and an order directing the hospital to perform the surgery. The court appointed a guardian ad litem and ordered the surgery, but the appellate court reversed, and New York's highest court affirmed this reversal, saying that the case should never have been permitted to go forward.[72]

While the state proceeding was ongoing, DHHS received an anonymous complaint that Baby Jane Doe was being discriminatorily denied medical care in violation of Section 504 of the Rehabilitation Act. The Surgeon General determined that immediate access to Baby Jane Doe's records was necessary in order to determine whether her care was "within the bounds of legitimate medical judgment rather than based solely on a handicapping condition which is not a medical contraindication to surgical treatment" and DHHS requested that the hospital make these records available for inspection.[73] The hospital refused this request and the government filed suit in the Eastern District of New York, alleging that the hospital's refusal violated Section 504. The court found that the hospital's treatment of Baby Jane Doe did not violate Section 504 and that it did not have to disclose her medical records. In late February 1984, the Court of Appeals for the Second Circuit affirmed the district court's judgment denying the government access to Baby Jane Doe's records in a broadly written opinion holding that Section 504 does not apply to treatment decisions involving critically ill newborns.[74]

On March 12, 1984, the American Medical Association and five other groups filed suit in the United States District Court for the Southern District of New York against DHHS and Margaret Heckler, challenging the Baby Doe II Rule on the theory that the Second Circuit's decision rendered the rule invalid.[75] In May 1984, Judge Charles Brieant of the U.S. District Court for the Southern District of New York ruled in favor of the plaintiffs and invalidated the Baby Doe II Rule, calling the rule "invalid, unlawful, and without statutory authority."[76] Apparently because of pending Congressional action,[77] the Justice Department deferred appeal of Judge Brieant's order.

During the litigation regarding the Baby Doe regulations and the Baby Jane Doe case in New York, House and Senate bills on the issues were introduced in the 98th Congress. In late September 1984, a compromise agreement was reached to amend the Child Abuse Prevention and Treatment Act of 1974.[78] The Child Abuse Amendments of 1984 (Public Law 98-457) create a new category of child abuse and neglect, that of medical neglect. The law requires states to put mechanisms in place for child protective agencies "to pursue any legal remedies," including court proceedings, "as may be necessary to prevent the withholding of medically indicated treatment from disabled infants with life-threatening conditions."

Withholding indicated treatment is defined by the Act as the failure to "provide treatment (including appropriate nutrition, hydration, and medication) which, in the treating physician's or physicians' reasonable medical judgment, will be most likely to be effective in ameliorating or correcting all such [life-threatening] conditions." Physicians are exempt from this legal responsibility to treat when (1) "the infant is chronically and irreversibly comatose"; (2) the "treatment would (i) merely prolong dying, (ii) not be effective in ameliorating or correcting all of the infant's life-threatening conditions, or (iii) otherwise be futile in terms of the survival of the infant"; or (3) the treatment would be "virtually futile" and "under the circumstances would be inhumane."

The Act was signed by President Reagan on October 9, 1984, and on April 15, 1985, the Department of Health and Human Services issued final regulations to implement the Child Abuse Amendments and model guidelines for the establishment of infant care review committees.[79] The text and appendix of the regulations attempt to further define cases in which treatment may be withheld. The exemption of required treatment where treatment would "merely prolong dying" refers to situations where death will occur "in the near future" and does not include diseases that involve more lingering death, such as Tay-Sachs. The exemption for treatment that would be "virtually futile" and "under the circumstances inhumane" covers situations where treatment involves significant pain and suffering that clearly outweigh the potential benefits "for an infant highly unlikely to survive."

There are significant philosophical and procedural differences between the final Child Abuse Amendment regulations and the earlier Section 504 regulations. Since the earlier regulations were based on laws prohibiting discrimination against the handicapped, they focused on ensuring that handicapped infants were provided the same care as nonhandicapped infants. The new rules, however, are based on laws prohibiting child abuse, and instead focus on ensuring that handicapped infants are provided the best care for their circumstances. In addition, while the 504 regulations demanded federal intervention, with hotlines and investigative squads working out of Washington, D.C., the new regulations delegate intervention to state authorities. Some state child abuse programs utilize hotlines and investigations, so these devices may still be used in some instances. A state's failure to adhere to the regulations will result in loss of its federal child abuse funds.

Analysis

Both the regulatory and legislative efforts to govern selective nontreatment decisions described above fail because (1) their substantive aspects are unnecessary in some respects and oversimplified in other respects and (2) their procedural aspects are inappropriate, ineffectual, and damaging to parties involved in such medical treatment decisions and to society at large.

Neither the Section 504 Baby Doe regulations, the 1984 Amendments, nor the proposed Child Abuse Amendment regulations give substantive guidance to families, doctors, ethics committees, or courts faced with difficult neonatal decision making. As we have seen, prognostication in cases of critically ill newborns is often extremely difficult. There may be little agreement on what constitutes medically indicated therapy in individual cases. The diagnosis of "irreversible coma" is controversial, especially in neonatal neurology. Terms like "effective" and "virtually futile" have little useful meaning. The definitions and requirements of the law are necessarily so vague as to be entirely dependent on idiosyncratic interpretation. The effect of the legislation, then, is to create fear and risk on the part of parents, physicians, and health care administrators without providing medical, moral, or clear legal direction.

Treatment decisions for impaired infants are difficult and are best made, within the confines of state law, by parents, who bear responsibility for protecting the best interests of their children, and physicians, who have a legal and ethical role in identifying and then counseling parents about treatment options. DHHS's required notices, anonymous hotline, and threat of federal prosecution under the Section 504 regulations, and the investigative

"Baby Doe" squads envisioned in both the Section 504 Rule and, conceivably, in the implementing regulations for the Child Abuse Amendments, inhibit decision making by parents and physicians and are an affront to professional performance and commitment and to parental love. Only in instances where parents breach their responsibility to care for the child should state intervention occur. As one author has pointed out, adequate state legislation regarding child abuse and neglect (by parents) already governs situations where such breaches are suspected.[80]

Further damage is done by classifying allegedly inappropriate medical treatment decisions as "child abuse" in the federal legislation. Such classification creates an impression that our pediatricians are so prone to starve and passively kill infants born with disabilities that they must be policed by hospitals, their states, and the federal government. It is well to remember that these same physicians have developed the sophisticated technology for combating infants' impairments and have pioneered its use. The penalty for "child abuse" is a state's loss of federal anti-child abuse funds. Thus, a medical treatment decision that violates the federal law, if it is classified as child abuse, will not lead to better medical care for the impaired infant in question. Rather, redress will only lead to fewer federal funds for use by the state in which the child lives to fight child beating, sexual abuse of children, and other behavior that is more appropriately classified as "child abuse." The impaired infant medical treatment dilemma is inappropriately placed within the federal child abuse legislation.

Ethics Committees

Finally, we must consider the procedural recommendation made by Congress and increasingly popular as an answer to the impaired infant medical treatment dilemma in medical, bioethics, and legal circles: institutional ethics committees. Under varying proposals, including the final version of the Section 504 Baby Doe regulations and the final regulations implementing the 1984 Child Abuse Amendments, such interdisciplinary committees would prospectively and/or retrospectively review treatment decisions agreed upon between parents and attending physicians. The committee meeting would provide a forum for the discussion of treatment concerns by those involved in the infant's case. The committee's consensus emerging from this discussion could lead to institutional acceptance or approval of the committee's advice or, in other cases, to a referral to child protective agencies or the courts.[81]

The attraction of these review panels would be easy and immediate access by parents or doctors seeking advice; "local control" with presumed good understanding of the medical, social, and other circumstances of the case and community resources; and less cumbersome, expensive, and disruptive review than might be accomplished by government bureaucracy or in the courts. Another advantage cited by proponents is that committees could relieve some of the emotional burden on stressed parents and/or committed physicians. In addition, some contend that dispassionate review by knowledgeable, impartial, emotionally stable, consistent committee members is superior to decision making by involved families and doctors.[82]

Nevertheless, important questions must be raised about the prospect of institutional review committees being "the" answer for the disabled infant dilemma. As we have seen, defining which cases would come up for review poses no small feat. Even assuming that committees would become involved only when a baby was suffering from a life-threatening condition and withdrawal or refusal of treatment was at issue, it is not clear what level of impairment would permit parents or physicians to agree to forego life-saving treatment. Take, for instance, the situation of a child with trisomy 18 and tracheoesophageal fistula, where the trachea and esophagus have an abnormal connection and the esophagus does not connect with the stomach. Most babies with this disorder die in the first few months of life, regardless of treatment. Would surgical repair "merely prolong dying?" Even if not operating were permissible under law, what are the limits of "appropriate nutrition, hydration, or medication," not excepted by the law?

Debate also surrounds the status of the review committees. What legal standing do they have? If the committee recommends a course of action contrary to that agreed upon by the family and the doctors, what are the obligations of the various parties? Must the committee contact child protective agencies, the district attorney, recommend that hospital administration seek court supervision of the baby's care, etc.?

There are other overriding concerns as well. It is a truism in sociological and political science that committee process tends to produce solutions to problems that minimize conflict within the group. Such an outcome, however, does not necessarily speak to the best interests of an impaired infant. Reinforcement for this skepticism arises from recent questions about the value of institutional review boards for research on human subjects.[83] We must be wary that decisions or recommendations from ethics committees will have more to do with power and authority in the institution and the community or economic considerations (such as Diagnostic Related Groups reimbursement schemes) than the upholding of moral or legal standards. This is especially true since physicians and others on such committees are likely to have minimal expertise in ethics. The popular notion that philosophy as applied to medicine can be "practiced" by anyone stands in stark contrast to an insistence in high-technology medical circles on subspecialty mastery of ever smaller areas of knowledge.

CONCLUSION

The birth of a critically ill infant may present parents and physicians with agonizing medical treatment dilemmas. The normal instinct to treat may conflict with fears of harm that such treatment may cause. To avoid such suffering, physicians may consider or parents may request withholding or withdrawal of treatment. The future of many impaired infants is very difficult to predict. For others, who are awaiting imminent and unavoidable death, it is often unclear what measures should be used to maintain comfort during the dying process. There is disagreement about the proper course of action in many of these cases, and legal requirements are not yet clear. In order for intelligent legal guidance to emerge, our society needs to develop a clearer consensus and, subsequently, social policy regarding the treatment of impaired infants.

While they are not a panacea for all ethical dilemmas, hospital ethics committees may play a useful role in generating discussion of the difficult medical, moral, and legal problems involving treatment of the critically ill infant. Until a more definitive societal consensus regarding the impaired infant emerges, examination of such cases of multidisciplinary institutional ethics committees increases the probability that such treatment decisions are informed and consistent with the broadest moral values of our society.

NOTES

1. Roth & Wild, *When the Patient Refuses Treatment: Some Observations and Proposals for Handling the Difficult Case*, 23 ST. LOUIS U.L.J. 429, 432 (1979). In Schloendorff v. Soc'y of N.Y. Hosp., 211 N.Y. 125, 129, 105 N.E. 92, 93 (1914), Judge Cardozo stated that "[e]very human being of adult years and sound mind has a right to determine what shall be done with his own body." And in Erickson v. Dilgard, 44 Misc.2d 27, 28, 252 N.Y.S.2d 705, 706 (Sup. Ct. 1962), the court said: "[T]he Court concludes that it is the individual who is the subject of a medical decision who has the final say and that this must necessarily be so in a system of government which gives the greatest possible protection to the individual in the furtherance of his own desires."

2. Brant, *Last Rights: An Analysis of Refusal and Withholding of Treatment Cases*, 46 ME. L. REV. 337, 341 (1981).

3. *Id.*

4. Clarke, *The Choice to Refuse or Withhold Medical Treatment: The Emerging Technology and Medical-Ethical Consensus*, 13 CREIGHTON L. REV. 795, 800 (1980).

5. *See* Superintendent of Belchertown State School v. Saikewicz, 373 Mass. 728, 370 N.E.2d 417 (1977) [hereinafter cited as Saikewicz]; In re Quinlan, 70 N.J. 10, 355 A.2d 647, *cert. denied*, 429 U.S. 922 (1976). In Griswold v. Connecticut, 381 U.S. 479 (1965), the Supreme Court declared that the unwritten constitutional right of privacy exists in the penumbra of specific guarantees of the Bill of Rights "formed by emanations from those guarantees that help give them life and substance." *Id.* at 484.

6. Saikewicz, 373 Mass. at 742, 370 N.E.2d at 426.

7. Courts should not leave young children destitute by allowing their parents to die. In re President & Directors of Georgetown College 331 F.2d 1000, 1008 (D.C. Cir.), *cert. denied*, 377 U.S. 978 (1964); *see* Byrn, *Compulsory Life-Saving Treatment for the Competent Adult*, 44 FORDHAM L. REV. 1, 33 (1975).

8. Saikewicz, 373 Mass. at 741, 370 N.E.2d at 425. These four interests were derived from In re President & Directors of Georgetown College, 331 F.2d 1000 (D.C. Cir.), *cert. denied*, 377 U.S. 978 (1964).

9. A dying, competent adult's refusal of medical treatment does not constitute suicide and does not threaten the integrity of the medical profession. It is not suicide because in refusing treatment, the patient may not have the specific intent to die. Moreover, even if he did have such an intent, to the extent that the cause of death was from natural causes, the patient did not set in motion the death-producing agent with the intent of causing his own death. *See* Byrn, *supra* note 7, at 17-18. Furthermore, such refusal does not threaten the state's interest in protecting the integrity of the medical profession, because prevailing medical ethical practice recognizes that the dying often are more in need of comfort than of treatment. Eichner v. Dillon, 73 A.D.2d 431, 426 N.Y.S.2d 517, 541-42 (1980); *see* Saikewicz, 373 Mass. at 742, 370 N.E.2d at 426.

10. Saikewicz, 373 Mass. at 741-42, 370 N.E.2d at 425-26.

11. *Id.* at 373 Mass. 745, 370 N.E.2d 427.

12. 70 N.J. 10, 55, 355 A.2d 647, 671-72, *cert. denied*, 429 U.S. 922 (1976).

13. *Id.* at 55, 355 A.2d at 671.

14. 373 Mass. 728, 752, 370 N.E.2d 417, 431 (1977).

15. *Id.* at 758, 370 N.E.2d at 434.

16. *Id.* at 759, 370 N.E.2d at 435.

17. 8 Mass. App. Ct. 831, 850, 399 N.E.2d 493, 502-03 (1979).

18. 380 Mass. 629, 633, 405 N.E.2d 115, 117 (1980).

19. 70 N.J. 10, 355 A.2d 647, *cert. denied*, 429 U.S. 922 (1976).

20. *Id.* at 51, 355 A.2d at 669.

21. *Id.* at 39, 355 A.2d at 663.

22. Saikewicz, 373 Mass. at 750-52, 370 N.E.2d at 430-31.

23. *Id.* at 753, 370 N.E.2d at 431.

24. 380 Mass. 629, 405 N.E.2d 115 (1980).

25. Wisconsin v. Yoder, 406 U.S. 205 (1972) (right of Amish to educate their children); Pierce v. Soc'y of Sisters, 268 U.S. 510, 534-35 (1925) (right to choose parochial schools over public schools); *see* United States v. Orito, 413 U.S. 139 (1973) (right of privacy extends to certain aspects of family relationship).

26. Prince v. Massachusetts, 321 U.S. 158, 160 (1944).

27. *Supra* note 2, at 362-63 (1981).

28. *See* Goldstein, Freud & Solnit, *Refusal by Parents to Authorize Lifesaving Medical Care*, in BEFORE THE BEST INTERESTS OF THE CHILD (1979); Capron, *The Authority of Others To Decide About Biomedical Interventions with Incompetents*, WHO SPEAKS FOR THE CHILD (W. Gaylin & R. Macklin, 1982).

29. In re Clark, 21 Ohio Op.2d 86, 90, 185 N.E.2d 128, 132 (1962).

30. *See, e.g.*, Custody of a Minor, 375 Mass. 733, 379 N.E.2d 1053 (1978) (ordering chemotherapy for leukemia-stricken child over parental objections); John F. Kennedy Memorial Hosp. v. Heston, 58 N.J. 576, 279 A.2d 670 (1971) (ordering transfusions for 22-year-old comatose patient over parental objections).

31. Custody of a Minor, 375 Mass. 733, 379 N.E.2d 1053 (1978).
32. 278 F. Supp. 488 (W.D. Wash. 1967), aff'd, 390 U.S. 598 (1968).
33. 411 Ill. 618, 104 N.E.2d 769, cert. denied, 344 U.S. 824 (1952).
34. 58 N.J. 576, 279 A.2d 670 (1971).
35. In re Hamilton, 657 S.W.2d 425 (Tenn. App. 1983).
36. Custody of a Minor, 378 Mass. 732, 393 N.E.2d 836 (1979).
37. Id. at 746, 393 N.E.2d at 845.
38. 199 N.W.2d 147 (Iowa 1972).
39. 85 Misc. 2d 846, 380 N.Y.S.2d 620 (1970).
40. 175 Misc. 948, 25 N.Y.S.2d 624 (1941).
41. 47 N.Y.2d 648, 393 N.E.2d 1009, 419 N.Y.S.2d 936 (1979).
42. 309 N.Y. 80, 127 N.E.2d 820 (1955).
43. Parental objections in In re Seiferth were based on a "philosophy" that there are "forces in the universe" that would close the cleft. The child apparently agreed with this philosophy and did not want the surgery.
44. 12 CRIME & DELINQ. 377 (Child Div., Milwaukee County Ct., Wis. 1966).
45. 385 Mass. 697, 434 N.E.2d 601 (1982).
46. 445 So.2d 365 (Fla. App. 2 Dist. 1984).
47. Behmran, *The Field of Neonatal-Perinatal Medicine*, in NEONATAL-PERINATAL MEDICINE (A. Fanaroff & R. Martin 3d ed. 1983) [hereinafter cited as NEONATAL-PERINATAL MEDICINE].
48. Sinclair & Tudehope, *Birth Weight, Gestational Age, and Neonatal Risk*, in NEONATAL-PERINATAL MEDICINE supra note 47.
49. Martin, Fanaroff, & Skalina, *The Respiratory Distress Syndrome and Its Management*, in NEONATAL-PERINATAL MEDICINE, supra note 47.
50. Brann Schwartz, & Schwartz, *Central Nervous System Disturbances*, in NEONATAL-PERINATAL MEDICINE, supra note 47.
51. Mangurten, *Birth Injuries*, in NEONATAL-PERINATAL MEDICINE, supra note 47.
52. Brann, supra note 50.
53. D. SMITH, RECOGNIZABLE PATTERNS OF HUMAN MALFORMATION (3d ed., 1982).
54. Id.
55. Id.
56. Nicholson, *Inborn Errors of Metabolism*, in NEONATAL-PERINATAL MEDICINE, supra note 47.
57. See Rowe, *Infanticide: Who Makes the Decision?*, 73 WIS. MED. J. 10 (May 1974).
58. In re Guardianship of Infant Doe, No. 1-782 A157 (Ind., April 14, 1982).
59. No. 74-145 (Super. Ct., Cumberland County, Me., Feb. 14, 1974).
60. 101 Misc. 2d 669, 421 N.Y.S.2d 965 (1979).
61. In re McNulty, No. 1960 (Probate Ct., Essex County, Mass.) (February 15, 1978).
62. See discussion of the case at page 78, infra.
63. 29 U.S.C. §794 (Supp. V, 1981), Section 504 of the Rehabilitation Act of 1973 states: "No otherwise qualified handicapped individual... shall, solely by reason of his handicap, be excluded from the participation in, be denied the benefits of, or be subjected to discrimination under any program or activity receiving Federal financial assistance...."

64. Smith, *Handicapped Newborns: Current Issues and Legislation,* CONG. RES. SERV. REP. (July 28, 1982).

65. Discriminating Against the Handicapped by Withholding Treatment or Nourishment; Notice to Health Care Providers, 47 Fed. Reg. 26,027 (June 16, 1982).

66. News release of the American Hospital Association, May 18, 1982.

67. Official statement of the American Academy of Pediatrics, June 21, 1982.

68. Interim Final Rule, Nondiscrimination on the Basis of Handicap, 48 Fed. Reg. 9,630-9,632 (March 7, 1983) (to be codified at 45 C.F.R. pt. 84).

69. American Academy of Pediatrics v. Heckler, 561 F. Supp. 395 (D. D.C. 1983). *See also* Annas, *Disconnecting the Baby Doe Hotline,* 3 HASTINGS CTR. REP. 14-16 (1983).

70. Nondiscrimination on the Basis of Handicap Relating to Health Care for Handicapped Infants, 48 Fed. Reg. 30,846-30,852 (1983).

71. Final Rule, Nondiscrimination on the Basis of Handicap, 49 Fed. Reg. 1,622 (Jan. 12, 1984).

72. Weber v. Stony Brook Hosp., 456 N.E.2d 1186 (N.Y. 1983).

73. United States v. Univ. Hosp., 729 F.2d 144, 147 (2d Cir. Feb. 23, 1984).

74. United States v. Univ. Hosp., 729 F.2d 144 (2d Cir. Feb. 23, 1984).

75. *See* American Medical Ass'n et al. v. Margaret M. Heckler, IP 84-1317C (1984).

76. *Id.*

77. *See* discussion at pages 79-80, *infra.*

78. Pub. L. 98-457.

79. 45 C.F.R. pt. 1340 (April 15, 1985). The model committee guidelines encourage hospitals to establish committees to educate hospital personnel and families of disabled infants with life-threatening conditions; to recommend institutional policies regarding withholding medical care from such infants; and to offer counsel in cases involving disabled infants with life-threatening conditions.

80. Holder, *Parents, Courts and Refusal of Treatment,* 103 J. PEDIATR. 515-21 (1983).

81. It has been suggested that states enact statutes to protect impaired infant medical treatment decisions that are concurred in by parents, attending physicians, and hospital ethics committees. In cases where parents and attending physicians and/or the ethics committee disagree, the matter would be expeditiously heard by a state Medical Treatment Panel comprised of a physician, a hospital administrator, an attorney, and two public members. The Panel decision could be appealed to the circuit court. *See* Shapiro, *Medical Treatment of Defective Newborns: An Answer to the "Baby Doe" Dilemma,* 20 HARV. J. ON LEGIS. 137 (Winter 1983).

82. R. WEIR, SELECTIVE NONTREATMENT OF HANDICAPPED INFANTS (1984).

83. Goldman & Katz, *Inconsistency and Institutional Review Boards,* 248 J. A.M.A. 197-202 (1982).

Chapter 5

The Economics of Intensive Care Units

Judith R. Lave and William A. Knaus

After two decades of rapid and largely unquestioned growth, the American medical system is entering a period where investment in new services and the value of existing practices will be carefully evaluated. This evaluation will take place because there is an increased perception that the large annual increases in the cost of medical care should be reduced and that the total amount of money provided for health care services could be allocated more judiciously.

In this time of change and increasing resource constraints, the practice of intensive care will receive special attention. Intensive care has grown rapidly; the cost of care provided while patients are in intensive care units now accounts for a large portion of total hospital costs. Yet fundamental questions concerning the scope and value of intensive care remain unanswered. This increased scrutiny will influence the medical and legal atmosphere in which intensive care is practiced.

This chapter will review some of the economic aspects of intensive care in the United States, its rapid expansion, and its current costs. It will then explain how new approaches to financing hospital care may influence intensive care practice. Finally, it will offer some suggestions that represent a positive response to new financial constraints.

THE GROWTH IN INTENSIVE CARE

Postoperative recovery rooms, the forerunners of modern intensive care units, were introduced in this country in the 1940s; coronary care units in the 1960s.[1] The most rapid growth in intensive care units, however, occurred during the past 20 years. In 1965, only 28.6 percent of the short-term hospitals had an intensive care unit. By 1982, 29 percent of these hospitals had a cardiac intensive care unit and 76.2 percent had a mixed intensive care unit. In 1972, the first year for which bed counts for intensive care units were available, 4 percent of total short-term hospital beds were ICU beds. By 1982, ICU beds accounted for 7.2 percent of all short-term hospital beds. In fact, 28.5 percent of the total increase in bed supply between 1972 and 1982 was in intensive care beds. The *types* of intensive care units have also proliferated. Some hospitals place all of their critically ill patients in a single unit; others use more specialized units such as medical, surgical, neurological, and respiratory ICUs.

The growth of intensive care relative to total hospital beds in the United States is represented in Table 5-1, which shows the increase in beds categorized by coronary care units and mixed general medical and surgical including pediatric, neonatal intensive care beds and burn unit beds.[2] (The pediatric beds are included with CCU/ICU beds because they were reported together prior to 1979.) From 1972 to 1982, ICU/CCU beds increased from 35,577 to 64,160 or at an annual rate of 6.2 percent; i.e., more than four times the 1.4 percent annual growth rate of all hospital beds. As a result, ICU/CCU beds increased from 4 percent of total beds to 6.3 percent, whereas all ICU beds increased from 4.8 percent to 7.2 percent. (Beds devoted to neonatal intensive care or to burn care may have been reported as ICU beds since they were not separately identified.) Hereafter, unless otherwise indicated, the term ICU will be used to represent all types of intensive care unit beds.

Intensive care units are now in hospitals of all sizes. Virtually every hospital with 100 beds or more has an ICU and more than 60 percent of hospitals with less than 100 beds also have one (Table 5-2). Since the large hospitals generally treat sicker and more complicated patients,[3] the proportion of ICU beds increases with the size of the hospital (Table 5-2).

FACTORS ASSOCIATED WITH THE GROWTH OF ICU/CCU BEDS

The rapid growth of ICUs is due to a number of factors. These include the changing character of American medical practice, the "technological imperative," and methods of financing medical services. Each is discussed below.

Regardless of the type of unit, a patient is admitted to the ICU for one of three reasons: (1) an immediate need for one or more of the approximately 35 active life-support therapies now routinely available and best performed within ICUs; (2) the need for continued observation and/or monitoring because the patient is perceived to be at risk of quickly needing one or more life-saving therapies; or (3) a perceived need for intensive nursing care not available on the general ward.

Table 5-1 Growth of Beds in Intensive Care Units of Short-Term Hospitals*—1972–1982

Year	Total Beds	Coronary Care Units and Other Intensive Care Beds	ICU Beds As % of Total	Neonatal Intensive Care Beds	Burn Beds	All ICU Beds % of Total
1972	883,681	35,577	4.0%	—	—	4.0%
1973	903,324	39,884	4.4	—	—	4.4
1974	931,172	42,048	4.6	—	—	4.6
1975	946,976	45,312	4.8	—	—	4.8
1976	961,175	47,540	4.9	6,477	—	5.6
1977	973,866	50,474	5.2	7,595	—	6.0
1978	979,659	52,811	5.4	6,404	—	6.0
1979	987,687	54,365	5.5	6,718	1,481	6.3
1980	992,020	58,140	5.9	6,305	1,376	6.6
1981	1,003,435	62,021	6.2	6,671	1,359	7.0
1982	1,015,180	64,160	6.3	7,496	1,416	7.2
Annual rate of growth 1972–1982	1.4%	6.2%				

*These beds include pediatric intensive care beds which were first reported separately in 1979.

Source: American Hospital Association, Hospital Statistics, various years. These data have been adjusted for nonreporting hospitals.

Table 5-2 Distribution of Intensive Care Beds in Short Term Non Federal Hospitals by Size of Hospital*—1982

Hospital Bed Size	Percent Hospitals with ICU	Percent Hospitals with CCU	ICU/CCU beds as a % of beds	All ICU beds as a % of beds
100 or less	28%	52%	3.8%	4.9%
100 – 199	18	90	5.2	6.5
200 – 299	45	98	6.0	7.3
300 – 399	65	98	6.0	7.7
400 – 499	77	98.5	6.0	7.9
500 or more	84	98.7	6.8	8.7

*ICUs excluding pediatric, neonatal, and burn.

Source: Statistics in table were compiled from data in *Hospital Statistics 1983*, American Hospital Association, ©1983.

As American medicine has changed, the number of patients in each of these categories has increased. The development and increased availability of new life-support techniques, ventilators, dialysis machines, intra-aortic balloon pumps, powerful vasoactive drugs, etc., have expanded the number of patients eligible for ICU admission. Furthermore, the physiologic abnormalities treated by these techniques are common to a wide variety of both medical and surgical diagnoses. More aggressive management of life-threatening trauma and the recent upsurge in new complex operations, such as open heart surgery, aggressive surgery for cancer, and organ transplantation, have also increased the demand for intensive care as patients recuperating from these conditions require sophisticated monitoring during the immediate postoperative period. The greater availability of sophisticated electrocardiographic and other monitoring practices has increased the number of "stable" patients for whom an ICU admission provides an additional measure of insurance.

Growth in intensive care also has been encouraged by what Fuchs has termed the "technological imperative"[4]—a social and medical tradition that emphasizes giving the best care that is technologically possible. The only legitimate and recognized constraint is the state-of-the-art! In addition, physicians have been trained to try and are rewarded by trying everything. This has benefited many persons. For some critically or terminally ill patients, however, this has meant more intensive and prolonged suffering during the last days of life. This idea has been expressed poetically by T.S. Eliot in *The Family Reunion:*

Not for the good that it will do but that nothing may be left undone
on the margin of the impossible[5]

Government and other third party funding sources for intensive care also have encouraged the growth of ICUs. Patients have been shielded from the cost of intensive care because they hold extensive health insurance that covers almost all of their costs.[6] In addition, insurance policies reimburse physicians more for undertaking procedures than for taking *time* to advise, consult, and care for the patient. Until recently, hospitals have been reimbursed for the services provided primarily on the basis of incurred costs or posted charges. The combination of the patient who is not concerned about cost, the physician who is trained and financially rewarded to do everything to sustain life, and the hospital that could recover costs and increase "profits" by building more ICUs sets the stage for continued expansion of intensive care services.

Government regulatory actions stimulated this growth further.[7] Under the Medicare reimbursement policy in existence from 1974 to 1982, limits were set on the amount of money Medicare would pay for routine hospital care (i.e., the costs of room, board, and nursing care rendered on a regular floor). These limits were significantly tightened in 1979. Since Medicare pays for approximately 27 percent of all hospital care, it was in the hospitals' financial interest to shift the relatively sicker Medicare patients to intensive care units where the full cost of care could be recovered more easily.

Finally, the concentration of both therapeutic and monitoring techniques in the intensive care unit encouraged many highly trained nursing graduates to seek ICU positions. This has helped to create the impression that the only reliable place to obtain adequate nursing care (which is frequently all many ICU patients need) is in an ICU. Thus, patients may be placed or kept in an ICU when they could do as well on the general floor.

There have been few analyses describing the rapid growth of ICUs and no statistical studies to determine the relative importance of the factors influencing their growth. A pioneering study by Russell[8] on the diffusion of ICUs indicated that, as expected, (1) large teaching hospitals were the first to adopt intensive care units; (2) voluntary hospitals adopted them before either public or proprietary institutions; and (3) their adoption was stimulated by grants made under the Regional Medical Programs. A more recent study by Cromwell and Kanak looked at the effect of various regulatory programs on the growth of ICUs.[9] The study showed that certificate-of-need programs (i.e., programs that require the approval of a state agency before a hospital can add a new service or acquire expensive new equipment) had no effect on the diffusion of ICUs. However, the study also showed that the existence of statewide hospital prospective payment systems slowed down the diffusion of ICUs.

THE EFFECTIVENESS OF INTENSIVE CARE

It is difficult to evaluate the effectiveness of intensive care or to separate the nature of care from the setting in which it is provided. The patient population is heterogeneous, and this complicates the ability to make any general observations about effectiveness. There have been no clinical trials in which patients were randomly allocated to an ICU or to general ward care; therefore, no confident estimates of the benefits and associated costs exist. Further, many of the individual therapies used in an ICU have not been subject to systematic evaluation.[10]

In March 1983, the National Institutes of Health (NIH) held a consensus development conference on critical care. One of the issues addressed was the nature of the empirical evidence that care provided in the ICU actually decreases patient morbidity or mortality. The conference participants concluded that for a large proportion of patients evidence is equivocal. Nonetheless, the weight of clinical opinion is that ICU care improves survival. It was also pointed out that for some patients, the risk of iatrogenic illness associated with ICU care may outweigh the benefits.[11]

The NIH panel noted that the relative effectiveness of ICU care differed by patient type. Three categories of patients were identified: (1) patients with acute reversible diseases (such as those with respiratory failure due to drug overdose) whose probability of survival is low without ICU intervention but high with it; (2) patients with a low probability of survival without intensive care, but for whom the potential benefit of ICU intervention is not clear; and (3) patients admitted to the ICU because they are at risk of becoming critically ill and requiring a prompt response to a potentially fatal complication—a response made possible by continuous monitoring of need for care and availability of specialized personnel to provide it.

The panel gave no indication of the relative size of each group. The distribution of patients in each category differs by type of hospital and unit. For example, a comparison study of a teaching hospital with a community hospital found that proportionally more patients were admitted for monitoring to the community hospital's ICU than to the teaching hospital's ICU.[12] In addition, a study of 2,613 consecutive admissions to medical ICU/CCUs at the Massachusetts General Hospital showed that 77 percent were admitted for monitoring.[13] By contrast, a study of 624 admissions to a multispecialty medical/surgical ICU at George Washington Medical Center (the hospital had a separate CCU) found that only 46 percent were admitted for monitoring.[14] In addition, the boundaries between the three groups are not clear-cut. With this background we discuss each of the three groups briefly.

There is little doubt that ICU treatment for most patients in group 1 is essential. However, these patients make up only a small proportion of patients in an ICU today.

Group 2 patients comprise a significant proportion of patients now admitted for treatment to an ICU. For this group, the benefits are less clear and the potential for harm and wasted spending is greater. As experience with intensive care has grown, it has become increasingly clear that the unique service an ICU provides, temporary correction of acute physiological abnormalities, is not, by itself, curative. This therapy buys time, time during which diagnosis can be established and treatment given to the primary disease. When patients with long-standing, poorly treated, or untreatable illnesses are admitted to ICUs, the efficacy of intensive care is limited. Failure to recognize these limits has been and still continues to be very frustrating for professionals working in intensive care units and for many of their patients. This is an area where further research into prognosis and outcome can provide substantial benefit.[15]

Group 3 patients not only comprise the majority of patients in the ICU but they also have been responsible for much of the growth of ICUs. The types of patients admitted for monitoring will vary from hospital to hospital. For example, in the comparison study of a university and a community hospital referred to above, it was found that at the former institution most surgical patients admitted to an ICU were neurological and cardiovascular patients; those in the latter facility were largely gastrointestinal patients. This difference was reflected in the extent to which patients needed an ICU intervention: 86 percent of the surgical patients in the community hospital received only monitoring or routine floor care during their initial 24 hours in the ICU, compared with 48 percent of those in the university hospital.[16] Clearly, the efficacy of intensive care will depend on the types of patients who are admitted to the unit.

Most analyses of the efficacy of intensive care have focused on its effect on patient mortality. However, the use of patient survival as the only outcome measure is frequently questioned. Many patients, for example, whose deaths are averted, survive only for a short period of time or survive to live a life of greatly reduced quality.[17] Nevertheless, it is reasonable to begin the analysis of ICU effectiveness with reduced mortality rates as the output measure. (In such an analysis, however, the analysts must control for the types of patients being treated.) Later information concerning quality and length of survival can and should be added. Indeed, from many existing surveys, it is possible to estimate the post-hospital survival rates of most types of ICU patients when information is available on their primary disease.[18]

COST OF INTENSIVE CARE

The NIH Consensus Development Conference on Critical Care Medicine established criteria for equipment and staff support for intensive care units.[19] The panel recommended that all intensive care units should have a physician identified as director of patient care and as administrator of the unit. It also recommended that specially trained nurses should be employed and that there should be one nurse for every one to three patients. In addition, the unit should provide a wide range of technological services, with the help of expert medical subspecialists and ancillary personnel. The unit should have access to 24-hour acute laboratory services. The cost of staffing and equipping units meeting these standards would be very high.

It is, however, difficult to determine the real cost associated with such care. Obviously, if intensive care units had never been developed, patients who are now in these units would have been treated in the wards. Many of the technologies that are concentrated in special units would be distributed throughout the hospital. As noted above, there have been no clinical trials in which patients were randomly allocated to an ICU or to ward care. Thus, estimates of the incremental costs and associated benefits have not been made. There is some evidence to suggest, however, that clinically similar patients are treated differently on the floor than in the ICU; in the latter, they are likely to receive more procedures.[20]

In estimating the aggregate costs associated with providing ICU care, most analysts have tended to examine charge data from the patient's bill. The average charge for a day in an intensive care unit—excluding the charges of ancillary services received while the patient is in the room—is roughly 2.5 times higher than that for a semiprivate room. This ratio has remained remarkably stable since 1975.[21] However, these data have limitations since billed prices may not reflect actual costs.[22] In particular, charge data may understate the true relative cost differences as many hospitals reduce ICU room and board charges relative to charges for regular beds. The extent of this reduction is not known.[23]

Piecing together information from various studies, Wagner et al. estimate that a day in the ICU is on average 3.8 times more expensive than a day in a regular bed.[24] (The day in the ICU is more expensive both because of the high cost associated with the unit and because the patients are sicker than ward patients and consequently they use more ancillary services.) Using reasonable assumptions, e.g., that the occupancy rate in intensive care units is on *average* lower than that on the regular floor,[25] they estimate that between 19 and 21 percent of the total cost of inpatient care is incurred while patients are in an intensive care unit, even though ICU days represent only 5.8 percent of total inpatient days.

Table 5-3 Resource Allocations among 4152 ICU Patients in 13 Tertiary Care Hospitals

Patient Category	Proportion of Patients	Proportion of Total TISS Points*
Patients who only were monitored first day	27.9%	9.0%
Patients actively treated first day	72.1	91.0
Some characteristics of a subset of these patients		
ICU died (no code)#	(4.2)	(11.6)
Other ICU deaths	(5.2)	(20.3)
Patient with both severe chronic and acute illness	(3.4)	(6.0)

These deaths exclude those among patients with both severe chronic and acute illness of whom 47 percent died while in the ICU.

* TISS Points measure the amount of resource use while in the ICU. See notes 27 and 28. Resource costs are measured by the number of TISS points a patient receives. (TISS assigns a score of 1 to 4 to a listing of therapeutic tasks routinely performed on ICU patients.)

Source: Adapted from "Improving the Productivity of Intensive Care: A National Sample" by D.P. Wagner, E.A. Draper, and W.A. Knaus, a paper presented at the NBER Conference on Productivity in Health, Stanford, California, 1983.

Further analysis of ICU patient care costs shows, not surprisingly, that (1) the more severely ill a patient, the more costly is the care rendered and (2) a large proportion of the costs are incurred by a small proportion of the patients.[26] This concentration of costs is documented in a recent study by Wagner, et al., one of the few studies reporting data from multiple sites.[27] Table 5-3 shows the distribution of the resource costs for 4,152 admissions to the ICUs in the 13 tertiary care hospitals that participated in the study.[28] Patients were classified by the type of care they received on the first day in the ICU, their risk of needing unique ICU services, and their survival. The data indicate that a significant proportion of the total patients (28 percent) received only monitoring services their first day in the ICU and that collectively they used 9 percent of the ICU resources allocated to all patients. The majority were at low risk of need for ICU services. On the other hand, the most seriously ill patients (those who died) represented only 9.4 percent of the patient population but received approximately 32 percent of total ICU resources. These data may reflect a need for intermediate monitoring units to provide care at lower cost than a fully staffed and equipped ICU.

Table 5-4 Distribution of Charges across the Medicare Patient Population by Length of Stay in a Special Care Unit—1980

Number of Days in ICU	Proportion of Patients	Proportion of Special Care Charges	Proportion of Total Ancillary Charges Incurred By Special Care Population
1	23.4%	5.5%	13.0%
2	22.0	10.2	14.4
3	15.5	10.6	12.0
4	10.3	9.4	9.3
5	6.8	7.8	7.1
6	4.9	6.8	5.8
7	3.5	5.7	4.7
8	2.6	4.8	3.9
9	2.0	4.0	3.2
10	1.5	3.2	2.6
11 +	7.5	32.0	24.0
	100.0%	100.0%	100.0%

Number of Medicare patients (ICU) 1,621,130

Total ICU Charges $1,996,529

Total Ancillary Charges $5,643,812

Source: Special tabulations prepared by Charles Helbing, Office of Research and Demonstrations, Health Care Financing Administration.

The disproportionate expenditure of ICU resources for a small number of patients can also be seen by examining the distribution of charges incurred by the Medicare population. Table 5-4 shows the distribution by length of stay in intensive care units (both ICU and CCU) of ICU and ancillary care charges incurred in a 20 percent national sample of Medicare patients. (The ancillary charges could be incurred at any time during the stay, not only during the entire hospital stay in the ICU.) These data indicate that the 23.4 percent of the patients who stayed one day accounted for 5.5 percent of ICU charges. The 7.4 percent of the population who stayed over 20 days accounted for 32 percent of the charges. These data probably underestimate the proportion of ICU resources allocated to long-stay patients because patients who stay only one day are more likely to be "monitor only" patients, while those who stay a longer period of time are more likely to have been actively treated. The patients who spent only one day in an ICU incurred 13 percent of the total ancillary charges of the Medicare population who spent any time in a special care unit. Those who stayed more than 20 days were responsible for 24 percent of the total ancillary charges. These data reflect the fact that most patients who stay in the ICU for a long time also stay in the hospital for a long time and will incur a higher percentage of ancillary charges in both the ICU and on the hospital floor.

CHANGES IN THE FINANCING ARRANGEMENTS FOR HOSPITAL SERVICES

As noted above, most patients who are hospitalized are covered by insurance. Until recently, public and private insurance companies paid hospitals for services provided either on the basis of incurred costs or posted charges. This method of paying for hospital care stimulated the rapid growth of the hospital sector.

Between 1972 and 1982, expenditures on hospital care grew at an annual rate of 18 percent.[29] The source of most of this increase was the rising cost of hospital care, not an increase in hospital utilization. In addition, the overall cost of a hospital stay rose much faster than the increase in the unit cost of hospital inputs—the wages paid for nurses, the price paid for food, the price paid for electricity, etc.[30] The term that is used to describe hospital inputs is the "hospital's market basket," introduced here because it is frequently used in hospital financing. In fact, between 1972 and 1982, the cost of a hospital stay increased 3 to 4 percentage points more than the cost of the hospital's market basket.[31] Other factors contributing to the increase in the cost of a hospital stay are the changing patient population, the adoption of cost-increasing technologies (such as those found in intensive care units), the use of more services per admission, and new treatment modalities making it possible to treat successfully those who were previously left to die (transplantation surgery, etc.).[32]

The organizations responsible for paying for a major portion of hospital care—the federal government (Medicare and Medicaid), the states (Medicaid), and employers (private health insurance)—are seeking methods to control rising health care costs as well as their financial responsibilities for these costs. For example, some states have implemented hospital rate-setting programs that cover all payers in the state. The Medicaid program in many states is limiting its payments by implementing some form of prospective payment system. Businesses are redesigning their health benefit packages by increasing the amount of patient cost sharing and by encouraging their employees to enroll in alternative delivery systems such as Health Maintenance Organizations (HMOs) or Preferred Provider Organizations (PPOs).

Medicare has radically changed its hospital reimbursement method. Instead of providing retrospective payment of costs, as Medicare had done since 1965, Medicare now pays a prospectively determined amount to cover the operating cost of each admission, that is, to cover all costs with the exception of capital costs and costs directly associated with education programs. Since the Medicare population makes up about 28 percent of the ICU population, this new payment system is likely to have a significant impact on hospital ICUs.[33]

Under Medicare's prospective payment system, patients are classified into one of 470 patient groups called Diagnostic Related Groups (DRGs) for purposes of payment. With limited exceptions, Medicare will pay a hospital a fixed price (which differs with the hospital's location, area wage rates, and the number of residents in training) for any patient in a given DRG. The price set for each DRG is based on an estimate of the average cost of treatment, which is equal to the sum of the special care costs (ICU/CCU), routine care costs, and ancillary costs. These cost estimates are derived from data on patient charges and hospital Medicare cost reports that are collected by the Health Care Financing Administration (HCFA), the federal agency that administers Medicare. The average estimated ICU cost for each DRG is equal to the sum of the average special care costs per day (as stated in the Medicare cost report) times the length of stay that each patient in the DRG spends in the ICU, divided by the number of patients in the DRG in the HCFA data base. Thus, the ICU costs are allocated to patients according to the average length of stay in an ICU. Hence, a hospital that keeps patients in a given DRG in an ICU longer than the average (either because its physicians tend to admit patients to the ICU more readily or because the patients treated in that hospital are sicker) is likely to experience financial pressure because it will be reimbursed by Medicare for less than the amount it actually costs to care for its ICU patients.

Under the new payment system, the rate of increase in DRG payments has become a political decision. In fiscal year 1985, the increase in DRG prices will be limited to the increase in the cost of the hospital's market basket. (The Reagan Administration has recommended that DRG payments be frozen for Fiscal Year 1986.) This new approach to hospital payment represents a major change in direction, for historically, as noted above, hospital costs (which were effectively the price paid by Medicare) increased three to four percentage points more than the cost of the hospital's market basket. Thus, in order for hospitals to remain financially healthy, they will have to seek ways to limit the increase in costs in their institutions and even to find ways to decrease them. Since the growth of ICUs has been responsible for much of the increase in costs and since ICUs account for about 20 percent of the total cost of hospital care, the care delivered in these units will come under close scrutiny. It will be essential to reduce the cost of intensive care without lowering its quality.[34] The next section of this chapter will outline some approaches to cost reduction.

INCREASING THE EFFICIENCY OF INTENSIVE CARE

The best way to improve the use of intensive care is to reduce the admission rates into the units by identifying those patients who are unlikely to benefit from such care. These patients come from two groups: those who are not critically ill and are unlikely to need an ICU intervention (low-risk admission) and those who are terminally ill and for whom intensive care will not improve the chance of survival (too ill). Patients with suspected acute myocardial infarction (AMI) are good examples of low-risk admissions. Considerable research has been undertaken to identify those patients with suspected AMI who are most likely to be true AMIs.[35] Based on this research, criteria have been developed that, when applied in clinical practice, result in an increase in the proportion of patients admitted to an ICU with true AMIs.[36] The "too ill" to benefit from an ICU admission usually reflects patients with end-stage cancer or other chronic untreatable primary disease. Treatment in an ICU may stabilize acute physiological abnormalities, but it has no effect on the underlying disease and only prolongs the dying process. The patients who are "too ill" should be treated on the general floor or in hospice settings.

Another approach to improve ICU efficiency is to identify those ICU patients who have not responded to initial aggressive efforts and for whom further treatment should be limited or terminated. Again, research such as that by Levy and his colleagues can provide the kind of information needed to facilitate such decision making.[37] The prognosis of 500 nontraumatic coma cases was studied and the clinical indices associated with probability of responding to treatment were identified. The findings—that if the patients had not responded in three days they were unlikely to respond—have been used by other physicians in their decisions to terminate life-support therapy.

A third approach is to assess the efficacy of care and to determine whether it is possible to increase ICU cost effectiveness, that is, to compare the treatment pattern of "similar patients" in different institutions. This type of comparison would help to assess whether some procedures are redundant or whether increasing the frequency with which a given procedure is done affects patient outcome. Unfortunately, with the exception of the work by Wagner et al.[38] to be discussed below, there are no relevant studies reported in the literature.

Finally, the optimum size intensive care unit can be determined and tested for increased cost effectiveness (where effectiveness is measured in terms of patient outcome). This information would be useful in deciding whether to consolidate units or to create smaller, special-purpose ICUs, and whether these ICUs should be grouped together in a Critical Care Center. While there are no published analytical studies on optimal size, conventional wisdom suggests that the appropriate size of an ICU is 8-12 beds.[39]

POTENTIAL FOR SAVINGS

Wagner et al.[40] estimated the potential savings that could be achieved by using the first three approaches discussed above: being more selective in admission and continued treatment decisions and delivering more cost-effective care. They based their estimates on an analysis of data obtained from a national sample of 4,152 admissions to intensive care units in 13 tertiary care hospitals alluded to earlier (see Table 5-3).

Of the 4,152 admissions, 1,159 received only monitoring services the first day. Of these patients, 923 were classified as low-risk patients, that is, patients who based on their admitting health status were estimated to have less than 1 percent chance of needing a unique ICU therapy. There were also 140 patients who were classified as being "too ill" to benefit from intensive care. These patients were terminally ill and had severe underlying chronic health problems.[41]

Within this study population, there were 201 other patients designated as "no-code" hopelessly ill patients for whom explicit decisions were made to limit care. These patients spent an average of seven days in the ICU before the "no-code" decision was made. They died an average of two days later. It is possible that many of these "no-code" decisions could have been made earlier. Two studies of hopelessly ill patients, the one mentioned earlier of nontraumatic coma patients[42] and one of patients in multiple organ system failure,[43] indicated that if patients did not respond within three days, survival was extraordinarily unlikely.

The treatment patterns of the patients in the study who survived and who did not fall into one of the three above groups were analyzed. The data indicated that there was substantial variation in the intensity and type of therapies provided patients even after controlling for severity, age, sex, and diagnosis. Thus in some hospitals it might be possible to reduce interventions (blood analyses, x-ray examinations, invasive monitoring management, etc.) without affecting patient outcome.

From the overall results of this study, the authors suggest that total resources allocated to ICU could be reduced by approximately 25 percent without affecting patient outcomes. Figure 5-1 shows the proposed ICU resource allocation they believe could reduce costs. About 37 percent of these savings would be generated by a more careful admission process—reducing the number of low-risk monitor admissions and not admitting patients who are too sick to benefit. About 24 percent of these savings would be generated by a less conservative policy for initiating "no-code" decisions. The remainder of the savings would come from greater efficiency in treating patients in the ICU to ensure that tests, procedures, etc., are indeed warranted.

The authors suggest that these reductions in the use of intensive care could be made without affecting patient outcomes. However, as pointed out below, in order for intensive care administrators to make the kinds of decisions suggested here, they need better data. We turn now to some of the steps that can be taken to encourage and facilitate more effective decision making.

RECOMMENDATIONS FOR CHANGE IN THE ICU

Current reimbursement systems are going to put increased financial pressure on hospitals. Under the new Medicare system, it is likely that the intensive care unit will become a source of financial loss, especially for the large teaching hospitals with substantial numbers of severely ill elderly patients. The first strategy to lower ICU costs should be to limit the growth of ICU beds and, perhaps, even try to reduce existing numbers. When this occurs, physicians directing ICUs will be forced to make more frequent triage decisions, that is, to spend more effort identifying the "low risk" and the "too ill" patients to ensure that patients admitted and kept in the unit are those most likely to benefit from the care. Increased triage pressure can be an effective tool in achieving this end, as emphasized by Sanders in discussing the effect of limiting cardiac surgery at the Massachusetts General Hospital:

> This has had a salutary effect in that a queue of sorts developed producing patient selection for application of all sorts of technology. In the case of cardiac surgery, operations are performed on those patients who have a reasonable chance of being helped. Alternatively, it is not difficult in such a milieu to deny surgery to the hopelessly ill.[44]

Another response to fiscal constraints should be efforts to increase the effectiveness of ICU care. Such efforts can be supported by new reporting systems that merge information from patient bills with that from medical records. These changes will allow administrators and physicians to compare treatment patterns and costs for similar patients. Used well, this information could lead to more efficient use of resources.

Figure 5-1 Resource Allocation among Patient Groups in a National Sample of 4,152 ICU Admissions to 13 Tertiary Care Hospitals

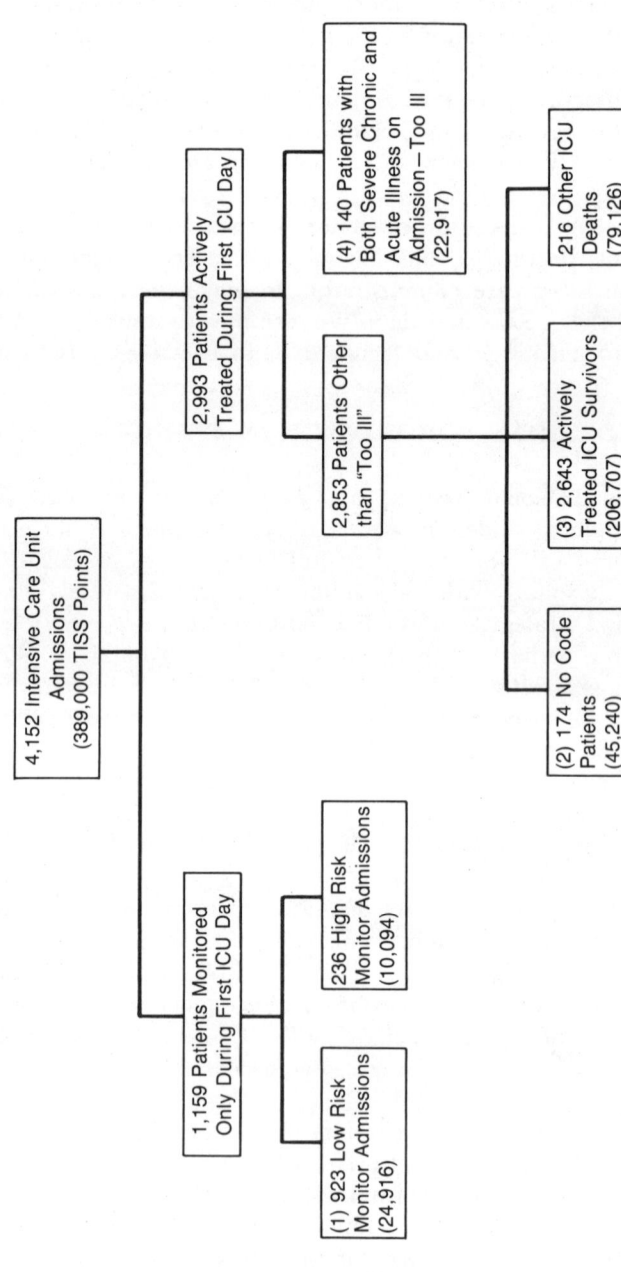

Patients have been classified as low risk, high risk, and too ill by use of the APACHE-II patient classification System. See note 40.

Source: Adapted from "Improving the Productivity of Intensive Care: A National Sample" by D.P. Wagner, E.A. Draper, and W.A. Knaus, a paper presented at the NBER Conference on Productivity in Health, Stanford, California, 1983.

For these strategies to be successful, however, the practicing physician and the hospital administrator must have more information about the relative benefits of ICU services. They must have methods to classify patients in order to make appropriate admission decisions. They must know more about severity of illness and prognosis. This will require an increased research effort and the development of new methodologies to match the new challenges. Much of this effort will require data collection on a large number of patients. Each ICU treats a limited number of cases and individual physicians have little way of gathering experience that would permit them to make confident prognoses or compare their performance with others. Levy could make estimates about prognosis of nontraumatic comas because he reviewed 500 cases from several hospitals. An individual physician, however, may see only one such patient a month. Given the emotional, ethical, legal, and financial issues surrounding intensive care, the collective knowledge of pooled experience is essential.

Limiting the amount of ICU resources inevitably raises the issue of rationing. This term implies, however, that resources will be denied or reduced to persons who need them. The policy strategies reviewed in this chapter are predominantly aimed at nonproductive ICU use. Realistically, we acknowledge that a few individual ICU patients may be harmed by more restrictive admission and treatment policies. Even so, it is hard to believe that any society could be so rich that it would not have to ration a service as expensive as intensive care. Moreover, unlimited commitments imply unlimited capabilities. It is clear from the information concerning effectiveness that the benefits of intensive care are limited.

In addition, it has long been recognized that commitment of resources to intensive care diminishes resources available for other hospital facilities or the acute care sector.[45] It is also true that the inexorable growth of the ICU harms other areas of health care that may be more effective in improving the overall health of the population, such as preventive health programs, prenatal clinics, nursing homes, and programs for the handicapped.

Until now the professional and public response to these allocation issues has always been to provide support for the dramatic and occasionally life-saving capabilities of intensive care and related specialties. Whether this new era of fiscal constraints will encourage a redistribution of these investments is unknown. The experience of the past two decades, however, suggests that at least within the professional community of intensive care, there is an increased desire for more prudent growth.

In his 1983 Presidential Address to the Critical Care Medical Society, Dr. Gregory said that there is a need to evaluate which ICU therapy works on whom. He asked (1) what kind of criteria should be established to determine who receives critical care, (2) what is the optimal staffing pattern, (3) what is the outcome of critical care in terms of death and quality of life, and (4) what is the optimal size unit?[46] These questions now demand answers.

SUMMARY AND CONCLUSIONS

Between 1965 and 1982, the proportion of hospitals with an ICU increased from 28.5 percent to about 78 percent. Between 1972 and 1982, ICU beds increased from 4 to 7.2 percent of total beds. Intensive care units are costly to set up and to staff. Intensive care is expensive to render and now accounts for about 20 percent of total hospital cost.

The growth of intensive care took place during a period of open-ended financing of hospital care. That period has now come to a close. Today, Medicare, Medicaid, and employers are seeking ways to limit outlays for hospital care. Constraints are being placed on payments for hospital care and hospitals will have to reduce costs in order to survive. Given the magnitude of costs generated in ICUs, these units will be scrutinized for savings.

This chapter has presented some approaches that could be used to increase the effectiveness of intensive care. Greater scrutiny of low-risk monitor patients is the most direct way of reducing the current demand for more ICU beds. Such efforts, combined with more realistic therapy for those who are hopelessly ill, can improve the efficiency of intensive care.

For efforts to be successful, it is necessary that professionals and the public view the ICU as an area within hospitals and medical practice where investment can and should be decreased. Such a change in attitude is taking place. These changes, however, can only be put into action if there is increased attention and effort devoted to research into severity of illness, prognosis, and outcome. The results of such research can guide better decision making and ensure that quality of care is maintained. If this is done, the new economic incentives could enhance effectiveness and improve knowledge of how intensive care works. Such knowledge is the only legitimate response to the current uncertainty.

NOTES

1. Hilberman, *The Evolution of Intensive Care Units*, 3(4) CRITICAL CARE MED., 159-65 (1975).

2. These data have been corrected for underreporting. The AHA gives data on total number of hospitals by bed class and the total number of hospitals that actually reported data on number of ICU beds. We corrected for underreporting by bed class by assuming that the hospitals that did not report their ICU beds had the same number of beds as those hospitals that did.

3. Horn, *Measuring Severity of Illness, Comparison Across Institutions*, 73(1) AM. J. PUBLIC HEALTH, 26-31 (1983); Pettengill & Vertrees, *Reliability and Validity in Hospital Case-Mix Measurement*, (4)2 HEALTH CARE FIN. REV., 101-29 (1982).

4. Fuchs, *The Growing Demand for Health Care*, in ESSAYS ON THE ECONOMICS OF HEALTH AND MEDICAL CARE (V. Fuchs, 61-68 1972).

5. Quoted by Bendixen, *The Cost of Intensive Care*, in COSTS, RISKS, AND BENEFITS OF SURGERY 373 (J. Bunker et al. 1977).

6. Gibson, Waldo, & Levit, *National Health Expenditures*, 1982, 5(1) HEALTH CARE FIN. REV., 1-31 (1983).

7. Derzon, *Influences of Reimbursement Policies on Technology*, in CRITICAL ISSUES IN MEDICAL TECHNOLOGY 139-50 (B. McNeil & E. Cravaldo, 1982).

8. L. RUSSELL, TECHNOLOGY IN HOSPITAL (1979).

9. Cromwell & Kanak, *The Effects of Prospective Reimbursement Programs on Hospital Adoption and Service Sharing*, 5(1) HEALTH CARE FIN. REV., 1-31 (1982).

10. See U.S. CONGRESS, OFFICE OF TECHNOLOGY ASSESSMENT, 1984, INTENSIVE CARE UNITS (ICU): CLINICAL OUTCOMES, COSTS AND DECISION MAKING, Health Technology Case Study 28, Washington D.C., 1984, for a comprehensive overview of the methods used to evaluate the effectiveness of ICUs. The most common approach has been before and after studies.

11. NIH Consensus Development Conference on Critical Care Medicine, 11(6) CRITICAL CARE MED. 466-69 (1983).

12. Draper, Wagner & Knaus, *The Use of Intensive Care: A Comparison of a University and a Community Hospital*, 3(2) HEALTH CARE FIN. REV. 466-69 (1981).

13. Thibault, et al., *Medical Intensive Care: Indications, Interventions, and Outcomes*, 302(17) NEW ENGL. J. MED. 938-942 (1980).

14. Knaus, et al., *The Range of Intensive Care Services Today*, 246 J. A.M.A., 2711-16 (Dec. 11, 1981).

15. Knaus, *Changing the Cause of Death—Editorial*, 249(8) J. A.M.A., 1059-60 (1983).

16. Chassin, *Costs and Outcomes of Medical Intensive Care*, 20(2) MEDICAL CARE 165-79 (1982).

17. Robin, *A Critical Look at Critical Care—Guest Editorial*, 11(2) CRITICAL CARE MED., 144-48 (1983); McPeek, Gilbert, & Mosteller, *The End Result Is the Quality of Life*, in COSTS RISKS AND BENEFITS OF SURGERY 170-75 (J. Bunker, et al., 1977); Epstein, *Responsibility of the Physician Is the Preservation of Life*, 139(8) ARCH. INTERN. MED. 919-20 (1979); and Baum, *L'Chaim*, 139(8) ARCH. INTERN. MED. 921 (1979).

18. Schmidt, et al., *Prolonged Mechanical Ventilation for Respiratory Failure: A Cost-Benefit Analysis*, 11(6) CRIT. CARE MED. 407-11 (1983).

19. *Supra* note 11.

20. Griner, *Treatment of Pulmonary Edema: Conventional or Intensive Care*, 77(4) ANN. INTERN. MED. 501-506 (1972).

21. This constancy can be seen by comparing data in a number of published and unpublished sources such as AMERICAN HOSPITAL ASSOCIATION, SURVEY OF CHARGES IN COMMUNITY HOSPITALS AS OF JANUARY 1, 1975 (1975); METROPOLITAN WASHINGTON COUNCIL OF GOVERNMENT'S HEALTH INFORMATION SYSTEM, METROPOLITAN WASHINGTON MONTHLY HOSPITAL/UTILIZATION REPORT (1979); and C. Helbing, Special Tabulations of ICU Data (unpublished, Health Care Financing Administration, 1984).

22. Finkler, *The Distinction Between Cost and Charges*, 96(1) ANN. INTERN. MED. 102-109 (1982).

23. Wagner, Wineland & Knaus, *The Hidden Costs of Treating Severely Ill Patients: Charges and Resource Consumption*, 5(1) HEALTH CARE FIN. REV. 81-86 (1983).

24. *Id.*

25. These estimates are based on the assumption that the occupancy rate of the intensive care unit is about 10 percent lower than that of the regular floor.

26. *See, e.g.*, Schroeder, Showstack, & Roberts, *Frequency and Clinical Description of High Cost Patients in 17 Acute Care Hospitals,* 300(23) NEW ENGL. J. MED. 1306-1309 (1978); Fedulo & Swinburne, *Relationship of Patient Age to Cost and Survival in the ICU,* 11(3) CRITICAL CARE MED. 155-1599 (1982); Zook & Moore, *High Cost Users of Medical Care,* 302(18) NEW ENGL. J. MED. 996-1002 (1980); and *supra* note 16.

27. Wagner DP, Draper EA, Knaus WA: Improving the Productivity of Intensive Care: A National Sample, paper presented at the NBER Conference on Productivity in Health, Stanford, California, 1983.

28. Resource costs are measured by TISS Points—*See* Cullen, et al., *Therapeutic Intervention Scoring System: A Method for Quantitative Comparison of Patient Care,* 2 CRITICAL CARE MED. 57-64 (1974).

29. *Supra* note 6.

30. The various components of the increase in hospital costs are presented in the annual report on *National Health Expenditures* in the HEALTH CARE FIN. REV. *See, e.g., supra* note 6.

31. Personal Communication, Mark Freeland, HCFA. For 1970-1978 comparisons see Freeland, Anderson & Schendler, *National Hospital Input Price Index,* 1(1) HEALTH CARE FIN. REV. 37-61 (1979).

32. U.S. CONGRESS, OFFICE OF TECHNOLOGY ASSESSMENT, MEDICAL TECHNOLOGY AND THE COSTS OF THE MEDICARE PROGRAM (1984).

33. *Federal Register,* Department of Health and Human Services, Health Care Financing Administration, Medicare Programs: Prospective Payment for Medicare, Inpatient Hospital Services, Final Rule, January 3, 1984. For a less bureaucratic description, see Lave, *Hospital Reimbursement Under Medicare,* 62(3) THE MILBANK MEMORIAL FUND Q. 251-68 (1984).

34. Many of these same issues are discussed in Knaus, Draper & Wagner, *The Use of Intensive Care: New Research Initiatives and Their Implications for National Health Policy,* 61(4) THE MILBANK MEMORIAL FUND Q. 561-83 (1983).

35. Fuchs & Scheidt, *Improved Criteria for Admission to Cardiac Care Units,* 246(18) J. A.M.A. 2037-41 (1981); Goldman, et al., *A Computer-Derived Protocol to Aid in the Diagnosis of Emergency Room Patients with Acute Chest Pain,* 307(10) NEW ENGL. J. MED. 588-95 (1982).

36. Pozen, D'Agostino & Mitchell, *The Usefulness of a Predictive Instrument to Reduce Inappropriate Admissions to the Coronary Care Unit,* 94(3) ANN. INTERN. MEDICINE 293-301 (1980).

37. Levy, et al., *Prognosis in Nontraumatic Coma,* 94(3) ANN. INTERN. MED. 293-301 (1981).

38. *Supra* note 27.

39. *Supra* note 11.

40. *Supra* note 27.

41. Patient health status is measured by a severity of illness system called APACHE-11 (Acute Physiologic and Chronic Health Evaluation). The underlying philosophy of APACHE-11 is that the one unifying characteristic of ICU patients is their acute severity of illness, which this system is designed to capture. See Knaus, et al., *APACHE-II—Final Form and National Validation Results,* Abstract, 12 CRITICAL CARE MED. 213 (March 1984).

42. *Supra* note 37.

43. Knaus, et al., *Evaluation Outcome from Intensive Care: A Preliminary Multihospital Comparison,* 10(8) CRITICAL CARE MED. 491-96 (1982).

44. Sanders, *Adoption of New Technologies in Hospitals,* in CRITICAL ISSUES IN MEDICAL TECHNOLOGY 31 (B. McNeil & E. Cravalho, 1982).

45. Hiatt, *Protecting the Medical Commons, Who Is Responsible?* 293(5) NEW ENGL. J. MED. 235-41 (1967).

46. Gregory, *Who Should Receive Intensive Care?* 11(10) CRITICAL CARE MED. 767-68 (1983).

Chapter 6

Determination of Death

Alexander Morgan Capron

Uncertainty and unresolved issues attend many aspects of medicine, especially the process of dying. Yet most readers of this volume—especially physicians—probably believe that one subject in this field has been well resolved for a number of years: the "definition" of death. In light of all the attention this subject has received, in both its clinical and public policy aspects, the extent to which it remains a topic of discussion and debate in American courtrooms and legislatures, however well settled it may be in health care settings, is somewhat surprising.

Nonetheless, the remaining questions are tangential rather than central, matters of disagreement and delay in state legislative processes, not basic doubts about the wisdom of updating the standards by which death is determined. The broadly held consensus on this subject was reflected in *Defining Death*, a report issued in July 1981 by the President's Commission for the Study of Ethical Problems in Medicine and Biomedical and Behavioral Research.[1] In response to its congressional mandate, the Commission recommended a statute, the Uniform Determination of Death Act (UDDA), which has since become the most widely accepted legal formulation of the standards for determining human death. It also provided an up-to-date formulation of the medical criteria for applying this standard,[2] which was hailed as a "landmark" when it was published.[3] These guidelines, which are now widely used by physicians and hospitals for clinical decision making, set forth procedures for using either the traditional circulatory/respiratory measures or the brain-based measures that are needed when mechanical ventilators and other artificial means of support preclude reliance on the traditional signs.

This chapter reviews the basis for this medical consensus on the determination of death, examines the progress toward uniform legal recognition of biomedical developments, and closes with a survey of the philosophical and scientific issues that remain. It also argues that physicians can play an important role in educating the public and its lawmakers by making clear the differences among patients who are often grouped together in law discussions—patients without any brain function (who are dead) and patients in a persistent vegetative state, like Karen Ann Quinlan in the last decade of her life (who are alive, albeit in an apparently minimal fashion). Opportunities for physicians to improve public understanding arise not only through testifying in court cases or before legislative committees, but also in counseling a dead person's family when permission is sought for organ donation and in being careful, when quoted by the media, to avoid the confusion created when one speaks of maintaining a "dead" person for hours or days on "life-support" devices while medical or legal procedures are carried out.

THE NEED FOR CHANGE IN STANDARDS

Diagnosis by Traditional Measures

Until recently, laymen were probably as comfortable with this subject as were physicians—a determination of death was based upon such manifest signs as an absence of pulse and breath, and fixed pupils. Surprisingly, while these criteria have been used to determine death since ancient times, they have not always been universally accepted. Horror over being buried alive is not merely an imaginary creation by the authors of macabre, nineteenth-century stories like Edgar Allan Poe where cemeteries are dug up and exhumed skeletons are found to indicate clawing at coffin lids. During the eighteenth and early nineteenth centuries, some people even took elaborate steps, using coffins with escape mechanisms and speaking tubes to the world above, to avoid such a ghastly end.[4] Well into the eighteenth century, physicians argued over whether putrefaction was the only sure sign of death.[5] Only in the nineteenth century did the debate gradually dissipate as physicians became more competent and the public gained greater faith in them.[6] Part of the confidence centered on the invention of the stethoscope in the mid-nineteenth century which enabled physicians to detect heartbeat with increased sensitivity. The public took reassurance from this technological means of measuring what had long been regarded as one of the central signs in the diagnosis of death.

Today the bases for determining death on circulatory/respiratory grounds are well established. First, circulatory and respiratory functions must have ceased, as discerned through clinical examination by the absence of responsiveness, heartbeat, and respiratory effort. Depending on the circumstances, the physician may find it advisable to perform confirmatory tests, such as an electrocardiogram. At the opposite extreme is the situation where lay people have to determine death, based on easily measured signs, when a physician is not available in a remote locale.

Second, cessation must be permanent and irreversible, as demonstrated through a trial of therapy or an appropriate period of observation, which will vary depending on the circumstances of the death. Generally, a more vigorous and extensive approach is required when an apparent death occurs unexpectedly or was unobserved. In such cases, resuscitative measures will usually be undertaken both to protect the body from any further damage and to test for cardiovascular responsiveness. On the other hand, "where death is expected, where the course has been gradual and where irregular agonal respiratory or heartbeat finally ceases, the period of observation following the cessation may be only the few minutes required to complete the examination."[7]

Traditional Legal Standards

Because the determination of death was for many years a matter of neither controversy among medical professionals nor of arcane confusion for the public, it seldom arose in court cases and was not explicitly addressed by legislation in the United States. Instead, the term "death" was employed by lawmakers as one with a manifest and settled meaning. When judges did opine on the subject it was, as summarized by *Black's Law Dictionary*, merely to repeat the self-apparent: that death is "the cessation of life," revealed primarily by "a total stoppage of the circulation of the blood."[8]

In a few cases, the facts about a death were contested, usually when the moment of death was important for legal reasons, as when the relative time of death of two people determined whose heirs would inherit what property. The moment of death was then regarded "as a question of fact," to be resolved by the jurors largely on the basis of expert testimony, but within standards set down "as a matter of law."[9]

Impact of New Medical Capabilities

In the past 20 years, however, a divergence between the popular perception of death and that applied by the medical profession in certain cases has been brought about by the development and widespread use of mechanical respirators, potent cardiovascular therapies, and related forms of treatment. Mechanical respirators are applied in some cases because of an interference with, or loss of function in, the respiratory centers of the medulla that leads respiration to stop, this in turn depriving the heart of needed oxygen and causing it to cease functioning. Mechanical ventilators are not a perfect substitute for the missing natural functions when the cessation of breathing is caused by absent or deficient neural impulses, since the machines have difficulty in regulating blood gas levels precisely. But they are able to take over regulation of the rate and depth of "breathing," which is normally controlled by the respiratory centers in the medulla. Once the lungs are forced to work again, the heart will usually beat since its basic pumping functions are not dependent upon external control, although impulses from the brain centers are needed to modulate the inherent rate and force of the heartbeat. When artificial respiration provides adequate oxygenation and associated medical treatments regulate essential plasma components and blood pressure, an intact heart will continue to beat despite loss of brain functions.

The resumption of respiration and circulation in patients on mechanical ventilators gives the appearance of the "vital signs" that common experience, as well as the law, accepted as the definition of life. Indeed, as recently as 1977, a state court reaffirmed the traditional view "that death means the permanent cessation of all vital functions,"[10] a standard that does not differentiate between spontaneous bodily functions and those that are created artificially once internal stimulation and regulation has been lost because all integrated neuronal brain functions have permanently stopped.

The most frequent causes of the irreversible cessation of functioning in the whole brain are (1) direct trauma to the head, (2) massive spontaneous hemorrhage into the brain, and (3) anoxic damage from cardiac or respiratory arrest or severely reduced blood pressure.[11] Those injuries that are traumatic typically cause a loss of blood flow to both the upper and lower portions of the brain because of cerebral edema. If deprived of blood flow for 10 to 15 minutes, the adult brain (including the brainstem) will—in the absence of certain drugs such as barbiturates or of hypothermia—completely cease functioning. Even in the absence of trauma, loss of functions of the brain neurons can also occur, if circulation is impaired.

Patients who have suffered a loss of circulation to the brain for either traumatic or nontraumatic reasons can be categorized into three groups. First are those in whom "all brain structures above the foramen magnum have irreversibly ceased to function."[12] Such bodies lack not only consciousness and cognitive, affective, and integrative functions, but also all reflexes controlled by the brainstem, such as the gag reflex and the drive to breathe (although some spinal cord reflexes may persist, as circulation to the cord is separate from that to the brain). In the absence of artificial respiration it would be apparent to all that such a person is dead. With mechanical support, however, respiration and circulation may be maintained for a limited period of time. Total cessation of heartbeat occurs within hours or a few days in most respirator-supported, "brain dead" adults, though it may persist in a few for several weeks given vigorous support.[13] One recent report of the survival of cardiopulmonary functions for 68 days of mechanical ventilation and extensive medical support does not contain sufficient data to establish whether the diagnosis of "brain death" met the criteria suggested by the medical consultants to the President's Commission.[14] "Theoretically, it is possible for extracranial organs in a brain-dead body to function indefinitely, until old age wears out the heart."[15]

The second group of patients who have suffered brain ischemia consists of those whose brain injury is less severe—victims of trauma who receive prompt medical attention and victims of cardiac arrest whose circulation is restored before irreversible damage has occurred throughout the brain. Since the cerebrum, particularly the cerebral cortex, is more easily injured by a loss of blood flow or oxygen than is the brainstem, a shorter period without respiration or circulation may damage the cerebral cortex permanently, although the more resistant brainstem may continue to function. Patients in this category usually require artificial support for only a limited period, after which they will be able to breathe on their own, but without recovering consciousness. In this condition, the "persistent vegetative state,"[16] they may exhibit spontaneous involuntary movements such as facial grimaces but will remain at best "awake but unaware." Physicians' ability to prognosticate for these patients is less precise than for those in the first group, but the irreversibility of their unconsciousness can be documented over several weeks of clinical examination, if cerebral arteriography and modified CT scanning of the brain reveal the total loss of cortical layers. With medical and nursing support, including artificial feeding and administration of antibiotics for recurrent pulmonary infections, such patients can survive for years—indeed the longest reported survival exceeded 37 years.[17]

Finally, the third group of patients are those for whom the damage has been less severe. Few who persist in an unconscious state beyond one month will recover fully, but there are some who do; in addition, a larger number of unconscious patients who need artificial support for only a brief period will recover fully.[18] Although small, it is the latter group that in effect explains the existence of the first two. The respirator is not merely one more example of the Sorcerer's Apprentice at work in modern medicine. It is not, in other words, a device that serves solely to confound physicians' ability to determine whether people are dead, nor a device which, when administered to the victims of accidents and heart attacks, produces only persistent unconsciousness. Rather, it and the accompanying medical techniques are essential in some cases to provide the life support that acutely ill or injured patients need if they are to recover.

A study undertaken by the President's Commission at four acute care hospitals in 1980 found 133 patients who were comatose and respirator-supported during a two-month period. Only 16 of these achieved a good to moderate recovery within 30 days. (Incidentally, those who achieved a good outcome were usually in a coma due to drug intoxication or metabolic failure, e.g., hepatic encephalopathy.) Similarly, a secondary analysis of computerized data on critically ill patients at three centers, each covering a one-year period, also revealed that 10 to 12 percent of comatose, respirator-supported patients recovered.[19]

Emergence of a Medical Consensus

It is plainly a matter of ethical and legal, as well as medical, concern that physicians be able to distinguish the first group of artificially maintained patients from the other two, because of their marked variation in prognosis. Thus, it is of general importance that accurate methods have been developed to differentiate these groups of patients—that is, to determine whether death has occurred, despite the persistence of artificially supported respiration, by using tests of brain functioning at the brainstem as well as at the cortical level.

The emergence of a consensus among physicians—both about the means for diagnosing the permanent loss of all functions of the brain (including the brainstem) and about the reliability of those means—is indicated by the publication in November 1981 of the *Guidelines for the Determination of Death* prepared for the President's Commission by more than 50 of the nation's leading medical experts on the subject drawn from neurology, neurosurgery, pediatrics, internal medicine, forensic and legal medicine, among other fields.[20] It was concluded that each medical facility may have a locally adopted protocol, but the tests used should:

(1) eliminate errors in classifying a living individual as dead;

(2) allow as few errors as possible in classifying a dead body as alive;

(3) allow a determination to be made without unreasonable delay;

(4) be adaptable to a variety of clinical situations; and

(5) be explicit and accessible to verification.[21]

As with a determination of death based on the loss of circulatory and respiratory functions, the criteria for a neurologically based determination should specify (1) means for establishing the *cessation* of the relevant functions and (2) means for establishing that this loss is *irreversible*. The first requirement includes absence of cerebral functions (measured clinically and *confirmed* when appropriate by studies such as an EEG—a "flat EEG" being often mistakenly thought by the lay public to be *the* criterion of death) and absence of brainstem functions (as shown by the absence of reflex responses to stimuli, including adequate testing for apnea).[22] The second requirement (irreversibility) is obviously crucial; it usually necessitates that physicians establish a cause of the patient's coma that is sufficient to account for the loss of brain functions and that they rule out any conditions—such as shock, sedation, hypothermia, hypovolemia, hypotension, and neuromuscular blockade—that could produce a seeming loss of brain functions that was actually correctable.

The careful application of accepted medical criteria and tests by a competent, unbiased physician is a reasonable expectation whenever any diagnosis or prognosis is rendered. But it is plainly a matter of special importance—and hence of ethical and legal concern—in determinations of death, for several reasons. First, the finality of the diagnosis and the potential for harm from mistakes is unusually pronounced. Many errors by physicians are self-correcting; even when not, they can usually be caught and remedied and seldom have immediately fatal consequences, as a misdiagnosis of death probably would have. For this reason, the *Guidelines* states "consultation with a physician experienced in this diagnosis is advisable."[23]

Second, some respirator-supported patients are potential organ donors. The possibility that a determination of death will be beneficial to someone else can undermine the single-minded fidelity to patients' interests that is supposed to characterize physicians' execution of their duties. Thus, it is important for hospitals to do all they can to reinforce the spirit as well as the letter of the Uniform Anatomical Gift Act, which requires that the physicians who pronounce death in an organ donor cannot be involved in the process of transplanting any organs.

The benefits of following both these precepts is illustrated by a case reported by Presbyterian-University Hospital in Pittsburgh. An 18-year-old male who had sustained multiple injuries in a motor vehicle accident was admitted in an unconscious and unresponsive condition to the Intensive Care Unit of an outlying hospital. After 12 hours of treatment, "his parents were told that he was brain dead and permission was obtained to remove his kidneys for transplantation."[24] Upon transfer to the university hospital (for the sole purpose of organ procurement), the patient was reevaluated and received more vigorous treatment; 57 days after the injury he was discharged, "his only residual neurologic deficit being a right hemiparesis and slight impairment of higher cognitive functions."[25] Thus, while the criteria for pronouncing death in a respirator-supported patient based upon neurologic measurements are at least as reliable as the traditional heart-lung criteria, cases such as this are reminders of the need for physicians to possess appropriate skill and training in the application of the criteria and for hospitals engaged in organ transplantation to have grounds for confidence in the procedures used by the hospitals from which "dead bodies" are received as organ donors.

TRANSLATING MEDICAL KNOWLEDGE INTO POLICY

As biomedical scientists and practitioners over the past several decades have developed the ability both to maintain comatose patients artificially and to determine which of the patients have become dead bodies, the public has come to recognize—particularly since heart transplantation began in 1967—that public policy has to be updated to take into account the ways the new medical knowledge and capabilities depart from traditional understanding and expectations. To translate medical knowledge into law and policy is not always a simple matter. More is at stake than a matter of interest solely to the medical profession. Indeed, while physicians and other scientists can explain the consequences of differing "definitions" of death, the decision about what concept of death to adopt is a basic philosophical issue, not a narrow technical one.

What Is the Concept of Death?

Most people view human death, like the death of any animal, as a natural event. Even in establishing their "definition," people start from the premise that death is an event whose existence rests on certain criteria recognized, rather than solely invented, by human beings. Indeed, there are good reasons for holding that what is being "defined" for humans ought not to diverge at its core from a "definition" that would be used for saying that any other animal is dead, while acknowledging that the special qualities that are valued in humans *might* require distinctive features not germane to "lower" species.

Despite the reasonableness of this starting point, it also seems intuitively appropriate to ask whether there are any distinctive human features that should lead to a radically different basis for determining human death from the death of other organisms. On the one hand, circulation and respiration appear to be *necessary* functions for human life; though their origin may be artificial (rather than from natural cardiac and pulmonary mechanisms), they must be present for any and all other organic functions (including those of the brain). On the other hand, does the mere existence of these functions amount to human life? Clearly not if their origin is totally artificial and not a result of any operations of the brain, any more than a functioning heart-lung machine by itself (or a decapitated corpse hooked up to a ventilator) would be a living person. But is the persistence of spontaneous cardiopulmonary activity in a comatose patient *sufficient* to say that human life remains?

Some commentators, most prominently bioethicist Robert Veatch,[26] have answered this question in the negative. They point first to those activities such as thinking, reasoning, feeling, and human intercourse that make human beings distinctive. Without higher brain functions, these attributes of "personhood" disappear; hence, death of the person occurs when the neocortex ceases functioning, even though a breathing body remains.[27]

Other philosophers have argued that a patient's "personal identity" disappears when the higher brain functions are lost because one's identity depends upon the persistence of mental processes. These processes supply the consistency in one's reactions to the world and one's memory of it; they are subject to gradual change but when a radical, destructive event occurs, the changes may be so grave as to destroy one's identity.

These "higher brain" formulations raise theoretical as well as practical questions, however. Nothing approaching agreement exists about what things are essential to "personhood," or about how to solve the philosophical problem of identity. Further, the implication of the neocortical standards is that a person in a persistent vegetative state (like Ms. Quinlan) is as dead as any other corpse, even though the lower brain is functional and hence the person breathes spontaneously. It is unlikely that many people would accept such a concept of death, which implies that breathing, albeit unconscious, patients could be buried or otherwise treated as dead.

Moreover, the scientific and clinical knowledge necessary to implement a "higher brain" standard is lacking.

> [I]t is not known which portions of the brain are responsible for cognition and consciousness; what little is known points to substantial interconnection among the brainstem, subcortical structures and the neocortex.[28]

Even when aspects of consciousness can be linked with particular sites in the cerebral cortex, the methods of assessing irreversible cessation in the functioning of these sites are not yet sufficiently accurate to provide for a dependable diagnosis of death.

The "whole brain" formulation, by comparison, is conceptually sounder and rests on a well-verified basis of diagnosing death (as described above). This formulation recognizes that the heart, lungs, and brain have special significance in maintaining the integrated functioning of the human organism as a whole because, unlike other "vital" organs (liver, kidney, skin, etc.), "their interrelationship is very close and the irreversible cessation of any one very quickly stops the other two."[29] Whether this interrelationship is regarded as basic to a living organism, or, alternatively, stress is placed on the centrality of the whole brain (including the brainstem) to the organism's regulation and integration, is not really important in terms of policy. In the former view, the irreversible loss of circulatory and respiratory functions amounts to death because it shows directly that the integrated functioning of the three essential organ systems has ended. In the latter view, "the heart and lungs are not important as basic prerequisites to continued life but rather because the irreversible cessation of their functions shows that the brain has ceased functioning."[30]

The strongest argument against the "whole brain" standard is that even though intensive medical support for patients without any brain functions cannot truly replace everything that a functioning brainstem achieves, and hence such patients cannot be maintained indefinitely, this proves only that such patients are dying, not that they are dead. Yet what remains in a respirator-supported body without any brainstem functions is not a human being but "merely a group of artificially maintained subsystems."[31] Though it may be hard to discern precisely, a patient without any brain functions is missing—in a way that a person who only lacks neocortical functions is not— that cluster of attributes essential to an organism's responsiveness to its internal and external environment.

> The startling contrast between bodies lacking *all* brain functions and patients with intact brainstems (despite severe neocortical damage) manifest this. The former lie with fixed pupils, motionless except for chest movements produced by their respirators. The latter cannot only breathe, metabolize, maintain temperature and blood pressure, and so forth, *on their own* but also sigh, yawn, track light with their eyes and react to pain or reflex stimulation.[32]

It is at this point that physicians sometimes grow puzzled—and the framers of public policy impatient—with philosophers' arguments. The conceptual debate may not lead to a clear answer, though even in conceptual terms, the "whole brain" standard seems to rest on a firmer footing than the "higher brain" formulation. Moreover, the former rests on more precise and easily applied clinical criteria, and does not have implications (i.e., declaring spontaneously respiring patients "dead") that would be unacceptable to most people. Perhaps most important in terms of policy, any body declared dead under a "whole brain" formulation would also be dead according to the "personhood" and "personal identity" theories that undergird the neocortical view of death. Thus, while philosophical objections may still be heard, the major debate has come to a close because a coherent and sensible conception of death is available as a basis for translating medical knowledge into public policy.

What Are the Objectives?

What objectives should guide the formulation of such a policy beyond being medically accurate and conceptually sound? The two that seem important are the policy's comprehensibility to members of the general public and its simplicity. A legal rule (whether regulation, statute, or common law) that may affect every ordinary person and that controls a matter as central to people's relations with each other (as parent, spouse, and friend) and with the state (as taxpayer, voter, beneficiary, etc.) as the "definition" of death should be comprehensible to the general public as well as to the medical profession.

To enhance public understanding, a "definition" of death should have two features. First, it ought to speak in terms that laypeople can comprehend in light of their present experience and understanding. For most people, death is signified by an absence of breathing and heartbeat. Since that will continue to be true for the foreseeable future for the overwhelming majority of people (who are not going to die under circumstances in which artificial support precludes reliance on the traditional signs of death), a legal rule ought to explicitly acknowledge "irreversible cessation of circulatory and respiratory functions" (in the absence of artificial substitution) as one basis for determining that death has occurred.

Second, to educate the public the statute ought to show the parallel between the cardiopulmonary standard and the brain-based standard. Linking these two closely demonstrates that they are two windows through which the *same* phraseology would create the misimpression that there are two separate and distinct phenomena. This problem occurred with the first statute "defining" death, adopted in Kansas in 1970.[33]

The surest way to achieve the objective of legal simplicity is for public policy to focus on the issue at hand and neither be overbroad nor attempt to encompass more than the problem area needing attention. The task involves making clear that a medical determination that death has occurred will be acceptable legally if it is based upon measurements of brain functioning—or rather, their absence—when the traditional life signs have been obscured by the use of artificial means of support. There is no need for the law to prescribe the medical, social, or religious behavior that should follow upon a determination that a person has died. The law need not, in fact, "define" death—or life—at all, since it is not really the issue, merely the recognition of an alternative means of diagnosing death.

Further, although a statute of the type drafted by the Law Reform Commission of Canada, which propounds the irreversible cessation of brain functions as the *sole* "definition," would appear to be simpler than one that recognizes cardiopulmonary cessation as an alternative; in fact it is not. Such a statute would require that conscientious physicians perform tests of brain functioning even in clear cases of cardiopulmonary cessation or, as in the Canadian proposal, the statute itself would have to recognize explicitly that the brain-based standard can also be met "by the prolonged absence of spontaneous circulatory and respiratory functions."[34] This concern with greater complexity, and even unclarity, is not merely hypothetical. A statutory proposal once endorsed by the American Bar Association set forth the single standard of "irreversible cessation of brain function." Because this single standard might appear to be irrelevant to death determination in most cases—in which the diagnosis will depend on measuring cardiopulmonary cessation, not brain cessation—several states amended the statute to permit determination made by "other usual and customary procedures," without explaining these procedures or their relationship to the brain-based standard. The result was thus a statute that was less clear than one that explicitly incorporated "irreversible cessation of circulatory and respiratory functions" as one means of diagnosing death.

Finally, for a legal policy on death to be simple and understandable it ought to apply to all people equally: it would be disconcerting to declare one person "dead" and another "alive" if their physical conditions were identical. Critics who challenge the need for uniformity have claimed that, in effect, no "definition" of death is necessary at all.[35] In many contexts this notion is sensible; in this view, each situation in which it could be relevant to determine that a person has died would be governed by a particular statement of criteria for declaring death for that purpose. There are several objections to this approach regarding the present topic, however. First, no legislature perceived any serious need for varying "definitions" in different contexts—such as inheritance, voting, and the criminal law.[36] No reason exists comparable to that which leads the law to declare a corporation a "person" for purposes of owning property while using a different definition of "person" (one that excludes corporations) for voting purposes.

More important, confusion rather than clarity would be introduced if different physical conditions were called by the same name, "death." For example, there are two possible solutions to the problem of the shortage of useful human organs for transplantation: (1) promulgating a statute with special procedures to prevent abuse that would permit organs to be removed from "pre-mortem organ donors" and (2) allowing people to request that if they are dying their organs be "harvested" at a point in the dying process before it would be appropriate to bury or mourn them, even though they are not dead by definition. The former proposal achieves a better solution to the problem than the latter. People who might elect either solution, however, need not be "defined" as dead. Keeping the categories distinct is not only theoretically sounder but would also facilitate using special procedures before acting in cases of "pre-mortem donation"—or other situations of treatment termination—which would be unnecessary when one is dealing with a dead body.

ADOPTING A LEGAL STANDARD

Several means exist for translating the concept of death from medical criteria into public policy. In the early 1970s, when the subject first became a matter of debate among policymakers, some people argued that the task of "defining" death should be left to physicians, without interference by legislators.[37] Physicians themselves soon rejected this position because it became apparent that even in the absence of legislation, there was "law" (in the form of court opinions) on the subject of death, and that law might or might not take into account a modern understanding of death, as physicians in Virginia discovered when they were sued for removing organs for transplantation from a body they had declared "dead" according to medical criteria (based on cessation of all brain functions) but that continued to have the traditional vital signs of breathing and heartbeat because of a mechanical ventilator.[38]

Judicial Decisions

This experience also suggests the central difficulty with relying on the judiciary to "update" the law on death: until a definitive ruling on the subject from the highest court of a state, those people—such as physicians and family members—who must make decisions about respirator-supported patients are forced to act in the face of uncertainty as to whether the "definition" of death that they are applying will turn out to be consistent with state law. Indeed, for a number of reasons, courts for many years were very slow to modify the common law "definition" (cessation of all vital functions, including respiration and circulation) to accept determinations of death based on the irreversible cessation of all functions of the brain.

Nevertheless, based upon the decisions of the highest courts in all the states that have ruled on the subject, physicians in the few remaining states without a legislative "definition" of death can feel reasonably confident in predicting that the courts in these states would also apply modern standards for determining death if the issue ever arose in litigation.[39]

Illustrative of the judicial updating of the common law is *People v. Eulo*, a 1984 decision by the Court of Appeals of New York, the state's highest court.[40] This decision involved a consolidated ruling on two separate criminal cases; in each, the defendant was convicted of manslaughter for shooting his victim in the head, which resulted in severe brain damage, a declaration of death based on irreversible cessation of all brain functions, removal of the victim's organs for transplantation, and subsequent discontinuation of the mechanical ventilator, at which point the victim's heart stopped. The court rejected defendants' claim that they should be relieved of liability for homicide because the physicians removed vital organs while the victims were still "alive" according to the traditional standards of heartbeat and respiration. The court cited the accepted legal rule that an assailant can be held guilty of homicide unless the causal chain between the attack and the victim's death is broken by the gross negligence or intentional wrongdoing of the victim's physicians. Since the court found that determining death on brain-based standards was an accepted medical practice, the use of this standard by the physicians in these cases did not break the causal chain. Further, the court recognized the medical reasons for explicitly adopting a new common-law conception of death.

> Ordinarily, death will be determined according to the traditional criteria of irreversible cardiopulmonary repose. When, however, the respiratory and circulatory functions are maintained by mechanical means, their significance, as signs of life, is at best ambiguous. Under such circumstances, death may nevertheless be deemed to occur when, according to accepted medical practice, it is determined that the entire brain's function has irreversibly ceased.[41]

As with other cases that have reached similar decisions, one difficulty is that the court's holding may be limited to the context in which it arises, such as a homicide prosecution[42] or an organ donation.[43] Fortunately, most of the courts that have "adopted" a new "definition" of death have at least recognized that the medical criteria and tests by which such a legal standard is translated into practice should be left to "accepted medical standards," since "[a]ny attempt to establish a specific procedure might inhibit the development and application of more sophisticated diagnostic methods."[44]

Statutory Changes

Most states have now adopted statutes that set forth the standards for determining that death has occurred. Indeed, it is now generally acknowledged that public policy on this subject ought to be set by the legislature, rather than waiting for judicial modification of the common law. Even courts that have had to rule on the "definition" have seen legislation as preferable. See, e.g., *Lovato v. District Court,* 601 P.2d 1072 (Colo. 1979) (*en banc*): "We recognize the authority of, and indeed encourage, the General Assembly to pronounce statutorily the standards by which death is to be determined in Colorado."

In the decade after the adoption of the first statute in Kansas in 1970, 26 states adopted legislation setting the standards for determining death.[45] In addition to the Kansas statute,[46] several other "model" laws were proposed: The Capron-Kass proposal of 1972 was the most widely adopted (seven states),[47] followed by a 1975 model law proposed by the American Bar Association (5 states),[48] the Uniform Brain Death Act, proposed in 1978 by the National Conference of Commissioners on Uniform State Laws (2 states),[49] and a proposal approved by the American Medical Association at its December 1979 interim meeting, which was not adopted in any state.[50] Despite—or perhaps because of—this wealth of model laws, action in the states toward uniformity had slowed by 1980. Despite the proposals' similarity and common purpose, they were perceived as competitive, and legislators understandably wanted to avoid offending one sponsoring group (such as the American Bar Association or the American Medical Association) by favoring another group's bill. After 1978, most of the states adopting a death-determination act crafted their own, unique statute—sometimes blending together provisions from several of the model laws.

The Congress of the United States charged the President's Commission with reporting on the "ethical and legal implications of the matter of defining death, including the advisability of developing a uniform definition of death."[51] Rather than simply adding one more model statute, the Commission worked with the other groups that had sponsored legislation to develop the Uniform Determination of Death Act (UDDA):

> An individual who has sustained either (1) irreversible cessation of circulatory and respiratory functions, or (2) irreversible cessation of all functions of the entire brain, including the brain stem, is dead. A determination of death must be made in accordance with accepted medical standards.

In addition to the Commission's endorsement, this model law was approved in 1981 by the American Bar Association, the American Medical Association, and the National Conference of Commissioners on Uniform State Laws in place of their earlier proposals. It has been adopted in 15 jurisdictions (two are judicial "adoptions").[52]

The two standards for determining death recognized by this statute are accepted by biomedical science as equivalent bases for diagnosing the same phenomenon. The circulatory and respiratory standard is familiar to lay people as well as physicians; it is included in the statute because it will continue to be the actual basis on which death will be declared for the overwhelming majority of persons for the foreseeable future. When respiration is provided artificially, the statute recognizes that medically accepted means of determining that "all functions of the brain have permanently and irreversibly ceased"[53] provide an alternative basis for declaring death. It is important to emphasize—given the attention sometimes paid in lay accounts to the use of an electroencephalograph in diagnosing death—that "functions" are not to be confused with "mere *activity* in cells or group of cells if such activity (metabolic, electrical, etc.) is not manifested in some way that has significance for the organism as a whole."[54] The diagnosis must rest on the loss of integrated brain functions, not loss of all activity in the brain cells, "since recovery of some metabolic and electrical activity in the brain following even 60 minutes of total ischemia has been demonstrated experimentally."[55]

Relationship to Other Medical Decisions

Two other medical decisions—termination of treatment and removal of organs for transplantation—are often linked with the determination of death but are actually discrete issues that should not be made a necessary part of the legal or medical rules on death determination. Indeed, when the subjects are linked, needless confusion and controversy has arisen.

Some of those who have urged a "higher brain" or "cerebral" standard for determining death have apparently conceived of such a statute as an appropriate way to avoid prolonged treatment of permanently unconscious (albeit spontaneously respiring) patients. Yet a "whole brain definition" does not imply that all people who breathe spontaneously are equivalent for all purposes. There are contexts in which it may make sense to draw distinctions based on the degree of mental functioning, so that a retarded or senile or comatose person is regarded as having different rights and responsibilities than a person capable of more "normal" mentation. For example, in its subsequent report on decision making about life-sustaining treatment, the President's Commission concluded that a patient (like Karen Quinlan) who is reliably diagnosed to have permanently lost consciousness is not owed as vigorous medical care as are patients with better prognosis. Since their disability is "total" and no return to "even a minimal level of human functioning is possible," such patients' only interest in continued maintenance is "the very small probability that the prognosis of permanence is incorrect."[56] The Commission therefore concluded that the extent of care provided to such patients ought to be determined by the wishes of, and the direct and indirect consequences for, others, including the patients' relatives, care givers, and society at large.[57]

Consequently, one ought not to assume that the decision to continue the traditional understanding of death (albeit using the new neurological methods when the old circulatory and respiratory ones are inapplicable) has any necessary implications regarding society's attitudes toward these "diminished persons" and its obligations toward them. Concerns about "too much" or "inappropriate" treatment of seriously ill patients are important components of the current reexamination of the limits of medicine, but they carry no special weight in the "definition of death" debate.

The arguments against mixing organ-transplant rules with the statutes on death determination are at least as compelling. Organ (particularly heart) transplantation was responsible for first focusing public attention on the need to update the standards for determining death. Yet, on a national basis, only about 15 percent of those persons who are declared dead based on neurologic criteria become organ donors.[58] Special protection for organ donors—including requirements about the number of physicians needed to apply the standards to make a determination of death and their independence from any involvement in organ removal—is an acceptable part of the Uniform Anatomical Gift Act.[59] Nonetheless, a special standard only for organ donors would thus fail to address the overwhelming majority of comatose, respirator-supported cases, leaving unchanged the present limbo vis-a-vis these dead bodies.

Moreover, since the status of "organ donor" is an imposed rather than inherent one, creating a separate standard of death for this group alone opens the door to abuse and confusion. This is illustrated by a Connecticut case. That state had adopted a "brain death" statute in 1979 but attached it to its anatomical gift act. A case arose of a young woman who had lost all brain functioning as a result of general anesthesia during dental surgery. She was not a potential organ donor, however, and the court held that she was therefore not dead—although she could have been so declared had she been a potential donor. Only when the public prosecutor revealed his original stand—for this one case—and agreed not to bring charges, did the physician feel he could follow through on his medical diagnosis of death and cease artificial support.[60]

THE FUTURE

Progress toward Uniform Laws

Although the trend is strongly toward the adoption of statutes "defining" death—and particularly toward the Uniform Determination of Death Act (UDDA)—the pace of statutory adoptions has slowed again and interstate uniformity has yet to be achieved. This seems to be more a result of disinterest than any strong opposition to the UDDA. To the extent there is opposition, it rests less with the proponents of "higher brain only definitions," whose proposals would be too radical for most legislators, than with a few religious groups that misinterpret the intent and effect of the proposed statute.

Probably the most groundless opposition is that based on the contention that loss of all brain *function* is not enough for death, which should be declared only upon proof of *organic destruction*.[61] The premise is that until an organ has been destroyed there is always the *possibility* that it might resume functioning, a standard that has not been applied in diagnosing death on cardiopulmonary grounds. It is enough that a determination of *irreversible* loss of functions take account of current medical capabilities—indeed, the methods for both measuring and reversing loss of cardiac functions have increased dramatically over the past 30 years. "Since the evidence ... indicates that brain criteria, properly applied, diagnose death as reliably as cardiopulmonary criteria," there is "no reason not to use the same standards of cessation for both."[62]

A second objection to the UDDA—this one based on policy implications rather than doubts about medical science—is that any statute that would permit death to be declared on a respirator-supported body encourages euthanasia (first passive and eventually active). This view, advanced by some right-to-life groups, has been most effectively rebutted by theologians and activists of the same ideological outlook. For example, a pro-life Catholic scholar argues that

> a correct definition of death, if it would eliminate some false classification of dead individuals [as being] among the living, could relieve some of the pressure for legalizing euthanasia—in this case, pressure arising from a right attitude toward individuals really dead and only considered alive due to conceptual confusion.[63]

Similarly, Dennis J. Horan, President of American Citizens United for Life, declares that a statute incorporating irreversible cessation of total brain functions would be "beneficial" and would "not undermine any of the values we seek to support."[64] Catholic organizations, such as state Catholic Conferences, have supported legislative adoption of the UDDA in several states.

The final source of opposition arises from a disagreement in the Orthodox Jewish community. Although the leading view is that complete cessation of brain function provides a basis for declaring death (by analogy to decapitation), some rabbis interpret the Jewish texts as requiring cessation of corporal blood flow, even though it is being artificially maintained in a manner not contemplated when those texts were set down.[65]

There are two responses to the concern of this latter group about "premature" declarations of death. The first is that in some cases personal beliefs must yield to the needs of the collective—just as objections to autopsy must give way in appropriate cases to the state's investigatory requirements. The answer to the question whether a person is alive or dead is so central to many matters of public concern (as reflected throughout the civil and criminal law) that it cannot be left to individual preferences, no matter how sincerely held. Some who once urged a general "conscience clause," which would permit an individual to specify the standard to be used for determining his or her death,[66] seem now to recognize the chaos that could result were people free to declare that their "death" had occurred when senility arrived, or conversely, only upon total putrefaction.[67] Instead, the suggestion has been narrowed: people should be allowed to choose from among a few socially sanctioned alternatives.[68] While eliminating the worst kinds of mischief, this proposal still proceeds on the false premise that society would find it acceptable to treat two physically identical individuals in radically different ways (i.e., one as dead and the other as alive).

More important, by restricting the range of "definitions," the proposal contradicts its own major selling point, namely that "defining" death is a matter best left to individual conscience. There should, of course, be opportunity for choice regarding death—in the sense of the process of dying and the extent of artificial intervention in bodily processes. But, as has already been established regarding those who are concerned with what they regard as excessive medical maintenance of patients who have lost cognitive capacity, a statute on the standards for determining death issues no commands—one way or the other—about whether or when treatment may be ceased. Thus, if Orthodox Jews disagree with a determination that death has occurred in a body with artificially maintained respiration and circulation but no brain functions, they are not precluded from continuing to provide medical support (just as a potential kidney donor is maintained temporarily after death occurs, until the donated organs have been removed).

Biomedical Developments

The Uniform Determination of Death Act, like the other statutes and judicial decisions, recognizes that the criteria and test "accepted" by physicians will evolve with new scientific findings and technical advances. The law does not preclude changes in the criteria by which the statutory standards are implemented; thus, the statute is not at risk of becoming out-of-date simply because the medical consensus about the methods to be used—such as those distilled in the *Guidelines* of the Commission's medical consultants—will certainly change. There is, however, nothing to indicate that those changes will not occur within the boundaries set by the statute, namely the two standards of irreversible cessation of cardiopulmonary functions or irreversible cessation of all brain functions.

Recent findings on the natural replacement of neurons in the brains of adult animals[69] and of the recovery of neurologic function after injuries[70] open exciting avenues for research on methods to reverse brain injuries previously thought to be permanent. This work is still at an experimental stage, and the initial clinical applications of any results that are validated through further research will probably be in conditions—like Alzheimer's disease—involving neocortical functions. Nonetheless, techniques may someday be developed to restore functions in the entire brain, including the brainstem. Yet such developments would not contradict the UDDA and similar statutes; rather, they would provide a new meaning to the phrase "irreversible cessation of all functions of the entire brain" and would likewise lead to new medical criteria and tests.

The possibility of such reversals does serve, however, as a reminder of the dangers in a reductionist approach to "defining" human life in terms of various organ systems. There is potential for considerable confusion here between what is being measured and the means of measurement. The term "brain death" illustrates this: it is often used in a way that suggests the speaker means "the death of the brain," when what is actually at issue is "the death of a human being, as determined by an examination of brain functioning." Should the day ever arise when functioning can be restored to a totally nonfunctioning brain, by medical or surgical treatment or by the implantation of a "neurologic pacemaker"—as today functioning can be restored to nonfunctioning heart and lungs—it will be advisable to be thinking in terms of "irreversible cessation" as a means of making a judgment about an *organism* rather than "brain death," which is a conclusion about an *organ*.[71]

NOTES

1. PRESIDENT'S COMMISSION FOR THE STUDY OF ETHICAL PROBLEMS IN MEDICINE AND BIOMEDICAL AND BEHAVIORAL RESEARCH, DEFINING DEATH (1981) [hereinafter cited as DEFINING DEATH].

2. *Guidelines for the Determination of Death: Report of the Medical Consultants on the Diagnosis of Death to the President's Commission for the Study of Ethical Problems in Medicine and Biomedical and Behavioral Research*, 246 J. A.M.A. 2184 (1981) [hereinafter cited as *Guidelines*].

3. Barclay, *Guidelines for the Determination of Death*, 246 J. A.M.A. 2194 (1981).

4. Arnold, Zimmerman & Martin, *Public Attitudes and the Diagnosis of Death*, 206 J. A.M.A. 1949 (1968).

5. Alexander, *The Rigid Embrace of the Narrow House: Premature Burial & the Signs of Death*, HASTINGS CTR. REP. 25, 26-27 (1980).

6. *Id.* at 30.

7. *Supra* note 2, at 2185.

8. BLACK'S LAW DICTIONARY 488 (4th ed. 1968). In its latest edition, BLACK'S (5th ed. 1979) now includes any entry under "brain death" at p. 170.

9. See, e.g., Smith v. Smith, 229 Ark. 579, 587, 313 S.W.2d 275, 279 (1958); In re Estate of Schmidt, 261 Cal. App.2d 262, 273, 67 Cal. Rptr. 847, 854 (1968).

10. State v. Johnson, 395 N.E.2d 368, 372 (Ohio 1977).

11. Cranford, & Smith, *Some Critical Distinctions Between Brain Death and Persistent Vegetative State*, 6 ETHICS IN SCI. & MED. 199, 201 (1979).

12. Grenvik, *Brain Death and Permanently Lost Consciousness*, in TEXTBOOK OF CRITICAL CARE 968 (W. Shoemaker, L. Thompson, & P. Holbrook, 1984).

13. See Black, *Brain Death*, 299 NEW ENGL. J. MED. 338 (1978).

14. Parisi, Kim, & Collins, et al., *Brain Death with Prolonged Somatic Survival*, 306 NEW ENGL. J. MED. 14 (1982).

15. Grenvik, *supra* note 12, at 969.

16. Jennett & Plum, *The Persistent Vegetative State: A Syndrome in Search of a Name*, LANCET 734 (1972).

17. N. MCWHIRTER, THE GUINESS BOOK OF WORLD RECORDS 42 (1981).

18. Heiden, et al., *Severe Head Injury and Outcome: A Prospective Study*, in NEURAL TRAUMA (A. Popp, et al., 1979); Levy, et al., *Prognosis in Nontraumatic Coma*, 94 ANN. INT. MED. 293 (1981).

19. DEFINING DEATH, *supra* note 1, at 89-101.

20. *Guidelines, supra* note 2.

21. *Id.* at 2185.

22. *See, e.g.*, Grenvik, *supra* note 12, at 969.

23. *Guidelines, supra* note 2, at 2185.

24. Jastremski, et al., *Problems in Brain Death Determination*, 11 FOREN. SCI., 201, 205 (1978).

25. *Id.* at 207.

26. *See, e.g.*, R. VEATCH, DEATH, DYING AND THE BIOLOGICAL REVOLUTION (1977); Veatch, *The Whole-Brain-Oriented Concept of Death: An Outmoded Philosophical Formulation*, 3 J. THANATOL. 13 (1975).

27. VEATCH, DEATH, DYING AND THE BIOLOGICAL REVOLUTION *supra* note 26, at 34-54; Englehardt, *Defining Death: A Philosophical Problem for Medicine and Law*, 112 ANN. REV. RESP. DIS. 587, 590-94 (1975).

28. DEFINING DEATH, *supra* note 1, at 40.

29. *Id.* at 33.

30. *Id.* at 34.

31. Bernat, Culver, & Gert, *On the Definition and Criterion of Death*, 94 ANN. INT. MED. 389, 391 (1981).

32. DEFINING DEATH, *supra* note 1, at 35.

33. *See* Capron & Kass, *A Statutory Definition of the Standards for Determining Human Death: An Appraisal and a Proposal*, 121 U. PA. L. REV. 87, 108-11 (1972).

34. LAW REFORM COMMISSION OF CANADA, REPORT ON THE CRITERIA FOR THE DETERMINATION OF DEATH 25 (1981).

35. Dworkin, *Death in Context*, 48 IND. L. J. 623 (1973); Brennan & Delgado, *Death: Multiple Definitions or a Single Standard?* 54 S. CAL. L. REV. 1323 (1981).

36. Capron, *The Purpose of Death: A Reply to Professor Dworkin*, 48 IND. L. J. 640, 645 (1973).

37. Kennedy, *The Kansas Statute on Death—An Appraisal*, 285 NEW ENG. J. MED. 946 (1971).
38. Tucker v. Lower, No. 2831 (Richmond, Va. Law & Eq., May 23, 1972).
39. Annas, *Defining Death: There Ought to Be a Law*, HASTINGS CTR. REP. 20 (1983).
40. People v. Eulo, 63 N.Y.2d 341, 482 N.Y.S.2d 436 (1984).
41. *Id.* at 356, 482 N.Y.S.2d at 445.
42. *See, e.g.*, Commonwealth v. Golston, 373 Mass. 249, 366 N.E.2d 744 (1977), *cert. denied*, 434 U.S. 1039 (1978).
43. New York City Health and Hosp. Corp. v. Sulsona, 81 Misc. 2d 1002, 367 N.Y.S.2d 686 (Sup. Ct. 1975).
44. People v. Eulo, 63 N.Y.2d 341, 357 n.29, 482 N.Y.S.2d 436, 446 n.29 (1984).
45. A review of the state statutes appears in DEFINING DEATH, *supra* note 1, at 62-67 and 109-134.
46. KAN. STAT. ANN. §77-202 (Cum. Supp. 1979).
47. Capron & Kass, *supra* note 33, as modified in Capron, *Legal Definition of Death*, 315 ANN. N.Y. ACAD. SCI. 349, 356 (1978).
48. 100 A.B.A. ANN. REP. 231 (1975).
49. *Uniform Laws (1980 Supplement), Vol. 12.* Chicago, Ill., National Conf. of Comm. on Unif. State Laws 5 (1980).
50. 243 J. A.M.A. 420 (1980).
51. Pub. L. No. 95-622 (1978) (codified at 43 U.S.C. §300v-1(a)(1)(B) (Supp. 1982)).
52. The following states have adopted laws on the determination of death that recognize cessation of total brain functions (B = AMA proposal (1975); C-K = Capron-Kass proposal (1972); K = Kansas Model (1970); M = ABA proposal (1979); N = nonstandard; UBDA = Uniform Brain Death Act (1978); and UDDA = Uniform Determination of Death Act (1981)):

N ALA. CODE §§22-31-1 to -4 (1979) (when part of body is to be used in transplantation, must have second confirmation of death; limits liability for civil/criminal actions).

C-K ALASKA STAT. §09.65.120 (1974).

N ARK. STAT. ANN. §82-537 to -538 (1979).

UDDA CAL. HEALTH & SAFETY CODE §§7180-7183 (1982) (includes section on confirmation and procedures for UAGA, and on patient records).

UDDA COLO. REV. STAT. §12-36-136 (1981).

N CONN. GEN. STAT. ANN. §19a-278(b), (c) (1983) (part of UAGA).

UDDA D.C. CODE ANN. §6-2401 (1982).

N FLA. STAT. §382.085 (1980) (determination must be made by two physicians—one a neurologist, neurosurgeon, internist, pediatrician, surgeon, or anesthesiologist; limits liability).

N GA. CODE ANN. §§8-1716 (1982) (limits legal liability; allows other, unspecified medically recognized criteria).

C-K HAWAII REV. STAT. §327 C-1 (1978, amend. 1979).

UDDA IDAHO CODE §54-1819 (1981).

B ILL. ANN. STAT. ch. 110 1/2, §302 (1975) (part of UAGA).

(UDDA) Ind. (*see* Swafford v. State, 421 N.E.2d 596, 602 (Ind. 1981) (homicide law)).

C-K IOWA CODE ANN. §702.8 (1976).

K KAN. STAT. ANN. §77-202 (1970, amend. 1979).

C-K LA. REV. STAT. ANN. §9:111 (1976).

UDDA Me. Rev. Stat. Ann. §§22-2811 to 2813 (1983).
UDDA Md. Ann. Code HG §§5-201 to 202 (1972, amend. 1983).
C-K Mich. Stat. Ann. §14.15 (1021-1023) (1979).
UDDA Miss. Laws ch. 410 (1981).
N Mo. §194.005 (1982).
UDDA Mont. Rev. Code Ann. §50-22-101 (1983).
UBDA Nev. Rev. Stat. §451.007 (1979).
K N.M. Stat. Ann. §12-2-4 (1978).
(C-K) People v. Eulo, N.Y. Ct. App., No. 402, decided 10-30-84.
N N.C. Gen. Stat. §9-323 (1979).
M Ohio §2108.30 (1982) (mentions brainstem and artificial support).
N Okla. Stat. Ann. tit. 63, §1-301(g) (1975).
N Or. Rev. Stat. §146.001 (1975).
UDDA Pa. Stat. Ann. 35 §§10201-10203 (1982).
UDDA R.I. Gen. Laws §23-4-16 (1983).
UDDA Tenn. Code Ann. §68-3-501 (1982).
C-K Tex. Rev. Civ. Stat. Ann. art. 4447t (1979).
UDDA Vt. Stat. Ann. tit. 18, §5218 (1981).
K Va. Code §54-325.7 (1973, amend. 1979).
(UDDA) Wash. (*see* In re Bowman, 94 Wash.2d 407, 421, 617 P.2d 731, 738 (1982)).
UBDA W. Va. Code §16-10-1 to -3 (1980).
UDDA Wis. Stat. §146.71 (1982).
N Wyo. Stat. §35-19-101 (1979).

53. Conference of Royal Colleges and Faculties of the United Kingdom: Memorandum on the Diagnosis of Death, in Working Party of the United Kingdom Health Department, The Removal of Cadaveric Organs for Transplantation: A Code of Practice 32-36 (1979).
54. Defining Death, *supra* note 1, at 28.
55. Grenvik, *supra* note 12, at 968.
56. President's Commission for the Study of Ethical Problems in Medicine and Biomedical and Behavioral Research, Deciding to Forego Life-Sustaining Treatment 182 (1983).
57. *Id.* at 183-86.
58. Defining Death, *supra* note 1, at 101.
59. *See* §7(b) of the Uniform Anatomical Gift Act.
60. *See* Fabro, *Bacchiochi v. Johnson Memorial Hospital*, 45 Conn. Med. 267 (1981); Fabro, *The Bacchiochi Case—Continued*, 45 Conn. Med. 334 (1981).
61. Byrne, O'Reilly, & Quay, *Brain Death: An Opposing Viewpoint*, 242 J. A.M.A. 1985 (1975).
62. Defining Death, *supra* note 1, at 76.
63. G. Grisez & J. Boyle, Life and Death with Liberty and Justice: A Contribution to the Euthanasia Debate 61 (1979).
64. Horan, *Definition of Death: An Emerging Consensus*, 16 Trial 26 (1980).
65. Defining Death, *supra* note 1, at 11.

66. Veatch, Death, Dying and the Biological Revolution, *supra* note 26, at 72-76.
67. Capron, *supra* note 47, at 356-57.
68. R. Veatch, Whole Brain and Higher Brain Related Concepts of Death (in press).
69. Kolata, *New Neuronic Form in Adulthood*, 224 Science 1325-26 (1984).
70. J. Sladek & D. Gash, Neural Transplants: Development and Function (1984).
71. The author was the Executive Director of the President's Commission that produced the reports cited in the text; the Commission's work on the definition of death is analyzed in Capron, *The Report of the President's Commission on the Uniform Determination of Death Act*, in Whole Brain And Neocortical Definitions of Death: A Critical Appraisal (R. Zaner & C. Scott, in press), on which this chapter draws.

Chapter 7

Human and Environmental Factors in Critical Care: Patients and Their Families

G.L. Wallace-Barnhill

Most people do not comprehend the workings of an ICU. To know it you must actually experience it, either as a patient or as a family member of an ICU patient. Hearing about it secondhand from others, viewing TV or movie portrayals is not the same as the real thing. Movie stars do not suffer the indignity of being intubated and connected to a ventilator for respiratory support. Actors are not forced to endure the torturous attack of having one's chest and back pounded with fists to relieve enough lung congestion so that a long pliable plastic tube can be placed down the throat and into sore, bruised lungs to suction out secretions. Movie script ICUs are pale and lifeless compared to the real-world struggles against death in modern ICUs.

The most absolute, overriding anxiety for ICU patients and their families is the fear of death. This fear may not be expressed verbally or confronted consciously. However, the behavior of all family members can be viewed as reflecting this concern. Physicians and nurses may have a tendency to overlook the effects of these threatening realities on patients and families because their focus is on treatment and cure. Physicians proceed with treatment as if their patients will all survive but they should not be surprised that families do not always share that conviction. On the other hand, when it becomes necessary for the health care team to apprise the family of the likely possibility that their loved one may not survive, it is just as important to understand that the family may deny that death could be the final outcome.

I dedicate this chapter to Jason, Craig, and Christy in memory of their father and my brother, Robert D. Barnhill (1945–1977). He showed courage and compassion during his suffering. He gave love to others when he knew he was dying. Confronting the ordeal of his death has enabled me to face life with a renewed sense of awareness and purpose.

ICU ENVIRONMENT AND THE PATIENT

An ICU is neither quiet nor private. There is constant activity. Ever-present monitoring equipment provides not only minute-to-minute but heartbeat-to-heartbeat data to the ICU team of physicians, nurses, and therapists. The modern ICU surrounds the patient with a cascading array of equipment that spouts forth a crescendo of data in various shapes, sights, and sounds.

By the time a patient arrives in an ICU he or she has survived the initial impact of serious disease or injury, which may include emergency medical intervention at the scene of the incident, transportation to the hospital, emergency department, stabilization, and possibly a surgical procedure in the operating room. Therefore, just making it to the ICU is to be considered a survival of sorts.

For patients, the ICU environment requires *major* adjustments both mentally and emotionally. Patients find themselves in an unknown environment for which they have no "frame of reference." They must struggle to gain a feeling of stability and self-control. Their reality becomes one of almost total dependency, i.e., loss of control over their environment and personal well-being. They are no longer in charge of even the simplest bodily function, including breathing, urination, and defecation. They are constantly subjected to physical examination and probing into even their most private parts, because the need for a constant stream of medical data far outweighs personal needs for privacy or control over body functions. Routine habits learned over years of practice like bathing, washing one's hair, and brushing one's teeth become someone's assignment on the morning shift. This total state of dependence on others is usually quite devastating to ICU patients.

ICU patients frequently suffer from severe sleep deprivation.[1] Often the members of the health care team are responsible for disrupting patients' sleep patterns. While the importance of sleep is generally recognized by health professionals, priorities are dictated by life-threatening physiological needs that outweigh the need for sleep. Sleep deprivation, in addition to other factors, often results in the ICU psychosis syndrome, a recurring problem in the ICU.

ICU PSYCHOSIS

Most patients who are ill enough to require admission to an ICU will manifest an emotional response, regardless of the reason for admission. These feelings may follow a pattern varying from intense fear and anxiety to denial and depression. If not relieved, these symptoms are followed by increasing dependency and a state of paranoia with the patient, fearing that his or her life support systems will fail or be disconnected. Occasionally, there is complete withdrawal into a psychotic state.[2]

ICU psychosis is a diagnosis often applied to patients exhibiting acute agitation varying from mild confusion to advanced delirium. Eisendrath[3] has defined the ICU psychosis as "an acute organic brain syndrome" involving impaired intellectual functioning that occurs in patients being treated in critical care units. Cassem,[4] however, states that the term ICU psychosis is a convenient diagnostic catchall term, and that it is meaningless and inaccurate. Kleck[5] has reported that there is a 20–30 percent risk of some significant mental aberration occurring in a patient who spends more than five to seven days in an ICU and the longer the stay the greater the risk. Noble[6] reports that patients may be lucid for the first three to five days in the ICU but then 30–70 percent of them begin to have perceptual distortions or illusions. Hackett[7] found that delirium occurs in 2–10 percent of all ICU patients.

Patients who have sustained severe trauma, prolonged surgical procedures, and lengthy anesthesia have a greater tendency to develop organic reactions. The common features of this ICU syndrome consist of clouding of consciousness, decreased ability to maintain attention, orientation difficulties, memory problems, and labile affect. The awake ICU patient also realizes that there is a significant chance of dying. The response of the normal person in this situation ranges from mild anxiety to severe panic. Occasionally, a patient's initial reaction is one of relief in the realization that he or she has survived a near-death encounter. This feeling may approach a delusionary sense of indestructibility. Alternatively, patients may display symptoms of altered time perception, lack of emotion, feelings of surrealism, attention deficits, a sense of detachment, loss of control, revival of memories, and a sense of ineffability.[8] Interestingly, these symptoms are also frequently found among the families of ICU patients, who vicariously share these death-related experiences with their loved ones.

ICU patients face not only constant concern about death but also fears for loved ones and concerns for those dependent on them either financially or emotionally. This stress, in addition to the reality of their physical state, can cause extreme despondency or depression. The accumulation of environmental and situational factors affects all ICU patients to various degrees, depending on their personality characteristics, physical state, extent of physical trauma, degree and severity of any surgery performed and subsequent responses, and length of stay in the ICU. These extreme emotional states may be alleviated by allowing patients to verbalize any fears and concerns with their families.

Whether ICU psychosis is a verifiable entity or whether it is actually a misdiagnosis, as some would suggest, the fact remains that the symptoms described do exist.[9] The problem of communication for these patients is extraordinary. The inability to orally express one's thoughts, feelings, questions, or concerns to ICU staff members regarding one's physical condition or to convey thoughts and feelings to loved ones creates severe emotional distress. The experience of being attached to monitoring machines, and particularly to the respirator for ventilatory support, seems to initiate a very real sense of personal paranoia. Total dependence on these machines for life support (as well as on ICU personnel) and their continuous undeniable presence sometimes generating almost unbearable noise, leads some patients to extremes of paranoia—even to the belief that certain therapists or nurses are going to kill them. This situation usually becomes acute during or following long monotonous hours with little or no interaction with or personal response from others. When nurses or respiratory therapists arrive at the bedside to change intravenous infusions or reset the respirator or make other patient care adjustments, they may be met with a hostile or fearful stare from the patient who at that moment may fear that their actions threaten his or her life. These patient responses occur with some frequency as well as visual and auditory hallucinations, which also may occur.

Whether these symptoms are diagnosed as ICU psychosis or not, health care professionals as well as family members must be aware that these reactions may occur. They must be prepared to deal with them. Even a patient who is intubated but mentally alert and awake can be given emotional support and reassurance regarding these episodes particularly by a trusted family member. For example, in my own experience when my brother Robert was a patient in an ICU, I assured him that there were no bugs or monsters floating around in the room. It appeared as if there were such visions before him and he would look to me for confirmation and at times make gestures as if there were objects floating above the bed. I would calmly explain to him that there were none. This reassurance seemed to help him pull things back into a sense of reality.

FAMILIES AND COPING

The emotional impact of the patient's admission to an ICU is an experience for which few families are prepared. To the family involved, the ICU events do not follow a logical sequence and do not provide a frame of reference of previous experiences or behaviors; rather, they produce a novel and sometimes eerie or unreal state of existence. While family members struggle to comprehend what is occurring they often appear dazed. During this unusual state of existence it is difficult to imagine the full recovery of their loved one, or to envision death. From the family's viewpoint, time often goes by without signs of visible progress. The family members often cannot clearly comprehend the medical information reported by the ICU staff. The relatives' perceptions of daily events are often inaccurate, partly because it takes time for treatment to show evidence of effect and partly because of their need to adjust psychologically to what is occurring.

Bouman[10] and Prowse[11] have reported that family member's greatest concerns are the quality of medical treatment and indications that the ICU staff members really care. The next most important factors are a need to talk to the doctor at least once daily and a desire to have a place for the family to be alone while at the hospital. West[12] recommends changes in the ICU environment to provide more privacy by using partitions instead of drapes, with large glass windows facing the nursing station. He feels that this increased privacy would add to patient comfort and be conducive to allowing more frequent visits by family members.

Personnel should be as supportive and reassuring as possible to the patients' families. Most people can eventually accept and deal with the gravest of situations if they are given some hope and if they believe that everything possible is being done. Family members usually want honest and complete information regarding the condition of their loved one. However, it is extremely difficult for physicians and nurses to accurately assess the psychological needs of every individual within each family. There are families that are not prepared for or not capable of accepting, hearing, or interpreting the truth. In this situation, emotional tension between the family and the health care team may develop. For these reasons, many health care professionals tend to limit the depth of information given to families unless details are specifically requested. Thus, a paradox may exist. Families may wish to have honest information about their loved one but at the same time they may wish to hear only good news.

For most family members, hope for survival is the most important factor in their ability to cope regardless of the medical odds. The constant burden of facing the reality of the crisis is at times excruciating. To endure, it is necessary to rely on their best psychological defenses, both conscious and unconscious. After the initial emotional shock and sense of disbelief, families begin to accept the reality of the critical illness of their loved one. The next phase of coping usually involves a temporary feeling of relief that their loved one is at least alive. However, despite this temporary relief, a dreaded feeling that the disease or injury might ultimately be fatal is constantly present, although usually unspoken. There are times when these combined feelings of relief and fear or dread are mixed with brief thoughts that perhaps the patient should die so that suffering would end.

Family Emotional Needs

If patient outcome is not determined quickly, a long, seemingly unproductive and exhaustive time period may ensue. The family's fear and anxiety regarding the patient's outcome may influence their perceptions about the quality of treatment.[13] Families may conclude that if the staff were providing proper treatment, the patient would be getting well. If the patient is deteriorating, they may assume that staff must not be providing adequate care. At times this thinking may even lead to behavioral displays of antagonism toward the staff. Individual family members may "act out" or display feelings of anger, fear, or guilt. It is difficult even for well-trained health care professionals to assess these family behaviors accurately. However, it is important for the ICU staff to recognize that a family's negative behavioral reactions are usually a reflection of feelings of uncertainty and dread and should not, therefore, be taken personally.

These stress factors affect families differently. Often a family member's individual responses reflect the quality of that person's relationship with the patient at the time of the event that caused hospitalization. Thus, the situation may be complicated by interpersonal problems within the family structure at the time of the ICU admission. Confronting these dire circumstances may create a climate of forgiveness among the family members and create feelings of closeness and strength. At times, however, chasms in family relationships become even more exaggerated and fragile family ties begin to break.[14] The mood of family members seems to affect the emotional stability of patients more than any other factor. Some families, especially those that become fragmented, cannot provide the emotional support to the patient that is necessary to cope with the ICU situation.

Families and ICU Staff

The lack of physical space and privacy and the overwhelming congestion and high noise level of the ICU cause particular problems for both patients and their families. However, the impact of these factors can be reduced if efforts are made by the staff to inform and familiarize families with the ICU. Some ICUs provide information booklets describing the various types of medical procedures, terminology, and equipment in this very unique environment. In the future, videotape presentations may be used for this purpose. The impact of the above-mentioned problems is reduced if the families are convinced that the patient is receiving the best treatment available for survival. Feelings of trust and confidence in the staff providing care are usually enhanced if the medical and nursing staff provide continuous information in a direct and honest manner. A good doctor-patient-family relationship is of paramount importance and usually minimizes the possibility of families developing resentment, suspicion, or hostility.

About one out of every four or five ICU patients dies in the hospital. To endure the psychological trauma of the ICU experience requires tremendous emotional stability and a conviction that the loved one will survive. This concerted effort may require that families concentrate their expectations on whatever chance their relative has for survival, no matter how small. It is difficult to tolerate the daily pressure of seeing a loved relative near death without some degree of optimism. Family members must focus so much energy on having a positive, hopeful attitude that often the bad news is either not heard or denied such that optimism still prevails.

At times, family members may resort to unusual behavior in response to stress and lack of support. One family had each member phone the ICU separately, during a 24-hour period, asking the same question about their loved one. It was not discovered until morning rounds that each nurse had spent a great deal of time and effort conscientiously trying to answer the same question to each of the eight family members. Other results of a family's inability or unwillingness to face the near-death situation of their loved one may be anger, accusations, or other demonstrations of frustration with the health care team. Such circumstances may lead to a lack of trust and general dissatisfaction with the ICU team and the hospital itself. Depending on the level of psychological sophistication of the physicians and nurses involved, this situation may require consultation with a social worker, clergy member, or mental health counselor, specially trained in dealing with these matters. Families may respond with despair and disbelief upon hearing from their loved one's physician that there is nothing more that can be done. Some families wish to continue treatment at any cost despite overwhelming odds against survival or continued life with dignity. Therefore, families and physicians not infrequently disagree over the appropriateness of specific therapy. Fortunately, such disagreements are usually resolved within the patient-physician-family triad.

Families should be allowed an expanded role in questions concerning the appropriate level of patient care.[15] Physicians should not feel threatened when patients or families assume a greater role in decision making regarding medical treatment. They should recognize that in a moral, ethical, and legal sense, families should be and are empowered to participate in this decision making. Although there will certainly continue to be situations that can be resolved only through legal processes, it is quite possible that many such problems can be resolved through more understanding by the physicians and nurses involved.

When the inevitability of impending death is apparent, the medical staff must recognize and provide for family needs to allow the acceptance of death.

Civetta[16] believes that "providing an environment in which families can learn to cope with this unpleasant reality should, indeed, be one of physicians' most important goals." However, when confronted with the reality that their loved one will not survive, families may not respond as expected. At such time, family members are forced to give up the hope and belief that have kept them together and helped them tolerate the ordeal. Thus, regardless of prior discussion and counseling, physicians should not be surprised by family reactions of denial and disbelief. Usually, time and patience will resolve this problem. Most families make appropriate psychological adjustments within 24 to 48 hours. If not, it is wise to use the service of an experienced counselor before any withdrawal of life-sustaining treatment. It is incumbent upon the physician treating critically ill patients to become psychologically more sophisticated in dealing with these circumstances. Physician certification in critical care medicine should include evaluation of skills in effectively communicating with patients and families.[17]

In most situations, time is the main requirement for family members to adjust and to accept the reality of the imminent death of their loved one. In addition to allowing the family time, another consideration required is restraint. Unless all ICU beds are occupied and a critically ill or injured but potentially viable patient is waiting for a bed, any urgency to act quickly to discontinue treatment may proceed without urgency. Medical training has taught physicians to act on the basis of factual data. It is understandable that when the facts show that a patient is no longer viable and that further treatment can no longer lead to a cure, physicians tend to accept this reality and act accordingly. However, it is precisely during this time period that physicians should shift their efforts to attend to the needs of the family. Only then should the responsible physician proceed as medically indicated. Through such consideration, feelings of antagonism and resistance from the family will be avoided.

In circumstances where the death of a patient follows prolonged ICU treatment, there may be an initial feeling of relief on the part of the family. Relatives may react in this way, not because their loved one has died, but because the apocalypse is finally over. Expressions of relief may be unspoken, inhibited by restrictions imposed by feelings of guilt. Nonetheless, it seems that the need for psychological closure is greater than our ability to endure the frustration of uncertainty. At such times, medical staff interactions with the family are needed and appropriate. The health care staff's responsibility should not terminate with the death of a patient.[18] Family members may want to know the manner in which the patient died. Was their loved one alone? Was the death peaceful or did he or she suffer? These communications also offer an opportunity for family members to share feelings of gratitude with the medical staff. Nurses and physicians often are left in doubt about the thoughts of family members. What did they think about how their loved one was treated? Is the family angry? Do they blame the staff? Do they think their loved one was tortured or do they think treatment was discontinued too soon or prolonged unnecessarily? Does the family understand that the medical and nursing staff really cared and tried their best? Answers to such questions may help foster acceptance of the death for families and staff alike.

GRIEF AND GRIEVING

Grief is personal and a wide range of responses is possible. These have been defined as normal (those responses that occur most often in the greatest number of people) or abnormal (those that occur very infrequently or to the least number of people). Many articles and books—personal, philosophical, religious, and psychological—have been written to help us understand the impact of grief.[19] Most agree that there is a normal process of grieving and recovery at the loss of a loved one.[20]

Janis[21] reported that for normal personalities grief reactions in general are roughly proportional to the perceived magnitude and importance of the loss. The common theme that seems to develop in the normal grieving process is despair followed by gradual detachment from the mourning responses. Freud[22] postulated that as we engage in reminiscing about our past life with one deceased we gradually accept the changes in our lives imposed by the loss. Jacobson[23] refers to a contrasting example of pathological grief. Here grief turns into a chronic state of depression, which is a temporary escape from external social reality as well as one's internal feelings of guilt and bereavement. This pathological grief can persist unchanged for a period of years. According to Janis[24] the constellation of repressed hostility and guilt felt toward the lost person appears to be at the core of the pathological depression evoked by bereavement. In the most extreme instances depressed mourners become preoccupied with feelings of worthlessness. Suicidal thoughts are not uncommon and there is usually some risk that the survivor actually will commit suicide.

Regardless of the time or extent of one's grief, it is commonly accepted that the death of a loved one will interfere with one's emotional feelings and behavioral performance for an extended period of time. Poor judgment is a customary experience after the death of a loved one. It is not unusual to experience temporarily the loss of one's ability to concentrate while driving a car or doing other routine tasks. During the initial months after the death of a loved one, depression, denial, social withdrawal, and isolation are frequent responses. This resulting psychological vulnerability makes major decisions, such as moving, selling one's house or other belongings, rushing into a relationship, or undertaking financial rearrangements usually inadvisable (although by necessity sometimes required) during this time period.

Often the most difficult feelings to deal with are the negative ones related to the deceased. For example, it is quite common for the mourner to become angry with the loved one for dying and it is difficult to feel, without guilt, the right to express these feelings. There are other common factors that exist during this time of recovery for the mourning person: depression and a devastating sense of loss, doubts about how to continue a normal life, an overinvestment of time and energy in thoughts about the deceased, guilt about the relationship and things left undone or unsaid, and an overidentification with the deceased leading to a temporary change in interests or hobbies to coincide with those of the deceased. Known illusionary experiences include seeing the deceased in public places, hearing the deceased talk to you, dreams of being together with the deceased and even being physically touched by the deceased. However, with time even the most severe of these symptoms subsides. Time is an important determinant in the grieving process and seems to have an acceptable societal limit that ends gradually at about one year. This generally accepted yet arbitrary one-year limit for mourning coincides with the passing of important landmarks that have emotional significance, such as a birthday, a wedding anniversary, the date of the incident or injury, and, of course, the date of death. Holidays like Christmas and Thanksgiving also are more difficult during the first year. However, it is important to recognize that even "normal" recovery from a loss may require longer than a year's time. Hendin also stated, "it is the progress of the course of grief that is the overriding factor, and not necessarily the length of time it takes."[25]

Despite mental preparation for a loved one's impending death, the actual impact of the death itself is devastating. "The loss of a loved person suddenly and violently alters one's view of the world and more importantly, provides drastic alterations in one's view of oneself."[26]

ROBERT

I will share with the reader an experience of my own which involved my brother and family. My brother, Robert, survived in an ICU for 2½ months following a car accident. A motorist lost control of his car and crossed six lanes of a major highway including a grassy median to hit my brother as he was entering the exit ramp. He was mentally alert and awake for most of the time in the ICU but in the end his body finally succumbed to the overwhelming demands placed on it.

Robert was transferred to the SICU from another hospital on November 30, 1976, with the following diagnoses secondary to the traumas of the automobile accident: aortic transection, ruptured spleen, lacerated liver, multiple rib fractures, paraplegia secondary to ischemia of the spinal cord, acute renal failure, left pleural effusion, atelectasis of the left lung, gastrointestinal bleeding secondary to stress ulcer, peritonitis secondary to breakdown of pyloroplasty, and acute respiratory insufficiency requiring a tracheostomy. He survived two additional surgical procedures before his last operation, which revealed widespread peritonitis. He suffered from septic shock, complete renal failure (no urinary output), worsening respiratory failure, and coma. Shortly before his death on January 2, 1977, our family agreed to discontinue therapy. Withholding further treatment was an act of accepting reality; he was no longer with us. The decision was for us, the surviving, not for Robert, who was unconscious and only exhibited the appearance of being alive.

The decision to terminate life-sustaining treatment caused us extreme emotional pain because it forced us to let go of someone we wanted desperately to hold on to. This experience allowed each of us to recognize more acutely our own mortality. Seeing a loved one die is as close as one can get to death without it being your own. Death with dignity has been a popular topic in recent years. To some it implies a relaxed, painless, serene state. In my opinion this interpretation places unnecessary emphasis on nonessential factors. Regardless of the hospital environment, the circumstances surrounding a loved one's death, or the atmosphere in which he or she dies, dignity can be maintained. Loving relatives of servicemen who have died in battle and descendents of those brave men and women who succumbed in concentration camps may attest to this. If we accept and believe this, in spite of the horrors sometimes surrounding death, one can die with dignity anywhere.

The actual ordeal of seeing a loved one die in an ICU cannot be adequately described. My feelings of desperation and helplessness during this time were the most devastating experiences I have ever had. Robert was paralyzed from his chest down, but he had full use of his arms. Initially he was mentally alert and his wife, Kathe, and I could talk to him. The exasperation of trying to communicate became more complicated when he was connected to a mechanical ventilator. The normal visiting policy of five minutes per hour was not enforced and I was permitted to stay with Robert throughout the day. I would arrive about 10 a.m. and stay until late at night. Kathe would visit in the morning and then leave to care for the children. There were days when Robert suffered from severe depression. His hands would grasp my arm as I leaned next to him and he would cry. Never have I felt so helpless. Invariably before I left, however, he would turn his face to look at me and then, with his hand, give me the thumbs-up signal. I still remember the feelings of those moments, his courage and never-ending desire to live.

Robert wanted desperately to see his children. He debated for days whether to allow them to visit. Finally, he painstakingly decided not to have his children see him in his miserable condition. He wanted them to remember their dad as he was before the accident. He hoped that some day they would accept and understand his decision.

Robert did not want to die. He was young and would have had to face life as a paraplegic, but still he wanted to live. He wanted to see his children grow up. His life could have been very full. His talents as an elementary school teacher and artist would not have been lost. Finally, though, he was forced to face and accept his death. Prior to his last trip to the OR he stated to Paula (a nurse who had befriended him and who had chosen to be assigned to his case at each of his previous surgical procedures) that he doubted he would survive that operation. Paula later recounted to me that he had his eyes shut, which was very unlike Robert. He had beautiful blue eyes and was always very alert. On previous visits he would interact with the OR personnel, but this time tears streamed down his cheeks and his eyes no longer danced.

My grief at the loss of my brother will last until I die. However the difference in my grieving now that time has passed is that it is no longer totally out of control. My continuing awareness of feelings related to his death is a constant reminder of our love for each other. These emotions support lasting memories and help me to live my life more fully.

NOTES:

1. Kleck, *ICU Syndrome: Onset, Manifestations, Treatment, Stressors and Prevention*, CRITICAL CARE Q. (March 1984); Gowan, *The Perceptual World of the Intensive Care Unit: An Overview of Some Environmental Considerations in the Helping Relationship*, 8 HEART AND LUNG 2 (1979); Poepsel, *Modified Nursing Routines: Their Effects on the Sleep of Patients in the Intensive Care Unit*, 13 HEART AND LUNG 3 (1984).

2. Kimball, *The Experience of Open-Heart Surgery*, 27(57) III ARCH. GEN. PSYCHIATRY (1972).

3. Eisendrath, *ICU Syndromes: Their Detection, Prevention and Treatment*, 7(4) CRITICAL CARE UPDATE 5-8 (1980).

4. Cassem, *Critical Care Psychiatry*, in TEXTBOOK OF CRITICAL CARE (W. Shoemaker, L. Thompson, & P. Holbrook, 1984).

5. Kleck, *Means to Forestall ICU Syndrome Explored*, 10(10) ANESTH. NEWS (1984).

6. Noble, *Communication in the ICU: Therapeutic or Disturbing?* NURSING OUTLOOK 195-98 (March 1970).

7. T. HACKETT & N. CASSEM, HANDBOOK OF GENERAL HOSPITAL PSYCHIATRY, MASSACHUSETTS GENERAL HOSPITAL (1978).

8. Brodland & Andreasen, *Adjustment Problems of the Family of the Burn Patient*, in STRESS AND SURVIVAL: THE EMOTIONAL REALITIES OF LIFE-THREATENING ILLNESS 230-35 (C. Garfield, 1979).

9. McKegney, *The Intensive Care Syndrome*, 30(9) COMM. MED. 633 (1966).

10. Bouman, *Self-Perceived Needs of Family Members of Critically Ill Patients*, 13(3) NTI RESEARCH ABSTRACTS (1984).

11. Prowse, *Needs of Family Members of Patients as Perceived by Family Members and Nurses in an ICU: An Exploratory Study*, 13(3) NTI RESEARCH ABSTRACTS (May 1984).

12. West, *Stresses Associated with ICUs Affect Patients, Families, Staff*, 49 HOSPITALS JAHA, 62-63 (December 1975).

13. Daley, *The Perceived Immediate Needs of Families with Relatives in the Intensive Care Setting*, 13(3) HEART AND LUNG (1984).

14. Olsen, *The Impact of Serious Illness on the Family System*, 47 POSTGRAD. MED. 169 (1970).

15. Geary, *Supporting Family Coping*, 10 SUPERVISOR NURSE, 52 (1979); Hymovich, *Incorporating the Family into Care*, 5 J. NEW YORK NURSES A. 332 (1974); Molter, *Needs of Relatives of Critically Ill Patients: A Descriptive Study*, 8 HEART AND LUNG 322 (1979).

16. Civetta, *Beyond Technology: Intensive Care in the 1980's*, 9 CRITICAL CARE MED. 11 (1981).

17. Grenvik, *Training and Certification in Critical Care Medicine*, in TEXTBOOK OF CRITICAL CARE, *supra* note 4.

18. Stillwell, *Importance of Visiting Needs as Perceived by Family Members of Patients in the Intensive Care Unit*, 13(3) HEART AND LUNG (1984); Hodovanic & Neardon, et al., *Family Crisis Intervention Program in the Medical Intensive Care Unit*, 13(3) HEART AND LUNG (1984).

19. A. LAZARE, UNRESOLVED GRIEF OF OUTPATIENT PSYCHIATRY: DIAGNOSIS AND TREATMENT (1979); C. PARKES, BEREAVEMENT: STUDIES IN ADULT GRIEF (1972); B. SIMOS, A TIME TO GRIEVE (1979).

20. Lindemann, *Symptomatology and Management of Acute Grief*, 101 AM. J. PSYCHIATRY (1944); 3 J. BOWLBY, ATTACHMENT AND LOSS: LOSS, SADNESS, AND DEPRESSION (1980); J. WORDEN, GRIEF COUNSELING AND GRIEF THERAPY (1982); Morris, *Research Studies of Bereaved Women*, in STRESS AND FRUSTRATION (I. Janis, 1971).

21. Janis, *Comparison of Normal and Pathological Grief*, in STRESS AND FRUSTRATION, *supra* note 20.

22. 14 S. FREUD, MOURNING AND MELANCHOLIA (std. ed. 1957).

23. Jacobson, *On Normal and Pathological Moods*, in 13 THE PSYCHOANALYTIC STUDY OF THE CHILD (R. Eisler ed. 1957).

24. *Supra* note 21.

25. D. HENDIN, DEATH AS A FACT OF LIFE (1974).

26. Cattell, *Psychiatric Implications*, in BEREAVEMENT IN DEATH AND BEREAVEMENT (Futscher ed., 1974).

Chapter 8

Human and Environmental Factors in Critical Care: Health Professionals

G.L. Wallace-Barnhill

Modern intensive care units are environments filled with extreme life-threatening situations where stress levels are elevated for staff, patients, and families. Most large hospitals have several intensive care units (ICUs) to provide specific treatment for patients within the various specialty disciplines. The number and types of ICUs in the United States has tripled since 1960. Types of ICUs include Coronary Care, Medical Intensive Care, Burn, Neonatal, Pediatric, Neurological, and Surgical Intensive Care Units. Four major groups of people interact within the ICU setting: physicians, nurses, patients, and patient families. All confront the daily uncertainty of a patient's life or death. The behavioral and psychological responses of these individuals often affect the stress level of those with whom they interact.

The problem of stress and its relationship to health is of practical as well as personal importance. The potential role of stress and its effects on health and productivity are recognized nationwide. Occupational stress has become an accepted factor in the pathogenesis of cardiovascular disorders, and stress-related illness is estimated to result in a loss of productivity of over $100 billion annually in the United States alone.[1]

THE STRESS CONCEPT

Contemporary interest in the stress concept originated with Hans Selye, a Canadian endocrinologist-physiologist. Selye sees stress as the state of the organism following failure of the normal homeostatic regulatory mechanisms

---

In memory of Edward F. McGuire (1923–1982). McGoo, the world was cheated by your passing.

"The guitar is quiet."

—Lillian McGuire

of adaptation to an externally present stimulus.[2] He equates stress with the general adaptation syndrome, a coordinated pattern of physiological responses that is evoked when demands are placed on the organism. However, Selye's approach to stress does not take into account individual differences. For example, factors that lead some individuals to respond to a noxious stimulus with mobilization and others to become immobilized for extended periods are largely ignored.[3]

Other authors have expanded the concept of stress to include psychological responses that may appear to be inappropriate if only the external physical stimuli present are considered. This extended concept of stress includes psychological stress.

In general, the stress-inducing property of a particular stimulus cannot be categorized on the basis of its ability to produce a precise degree of stress. It would be impossible to set forth a table of standards that associate a given level of stress with a specific stimulus. For instance, it has been shown that psychological stress factors fail to be universally effective because different individuals are not equally vulnerable to all types of stressor agents.[4]

Dato has proposed that stress, whether physical or psychological, can be conceptualized as a neutral law.[5] Dato's Law of Stress postulates that stress (S) is the difference between pressure (P) and adaptability (A), as expressed by the formula, $S=P-A$. According to this law, the greater the adaptability to any particular pressure, the lesser the resulting stress. Implied in the formula is the concept that stress represents the gap between pressure and adaptability and that stress may be managed successfully either by reducing pressure or increasing adaptability in order to close the stress gap.

Anxiety is a commonly agreed upon component of psychological stress. The term "anxiety" was coined by Freud in 1894 to specify that the "state of being" is associated with feelings of apprehension.[6] Freud also differentiated between objective anxiety (external) and neurotic anxiety (internal).

With the possible exception of extreme and sudden life-threatening situations, no single stimulus is a stressor to every individual exposed to it. Individuals may respond to similar situations in different ways.[7] Other theorists conclude that "stress occurs when a particular situation threatens the attainment of some goal, or when a threatening situation causes some significant change in behavior."[8]

ENVIRONMENT

Prior to World War II, most people died at home. Today 80 percent of all deaths occur in hospitals or nursing homes.[9] Physicians and nurses have become society's custodians of death. As a result of the rapid appearance and growth of ICUs, the role of physicians and nurses has become more complicated. Health care professionals who work in critical care are expected to be experts in the psychosocial issues that surround life and death. Unfortunately, these health professionals are not specifically trained or experienced to help others face death. When called upon to buffer the powerful impact of grief, to make sense out of death to family members, they are often unsuccessful.

The demands of intensive care are unrelenting and at times hectic. Tasks are accomplished under high personal and professional tension. The ICU fosters an increased awareness of physical pain, emotional terror, and often death. Advances in medical science and technology frequently allow the saving of a life and the return to society of a patient who would have surely expired under the same circumstances in a previous era. On the other hand, sometimes these medical advances may only delay an inevitable death or result in a prolonged existence with little "quality of life."

All ICU patients are in serious to critical condition. Patients arrive in an ICU for various reasons. Some have had very complicated or extensive surgery and may be admitted only for 24-48 hours of close observation. Others may have developed intraoperative complications that necessitated ICU admittance. Some patients have suffered emergency trauma from an automobile accident, blunt injury, or a stabbing or shooting incident. Still others may have extensive or complicated medical illness with acute deterioration.

Many patients treated in ICUs suffer from multiple organ failure. They are usually intubated for airway control and mechanical respiratory assistance. Because they have a tracheal tube passing between the vocal cords, these patients are unable to communicate orally with the health care team providing their care. Treatments and medications must be given continuously or at frequent intervals. Increasing use of invasive, highly technical monitoring and the addition of new experimental medical procedures is commonplace. Nursing duties associated with such patient care are intense, time consuming, and physically exhausting.

NURSING STRESS

Bailey and Steffen[10] reported results from a study of 1,800 ICU nurses nationwide which showed that the three most stressful factors in the ICU were (1) conflicts with other health care professionals, (2) inadequate staffing, and (3) lack of support in dealing with death and dying. Gentry[11] found that ICU nurses tend to show more objective signs of anxiety, depression, and hostility than non-ICU nurses. This increased level of psychological strain in ICU nurses appeared to be a result of situational factors, not of personality differences between the two nursing groups. The situational stressors reported by Gentry were overwhelming work load, excessive responsibility, poor communication with fellow professionals, and overcrowded facilities with limited work space.

Anderson and Basteyns[12] have reaffirmed that ICUs present a highly stressful environment for even the best prepared nurses. Their report also identified key ICU stressors to be staffing problems, heavy work load, and communication problems with physicians. In a more comprehensive review of critical care nursing stress, Stehle[13] reviewed 28 articles representing 19 investigations of ICU stress. However, Stehle found that ICUs, although generally portrayed as highly stressful, were not shown to be more stressful than other types of nursing units.

The growth of life-prolonging or death-avoiding technology has clearly altered the work performed by nurses in ICUs. The skills needed to function in the state-of-the-art ICU as well as the number of people needing these specialized nursing skills have increased considerably.

Patients categorized as "merely" seriously ill are often the healthiest patients in an ICU. Uncertainty of prognosis is a common observation. Most ICUs are spatially arranged to allow for constant vigilance, often sacrificing the privacy of the patient in the process. The need for easy access to patients forces nurses to perform their duties in a "fishbowl" situation. Continuous visual contact and easy access to all patients is paramount for maximum care. The uncertainty of patient outcome requires all personnel, and specifically nurses, to be constantly prepared for the unexpected. The unpredictability of complicating factors in the ICU can induce internal tension, personal concerns about one's performance, and self-doubt.

Despite advancements to improve patients' chances for survival, ICU nurses repeatedly are exposed to patients' near-deaths when trying their best to save them. Further, disagreements or misunderstandings over complex and ever-changing orders require ICU nurses to be able to cope with sometimes conflicting expectations and demands from physicians involved.

For a new intensive care nurse to feel insecure, threatened, or foolish is not uncommon. The first job-related experience that these nurses face is the emotional impact of the unit itself.[14] The lack of adequate physical space and the appearance of confusion when the critical care team is functioning at peak technical proficiency can be overwhelming. It takes 6 to 12 months to integrate the additional technical skills and applied physiological information needed to confidently assess the critically ill patients' pathophysiology and perform adequately.[15]

It is impossible to provide the level of care necessary in ICU areas without close working relationships and mutual interdependence among the nursing staff. At any given time the nurses on duty will have varying amounts of experience. Therefore, when unexpected emergencies occur, the more knowledgeable nurses must be available to help those with less experience. High turnover of nurses results in the loss of valuable staff time while training and educating new nurses and decreases the quality of care given to critically ill patients when fully qualified nurses are not available.[16]

Caring for patients who are expected to die is, however, not the most stressful event. Occurrences that are unexpected cause the greatest increase in tension, anxiety, and fear (e.g., when a young patient who is expected to survive abruptly deteriorates and dies). Unexpected changes in a patient's condition, particularly for a new nurse, may create concerns about his or her real or imagined contribution to the event. It may also create uneasiness among other staff members about the new nurse's ability to cope with the ICU. These feelings may lead to anger and frustration, as well as depression, self-doubt, and sometimes social isolation from others.

Patient families provide an additional drain on the ICU nurse's emotional resources. ICU visiting time is often restricted to approximately five to ten minutes an hour and only immediate family members may be admitted. The purpose of time restriction is to allow continuous uninterrupted care of the critically ill patient, to protect families from the overwhelming emotional burden of prolonged exposure to this stressful and unfamiliar environment, and to protect the staff from the constant pressure of having to answer the family's questions. Naturally, relatives want information and often the nurse is the only readily available source of information. He or she may be pressured with questions to which no answers exist. In addition, the nurse may not know what the doctor has already told the family. It is even more difficult to determine what the family has actually understood.

Research indicates that nurses' perceptions in intensive care come into direct conflict with the realities of their work environment.[17] The higher rate of patient deaths in the ICU is one of the distinguishing features that separates ICU nursing from other nursing experiences. Surviving patients reside in the ICU for less time than nonsurvivors. The majority of patients that survive usually leave within 24–72 hours from admission to the unit. In fact 95 percent of the patients that survive are discharged within the first seven days.[18] The longer a patient stays in the ICU the more uncertain is the outcome. ICU nurses, therefore, spend most of their time caring for patients who are probably going to die. Intensive care nurses expect a short-term involvement with their critically ill patients. They believe that technical expertise is the most important job qualification. They often begin work believing that they are totally prepared both educationally and professionally.

These expectations and perceptions are learned emotional and professional defenses against the realities they must face. Some ICU nurses will not "make it" beyond six months and will leave ICU nursing. Others will endure the process of adaptation to the real ICU environment and learn to cope effectively. Still others will stay but pay a personal price for their adjustment through the experience of emotional difficulties, interpersonal problems, job dissatisfaction, etc. Most ICU nurses will experience the stresses particularly indicative of providing this type of nursing care. There are those who will find effective ways of decreasing stress by decreasing external pressures (work load, responsibilities, time pressure, etc.) and/or minimize their personal responses to stress by acquiring new approaches to coping with fear, depression, and anxiety. The outcomes for the unique group of nurses who work in this environment are as different as individual nurses are from one another.

In small community hospitals where ICUs do not exist, the overall mortality rates are approximately 4–5 percent. To larger medical centers with ICUs and more advanced technology comes the burden of caring for sicker patients. The ideal size of a modern ICU is between eight and twelve beds. These specialized units care for about 600–800 critically ill patients per year with a mortality rate of about 20–25 percent. This means that an average ICU could have three to four patient deaths per week.

Unlike the case of oncology nurses, who expect a fatal outcome and are therefore resigned to caring for terminally ill patients, the most oft-stated reasons why nurses choose ICU assignment are educational advancement, one-to-one patient care, and opportunities for learning.[19] At times the dying process is much more stressful for the ICU nurse than the final moment of death. Nurses who remain on their jobs eventually adjust to the fact that they cannot control all the factors affecting their patients. The process of recognizing and accepting one's limitations in the control of life and death is essential to professional longevity in an ICU. This ability seems related to personality factors that have already been set by previous life experience. Nurses who cannot "make it" in an ICU environment can be identified within four to six months. Interviewing programs should be arranged to try to identify such nurses in advance.

PHYSICIAN STRESS

We have come to the point where death is often viewed as a failure of technology, and technological failure is potentially avoidable with increased research. This may also include, in part, a feeling that the physician has failed as well. All too often, the physician confuses "to care for" with "to cure" and is left feeling helpless in dealing with the dying patient. The illusion of the omnipotence of modern technology tends to result in an unrealistic belief in its ability to resolve any complex medical problem.

One ironic aspect of the hospital setting is that the medical professional lacks training in the psychological process of facing dying patients and their families. Advances in innovative medical technology have altered, perhaps forever, the character of dying and have forced us to look more resolutely at death. Physicians seem to have become desensitized, not to death, but to the environment surrounding death. The technical and procedural aspects of providing medical diagnosis, prescribing a treatment plan, and implementing therapy, even to critically ill patients, have become routine. Today, medical knowledge, skills, and the challenge of critical illness are the physician's primary focus rather than the care and comfort of the patient and his or her family. Even the most dedicated physician may get so caught up in the treatment aspects of caring for patients that the personal problems of the patient and family are inadvertently dismissed.

It has been suggested that many physicians experience irrational and unrealistic feelings of power, superiority, and control as a result of the constant exercise of authority.[20] However, the studies of Livingston and Zinet have indicated that health care personnel harbor unresolved emotions surrounding life and death issues. Results demonstrate that a significant portion of health care professionals choose their field in response to some personal loss. Thus, a common interpretation is that this reaction probably constitutes an attempt to achieve control over the fatal outcomes that make them feel powerless.[21]

There are times when the psychological vulnerability of physicians becomes acute. A study by Vaillant[22] comparing physicians with a socioeconomically matching control group reported that physicians involved in direct patient care were more likely to have relatively poor marriages, to abuse drugs and alcohol, and to obtain psychotherapy. Physicians also display other human frailties and may on occasion exhibit dependency, pessimism, passivity, or self-doubt. Terman reported in a prospective study of 800 gifted men that feelings of inferiority are relatively common among physicians.[23] Perhaps physicians in need of support themselves are not, under extreme emotional circumstances, capable of giving support to a patient's family. Is it not possible in some instances that a physician may protect his or her personal needs for love and dependence by caring for others as a superb form of adaptation? At times of death, a physician's dependency needs may compete with similar needs of the patient's family, thus placing the physician in a position of emotional conflict.

In a study of the stresses of graduate medical training, McCue has reported that the ultimate effect of residency training on the personal lives and future medical practices of physicians is largely unknown.[24] There are opposing views presented as to whether or not physicians are encouraged to be compassionate and dedicated or cold and uncaring.[25] The single-minded goal of becoming a physician may cause some to ignore personal development as they dedicate themselves to their professional development.[26] Physicians today are probably no more emotionally sophisticated or mature than they were in previous decades. They generally believe that the practice of medicine is more difficult and less enjoyable than it was 20 years ago.[27]

It takes more than high intelligence to be a competent physician. The importance of traits such as honesty, emotional stability, maturity, and interpersonal skills, as well as technical ability and good clinical judgment are necessary for complete medical competence. A few residency programs have incorporated data collection, psychological screening, and sophisticated evaluation programs to help identify residents with these qualities. These data are being collected throughout the residency period to help improve the chances of predicting good residents who will become successful attending physicians. The long-term benefits of this more sophisticated screening approach are as yet unknown. One short-term benefit, however, is the ability to identify physicians with personality problems before they are selected for residency programs. The identification of the impaired physician has become increasingly important. The key to detection of these physicians is the recognition of frequent and significant changes in physical, emotional, attitudinal, or behavioral responses.

Success in the medical profession is primarily measured in terms of curing patients of disease or injury. Health-care professionals undergo extensive training and develop confidence in the concept that if correct treatment is provided, all patients will survive. Prevention of death rather than comforting the dying has attained such a high priority that it has replaced efforts to address the reality of the dying person and his or her specific needs at that time.

The physician is trained to cure all who come under his or her care. Indeed, cure of all diseases is the ultimate goal of the medical profession. Nonetheless, death remains the obvious end of life, although there is a significant amount of denial regarding death in today's society. If a competent physician recognizes and believes that nothing can be done to save a patient, he or she should not initiate treatment. However, if there is any evidence to suggest that medical intervention has at least some chance of prolonging meaningful life, then treatment must be initiated, unless the competent patient refuses to undergo this form of therapy. (See Chapter 6.)

Physicians realize that despite the plethora of technologically sophisticated monitoring and therapeutic equipment, and computerized data at their disposal, much is still unknown. At times of crisis, the exact data necessary to make optimal treatment decisions for a specific patient may be lacking. While the course of medical treatment for most diseases is known, critically ill patients often have multiple organ failure causing many variables that defy the possibility for accurate assessment and interpretation, optimal treatment, and prediction of outcome. Immediate decisions about life-sustaining therapy must be based on available information, as well as the patient's condition.

When a patient dies, the loss of the patient may be experienced intensely. At times, however, it is the realization of failure that initially disturbs physicians. What went wrong? What could have been done differently? Is there something that another physician would have done that I missed? This frustration is very personal and is difficult to assuage even if nothing more could have been done.

Other factors that affect nurses and physicians include threats to one's self-esteem, personal conflict with peers, ambiguity in the assessment and treatment of patients, lack of accurate communication, and professional concerns about accountability for life and death decisions. Health care personnel need to let go of the perception of failure and move on to the next patient, not as a denial of the event, but as a healthy acceptance of the reality of the situation.

STANDARDS AND STAFFING PROBLEMS

It is clearly understood that working in an ICU imposes physical, mental, and emotional strains on nurses and physicians. The overall quality of care for critically ill patients, however, depends on a unit's organization to function optimally.

Gentry and Parks[28] have reported that the primary source of stress for ICU nurses is work overload, which in most cases is related directly to inadequate staffing. The result is pressure on nurses to complete each day's work assignment in a timely fashion. This can be physically and mentally exhausting.

The Joint Commission on Accreditation of Hospitals (JCAH), in its hospital accreditation manual, provides standards for the establishment of individual intensive or special care units.[29] These units shall be established for patients requiring extraordinary care on a concentrated and continuous basis. Each unit must be properly directed and staffed according to the nature of anticipated patient needs and the scope of services offered. All personnel must be provided appropriate initial orientation, in-service training, and continuing education programs. The quality and appropriateness of patient care must be monitored and evaluated with identified problems resolved. Finally, specific-purpose units (e.g., Burn Unit, CCU, Surgical ICU) may be established as determined by patient needs in the community and as resources allow. Clearly defined roles for each ICU within the hospital have not been established, but general guidelines have been published in the National Institutes of Health *Consensus Report on Critical Care.*[30] Each hospital must establish its own specific guidelines, procedures, and policies to adequately satisfy and ensure minimum medical standards of care.

Another factor to be considered is nursing and physician turnover. Although the problem of rapid turnover of nurses in ICUs nationwide seems to have abated, it has not disappeared. Many ICUs, particularly neonatal units, have reported continual nursing shortages. In most institutions, the retention rate of experienced critical care nurses has declined steadily over the last five years. Similarly, Greenbaum has reported that 15–20 percent of trained critical care physicians leave the field each year.[31]

STAFF INTERACTION

Interprofessional tensions, a major source of stress in ICUs, seem to stem primarily from the decision-making process in these units. Problems frequently concern ethical or personal factors related to the care of a critically ill patient. Situations most likely to elicit conflict are those that do not involve clear-cut medical decisions but rather patient care problems that are not covered in the policy and procedures manual, usually a life or death decision regarding a patient whose ultimate outcome is unknown. These cases seem to defy accurate assessment and therefore do not lend themselves to clear-cut medical, ethical, or legal guidelines.

There have been creditable efforts to increase the accuracy of predictions of outcome of ICU patients. Tagge[32] developed a formal classification system to help define overall therapeutic goals in critically ill patients. Cullen et al[33] developed the Therapeutic Intervention Scoring System (TISS), which quantifies the intensity of effort invested in a critically ill patient to provide useful data in making decisions to withhold or withdraw treatment. Youngner and Jackson[34] studied staff attitudes toward the care of critically ill patients in a medical intensive care unit (MICU) and attempted to determine the basis for conflict and tension surrounding decision making in MICU settings. A total of 36 house officers and 32 staff nurses responded to a questionnaire covering four major areas: (1) ethical issues, (2) the decision-making process, (3) communications, and (4) emotional reactions of the staff.

The results of this study revealed no clear difference in ethical position between physicians and nurses. In fact, there was a very high agreement in ranking various social issues that influence the decision to forego treatment. Both groups agreed that feelings of patient and family should be accorded high priority. There was a strong agreement that improving the quality of life, not only prolonging life but also improving its quality, is the central goal of critical care medicine. However, the authors found marked differences regarding criteria for withdrawing or withholding life support and the vigor with which heroic care measures should be pursued. Physicians felt strongly that evidence of permanent and severe cerebral deterioration should be considered in support of a decision to forego life support. A much smaller percentage of nurses believed that this was an important factor. On the issue of euthanasia, on the other hand, there were no significant differences between physicians and nurses. Ten of the 32 nurses reported they consider euthanasia unacceptable, even in patients with an extremely poor quality of existence (e.g., a terminal cancer patient with severe, intractable pain). Seven of the 35 physicians answered the same. However, when vigorous life support has already been stopped for that patient, 9 of 30 nurses and 3 of 33 physicians responded that they would take active steps to shorten the patient's life.

There was general agreement that the physicians actually make the final decision regarding withholding or withdrawing treatment for patients in the MICU. However, nurses tended to favor decisions by consensus of both groups. Nurses more than physicians favored strict legal guidelines for defining death and withholding treatment. Half of the nurses surveyed and 10 of 24 physicians were concerned about the potential for legal issues interfering with sound, independent medical judgment. The groups differed on whether agreement on these life and death decisions was actually reached. A majority of the physicians (18 of 24) believed that there was general agreement between the professional staff of the MICU and the involved patient families regarding foregoing futile life support, but half (13 of 24) of the nurses believed there were significantly different opinions between health professionals and the families involved.

Both the physicians and nurses in the above study acknowledged feeling intense emotional reactions to the ICU, although a majority of physicians (22 of 34) reported that the MICU was not more stressful for them than working on a regular medical floor. The nurses felt that liaison consultation and team meetings were helpful in dealing with work-related stress; the physicians did not. Finally, both of these study groups reported that professional background exerted a more profound influence on their attitudes toward life and death decision making than any formal, specific religious upbringing.

LEGAL CONSIDERATIONS AND ETHICS COMMITTEES

It is difficult to assess quickly and accurately all of the medical, technical, clinical, and emotional responses that are demanded in ICUs on a daily basis. Technology cannot resolve the human difficulties associated with critical care. The advances in medicine have altered, perhaps forever, our way of dying in America. At times, it becomes evident to all concerned that prolonging a life is not in the best interest of anyone involved, including the patient in question. Under these circumstances the issues of law and ethics become powerful and potentially stressful considerations.

The law usually does not seek involvement in medical treatment decisions unless there is disagreement between the physician and the family, disagreement among the family members, or the physician needs but cannot otherwise obtain consent to a specific course of action. (See Chapter 6.)

Occasionally, families insist on an all-out effort to save their loved one, while the medical/nursing team is convinced of the patient's impending death and that all treatment will be futile. At other times, patients who have been cared for in an ICU for weeks or months desperately appeal to the nurses to be left to die in peace and with dignity. Usually, these appeals are nonverbal, but experienced nurses become astute at understanding visual and behavioral messages from intubated patients.

Increased public awareness has catapulted ICU physicians into an area of public, legal, governmental, and medical scrutiny. Court decisions regarding ICU patients have influenced physicians to exercise extreme caution in deciding to forego life-sustaining treatment.[35] Two important basic concepts have been established: the patient's role in decision making is paramount; and a decrease in aggressive treatment of the hopelessly ill patient is advisable when such treatment would only prolong a difficult and uncomfortable process of dying.[36]

Physicians are understandably skeptical of the appropriateness of the court's involvement in the resolutions of complex life-death decisions. Regardless of the sagacity of court decisions, they usually are made too late to have any impact on the case in question, as the patient involved often dies in the interim. In practice, most ICU decisions involving the termination of futile life-supporting therapy are finalized without judicial involvement. A recent article (one of whose author's is Christopher J. Armstrong, Associate Justice of the Massachusetts Appeals Court) has stated, "it is not a general requirement of law . . . that judicial approval is legally required before life-sustaining treatment may be terminated." The article further states, "Physicians expect the courts to be wiser than society and to understand the realities of [complex ICU] situations, which are commonplace to the medical profession. But these expectations are ill founded. Courts, like most governmental institutions in a democratic society, reflect with great fidelity the views and attitudes of that society, with its confusion, its ignorance, and its prejudices."[37]

An alternative for the resolution of these complex medicolegal decisions is the utilization of hospital ethics committees. However, the rationale for their use is uncertain and ambiguous.[38] Ethics committees create additional stress for those involved. There are some who suggest the use of ethics committees as a tool to protect the critically or terminally ill from infringement of their guarantees of medical self-determination and the right to die with dignity.[39] Some hospitals have established such committees as a precaution against potential litigation. However, only 1 percent of all American hospitals and 4 percent of hospitals with over 200 beds have been reported to use ethics committees.[40] The President's Commission recommended decisions to forego life-sustaining treatment be made collaboratively by the patient and, if incompetent, by his or her surrogate and members of the health care team. Regularly assigning the task of making decisions regarding life-sustaining treatment to ethics committees could undermine the recognition of obligations by those who should be principally responsible.[41]

Creating ethics committees complicates, and does not improve, the process of medical decision making. The review process may be of less value if the ultimate authority for these responsibilities is taken from the health care team. The larger group of the ethics committee diffuses accountability so that no one individual accepts personal responsibility for the choices being made.[42] The concern that ethics committees will simply act either as rubber stamps for decisions made by others or as debating forums also has been raised.

Who has the right and responsibility to establish and appoint members to ethics committees in health care institutions is another issue that the Commission felt needs clarification. The utilization of ethics committees also creates serious privacy problems that apply to the keeping of records of committee deliberations and to the identification of and information on any cases discussed. Patients (or their families) could be unhappy about having their medical records revealed to ethics committee members without their consent. This is especially true if neither the patients nor their families are entitled to attend the meetings of the committee.[43] The President's Commission has not recommended that the formation of ethics committees be widely adopted, much less that it become a uniform requirement imposed by the federal government or by hospital accreditation bodies.[44] It is unlikely that any committee, no matter how well conceived, can resolve the medical, ethical, moral, social, and personal uncertainty when the bottom line is death. The decision is most appropriately left to those directly involved. Ultimately, it is the physician-patient-family triad that makes the final decision in most situations.

Physicians and nurses must learn to accept the fact that the death of a patient need not mean failure or loss of self-esteem. Health care professionals are also mortal, are entitled to personal and emotional reactions, and at times are in need of their own support and understanding. The conclusion that during a crisis everything medically possible was done for the patient usually is an acceptable outcome. In the end, the only recourse is to turn the responsibility back to the collective conscience of those directly involved and trust that they can make sane choices.

CONCLUSION AND RECOMMENDATIONS

Apathy toward a critically ill patient is a frequent means of personal defense against emotional involvement. It is virtually impossible to invest the same amount of personal energy and feelings in each ICU patient. Those who try usually pay for their vulnerability by a much shortened ICU career. The nurses and physicians who "make it" beyond a few years have managed to control their personal investment in patients and families. This protective mechanism is not cold and calculative. It is a measure of emotional insulation that allows ICU staff to provide care for all critically ill patients.

While care for all ICU patients is equivalent, on an individual basis the feelings toward particular patients are not. The staff's feelings are more sympathetic toward innocent victims than they are to perpetrators of crime. There is more emotional concern for young children. Patients with deeply involved, loving families tend to elicit more personal feelings from staff members. Also, if the patient reminds a staff member of someone he or she knows, regardless of age, there is a higher emotional response. And sometimes the staff member evaluates the patient's circumstances and concludes that "it could have been me."

It is difficult to become reconciled to the death of a patient who was expected to survive. The staff members may turn feelings of anxiety, disappointment, and frustration into anger or withdrawal. It is not uncommon for ICU personnel to physically and psychologically avoid a patient's family after the death of its relative. This behavioral reaction by the staff is often felt or interpreted as rejection by families. Many health care professionals and physicians particularly feel inept at coping with the emotional components of these affect-laden situations.

Most medical school training is focused primarily on education, science, and technology, not on human or personal aspects of patient care. Although some maintain that constant exposure to death is more than the normal defense mechanism can withstand, how to cope with the death of a patient is not included in most nursing or medical school curricula.[45] Unfortunately, both physicians and family members suffer from this lack of physician training. Physicians lose an opportunity to relate to the family members in an open and honest interchange. This interchange could provide a chance for families to give support and thanks to the health care team for their efforts on behalf of their loved ones. In addition, this process could provide a chance to defuse some of the guilt and feelings of responsibility regarding a patient's death. Health care providers may make their jobs less difficult if they become more sensitive to the psychological effects on those whose lives have been disrupted by critical illness.

Although there are efforts to establish standards for practitioners of Critical Care Medicine, there are no requirements for any educational background or training in the psychological dynamics involved. In this regard, some health care professionals believe (or act as if) there is a negative correlation between emotions and the ability to perform their duties. Health professionals need to know that sharing and/or showing thoughts and feelings about a patient does not imply weakness, unprofessionalism, or the inability to effectively complete work assignments.

Patient conferences afford an excellent opportunity to get specific medical information needed to provide care to a particular patient. These conferences also provide a unique opportunity to discuss the psychological problems of the patient and the patient's family. However, some ICUs function as if patients do not have families. It would be valuable to have professional mental health counselors, whether psychiatrists, psychologists, social workers, or clergy, to provide an assessment of the "psychological state" of the family as well as of the patient.

In the past, many psychological reports were less than helpful. They provided data that was already obvious or made recommendations that were impractical or both. These reports generally included a simple evaluation of the patient's mental status, usually finding the patients appropriately depressed, frightened, and worried about how their families would survive if they should die. Often a prescription for antidepressant medications was recommended, and just as often these medications were not given, mainly because of the already compromised physiological condition of the patient. Today, more appropriate psychological evaluation provides a bridge of information and understanding between the hospital staff, the patient, and the patient's family. This clarification of perceptions between staff and family can increase mutual trust and help lessen the tensions so often present in ICU situations.

The increased levels of situational stress on ICU nurses suggest the need for specific programs to reduce anxiety and to increase retention of ICU nurses. Kramer[46] supports the development of socialization programs to help nurses cope with job conflicts and stress. Implementation of organized programs with administrative support may lead to overall improvement in direct patient care, in staff morale, and in feelings of self-competence for new ICU nurses. Realistic job interviews may be appropriate and necessary for more effective screening of ICU nursing personnel. In addition, knowledge regarding nursing turnover could be increased if more carefully quantified and qualified interviews were conducted at the time of termination of employment.

There are those who support and encourage the need for the establishment of acceptable universal guidelines for physicians treating critically ill and dying patients. These efforts should be accomplished on behalf of all persons who may need access to these services. As Hilfiker states, "it is time we publicly examine our role in these situations, offer each other guidelines, and come to some consensus about our responsibilities."[47]

Despite the deluge of psycho-medico-legal complexities that encroach upon one's mind and body, the end result of what happens in an ICU depends on the process of interaction and communication among people. The questions raised go far beyond attitudes within an ICU; death and dying remain the most important issues in the lives of almost every thinking person.[48]

NOTES

1. K. PELLETIER, MIND AS HEALER, MIND AS SLAYER 7 (1977).

2. H. SELYE, THE STRESS OF LIFE (1956).

3. A. MEARES, THE MANAGEMENT OF THE ANXIOUS PATIENT (1963).

4. C. COFER & M. APPLEY, MOTIVATION: THEORY AND RESEARCH (1964).

5. Dato, *The Law of Stress*, Personal Communication, Philadelphia, 1980.

6. S. FREUD, THE PROBLEM OF ANXIETY (H. Bunker trans.). (Originally published under the title INHIBITIONS, SYMPTOMS AND ANXIETY by the Psychoanalytic Institute, Stamford, Conn., 1927).

7. Mahl, *Anxiety, HCL Excretion and Peptic Ulcer Etiology*, 11 PSYCHOSOM. MED. 30-44 (1949).

8. Lazarus, Deese & Osler, *The Effects of Psychological Stress upon Performance*, 49 PSYCHOL. BULL. 293-317 (1952); Miller, *The Development of Experimental Stress-Sensitive Tests for Predicting Performance in Military Tasks*, PRB Tech. Rep. 1079, Washington, DC, Psychological Research Associates, 449-450 (1953).

9. Abram & Wolf, *Public Involvement in Medical Ethics: A Model for Government Action*, 310(10) NEW ENGL. J. MED. 627-31 (1984).

10. Steffen, *Perceptions of Stress: 1800 Nurses Tell Their Stories*, in LIVING WITH STRESS AND PROMOTING WELL BEING: A HANDBOOK FOR NURSES (K. Claus & J. Baily eds., 1979).

11. Gentry, Foster, & Froehling, *Psychological Response to Situational Stress in Intensive and Non-Intensive Nursing*, HEART AND LUNG 793 (1972).

12. Anderson & Basteyns, *Stress and Critical Care Nurse Reaffirmed*, J. NURSING ADMIN. (Jan. 1981).

13. Stehle, *Critical Care Nursing Stress: The Findings Revisited*, 30(3) NURSING RESEARCH 182-86 (1981).

14. Kramer, McDonnel, & Reed, *Self-Actualization and Role Adaption of Baccalaureate Degree Nurses*, 21 NURSING RESEARCH 111-23 (March-April, 1981).

15. Hudson, Etling, & Lantiegne, *Intensive Care Nursing Requirements: Resource Allocation According to Patient Status*, 6(2) CRITICAL CARE MED. 115-16 (1978).

16. Wallace-Barnhill, *Comparison of Intensive Care Unit Nurses, Non-Intensive Care Unit Nurses and Non-Nursing Personnel with Regard to Personality Variables and Job Satisfaction*, 42(8) DISSERTATION ABSTRACTS INTERNATIONAL (1982).

17. *Supra* note 10.
18. Greenburg, Civetta & Wallace-Barnhill, *Neglected Components of Intensive Care*, 26 J. SURGICAL RESEARCH 494-98 (1979).
19. *Supra* note 16.
20. Marmor, *The Feeling of Superiority: An Occupational Hazard in the Practice of Psychotherapy*, 110 AM. J. PSYCHIATRY 370-76 (Nov. 1953).
21. Livingston & Zinet, *Death Anxiety, Authoritarianism, and Choice of Specialty in Medical Students*, 140 J. NERVOUS & MENTAL DISORDERS 222-30 (1965).
22. Vaillant, Sobowale, & McArthur, *Some Psychologic Vulnerabilities of Physicians*, 287(8) NEW ENGL. J. MED. 372-75 (1972).
23. Terman, *Scientists and Nonscientists in a Group of 800 Gifted Men*, 68 PSYCHOL. MONOGR. 1-44 (1954).
24. McCue, *The Effects of Stress on Physicians and Their Medical Practice*, 306(8) NEW ENGL. J. MED. 458-63 (Feb. 1982).
25. Cousins, *Internship: Preparation or Hazing?* 245 J. A.M.A. 377 (1981); *Internship: Physicians Respond to Norman Cousins*, 246 J. A.M.A. 2141 (1981).
26. Ford, *The Emotional Distress of Interns and Residents.* Presented at the 134th American Psychiatric Association Annual Meeting, New Orleans, La., May 1981.
27. *Medical Practice in the 1980's. Physicians Look at Their Changing Profession*, Lew Harris Poll, 1981.
28. Gentry & Parkes, *Psychologic Stress in Intensive Care Unit and Non-Intensive Care Unit Nursing: A Review of the Past Decade*, 11(1) HEART AND LUNG 43-47 (1982).
29. *Special Care Units*, ACCREDITATION MANUAL FOR HOSPITALS 181-91 (1984).
30. National Institutes of Health, *Consensus Development Conference on Critical Care Medicine*, 11 J. CRITICAL CARE MED. 466 (1983).
31. Greenbaum, *Availability of Critical Care Personnel, Facilities, and Services in the United States*, 12 CRITICAL CARE MED. 12 (1984).
32. Tagge, Adler & Bryan-Brown, et al., *Relationship of Therapy to Prognosis in Critically Ill Patients*, 2 CRITICAL CARE MED. 61 (1974).
33. Cullen, Civetta & Briggs, et al., *Therapeutic Intervention Scoring System: A Method for Quantitative Comparison of Patient Care*, 2 CRITICAL CARE MED. 57 (1974).
34. Youngner, Jackson & Allen, *Staff Attitudes Towards the Care of Critically Ill in the Medical Intensive Care Unit*, 7(2) CRITICAL CARE MED. 35-40 (1979).
35. Wallace-Barnhill, et al., *Medical, Legal and Ethical Issues in Critical Care*, 10(1) CRITICAL CARE MED. 57-61 (1982).
36. Wanzer, et al., *The Physician's Responsibility Toward Hopelessly Ill Patients*, 310(15) NEW ENGL. J. MED. 955-959 (1984).
37. Wallace-Barnhill, et al., *Health Care Law Update: Legal Protection for Critical Care Physicians; State of the Art in Termination of Life Support and Living Will Legislation*, 12(1) CRITICAL CARE MED. 56-61 (1984).
38. Veatch, *Hospital Ethics Committees: Is There a Role?* 7 HASTINGS CTR. REP. 22 (1977).
39. Cohen, *Interdisciplinary Consultation on the Care of the Critically Ill and Dying: The Role of One Hospital Ethics Committee*, 10(11) CRITICAL CARE MED. 776-84 (1982); Crawford & Doudera, *The Emergence of Institutional Ethics Committees*, 12(1) LAW, MED. & HEALTH CARE 13-20 (1984).

40. Younger, et al., *A National Survey of Hospital Ethics Committees*, 11(11) CRITICAL CARE MED. 902-05 (1983).

41. PRESIDENT'S COMMISSION FOR THE STUDY OF ETHICAL PROBLEMS IN MEDICINE AND BIOMEDICAL AND BEHAVIORAL RESEARCH, DECIDING TO FOREGO LIFE-SUSTAINING TREATMENT 160-170 (1983).

42. *Id.*

43. *Id.*

44. *Id.* at 452 App. F.

45. Hoggatt & Spilka, *The Nurse and the Terminally Ill Patient: Some Perspectives and Projected Actions*, 9 OMEGA 3 (1978-79).

46. *Supra* note 14.

47. Hilfiker, *Allowing the Debilitated to Die: Facing Our Ethical Choices*, 308 NEW ENGL. J. MED. 716-19 (1983).

48. McGuire, Personal Communication, July 1978.

Chapter 9

Deciding about Life-Sustaining Treatment: The Role of Hospital Guidelines*

Alan Meisel, Ake Grenvik, Rosa Lynn Pinkus, and James V. Snyder

A combination of circumstances over the last decade or two has led to an increasing recognition both within the health professions and in society at large that the devotion of more medical resources to a particular instance of illness or injury is not always better than less.[1] Nowhere has this been more clearly and poignantly recognized than in the case of hopelessly ill patients. There is a slowly growing realization that the quality of life of a hopelessly ill or injured person, *to that person,* must be considered an important criterion along with existence itself for determining when treatment should be administered.[2]

Since the Quinlan case in 1976, the courts of 11 states have been confronted with issues concerning the discontinuation of life-sustaining treatment from terminally ill patients. In addition, almost 40 states have enacted statutes (often referred to as "natural death acts") permitting terminally ill patients to sign directives authorizing the withholding of life-sustaining treatment. However, because these statutes are extremely limited in their applicability and because most states have not yet had any court cases on this subject, let alone a judicial decision that gives broad and clear guidance, health care professionals in most states lack a clear idea of when it is legally permissible to withhold or withdraw life-sustaining treatment.

Faced with such uncertainty, health care institutions—most notably hospitals and nursing homes—should adopt their own internal policies on foregoing life-sustaining treatment. These policies should reflect the law as it is developing nationally as well as the principles articulated by leading writers in the field. Internal institutional policies or guidelines not only encourage consistency within the institution, but should litigation ever occur they also provide evidence to a court that decisions to forego life-sustaining treatment

---

*The chapter is based on an article that appeared in *Critical Care Medicine* (1986;14), Copyright © 1986, Williams & Wilkins Company.

are undertaken only on the basis of considered judgment. Courts that are presented with these issues are more likely to approve decisions to withhold or withdraw life-sustaining treatment from terminally ill patients when made in accordance with preexisting policies that reflect the developing legal trends in other jurisdictions and the policy pronouncements of professional organizations and governmental commissions.

THE EFFECT OF TECHNOLOGY

Until recently, the question of when to stop life-sustaining treatment did not consciously arise with much frequency. The limitations of medical interventions compared with the potency of illness and injury meant that all that could be done usually was. When all that could be done was inadequate to preserve life, that fact was plain for all to see. Although it is no surprise that death has not yet been conquered, death can be held in abeyance for long periods of time. While death may be forestalled, often almost indefinitely, many illnesses and injuries remain irreversible. The net result is that medicine can now keep large numbers of people in a state of health "limbo." The nature of this state varies greatly from persons in a persistent vegetative state to conscious and alert persons in the later stages of carcinoma. The former require constant medication, artificial ventilation and feeding, while the latter may be significantly disabled and suffering from pain, nausea, vomiting, diarrhea, and other unpleasant symptoms, but still may have some small satisfaction from their daily lives.

THE INFLUENCE OF LAW

Along with the advances in medical technology, there has been an increasing concern by many people that patients themselves ought to have the opportunity to play a greater role, if not the predominant role, in making decisions about the kinds of health care they do and do not wish to have. These views are supported by and reflect the law governing medical decision making—i.e., the doctrine of informed consent.[3]

Although, as an abstract principle of law, individuals have always had the right to refuse to undergo medical therapy, prior to the last two decades requests to enforce this right have been rare. The consent requirement has metamorphosed into the doctrine of informed consent—which, as we have seen, prescribes that a physician has a legal obligation to provide patients with a range of information about treatment options, including the option of no treatment, before seeking the patient's consent to treatment. Concurrently, courts have been more willing to enforce a patient's right to choose whether or not to accept therapy. As more patients realize that they are not obliged to accept treatment just because it is available, more may choose not to prolong dying.

THE COST OF CARE

The third circumstance contributing to the realization that more treatment does not necessarily mean better existence is one we have become increasingly aware of during the last two decades: the cost of medical care. In 1970, expenditures on health care accounted for approximately 7.2 percent of the gross national product. Today, these expenditures consume in excess of 10 percent of the GNP.[4] In absolute terms, neither the level of spending on health care nor the rate of increase is particularly significant. Rather, it is the fact that, in the aggregate, each additional dollar spent on health care may not yield as much benefit as prior expenditures. A related concern is that even if additional funds are spent for medical care, they might yield greater benefit if directed to other areas, such as basic research or preventive health care, rather than to persons in the final months, weeks, or moments of life.[5]

THE PRESIDENT'S COMMISSION

Concerns such as these were the impetus behind the creation by Congress in the late 1970s of the President's Commission for the Study of Ethical Problems in Medicine and Biomedical and Behavioral Research ("President's Commission"), and the Commission's issuance in March 1983 of its report entitled *Deciding to Forego Life-Sustaining Treatment* (DFT Report).[6]

At this time, implementation of the recommendations of the DFT Report depends almost entirely upon the initiative of individual hospitals (and other health care institutions such as nursing homes). There are exceedingly few laws dictating specific procedures and standards that hospitals must follow. Only 11 states have one or more court decisions on the matter of foregoing life-sustaining treatment (California, Connecticut, Delaware, Florida, Georgia, Massachusetts, Minnesota, New Jersey, New York, Ohio, Washington). Some of these decisions do little more than establish the existence of the right while others are more thorough in prescribing the procedures to be followed in implementing it. In about three dozen states, legislatures have enacted "natural death acts." Although these acts provide more certainty in terms of the procedures to be followed, they are extremely limited as to the class of persons to whom they apply.

Thus, with the exception of a very few states, most health care providers are forced to make or effectuate decisions to forego life-sustaining treatment with little in the way of express legal guidance. In such an environment, the options that exist are (1) to refuse to withdraw life-sustaining treatment, a policy that may also impose legal risks; (2) to operate on an ad hoc basis, which may lead to a great deal of inconsistency and arbitrariness, with attendant legal risks, staff demoralization, and patient and family dissatisfaction; or (3) to develop a body of professional custom that will lead to more consistent decision making, greater fairness to staff, patients, and families, and which may serve as a basis for guiding courts when called upon to decide cases.

In light of the recommendations of the DFT Report, and the pervasive concerns on which they are based, the Executive Committee of the Medical Staff of Presbyterian-University Hospital (PUH), a University of Pittsburgh Health Center hospital, appointed an Ethics and Human Rights Committee. One task of this committee was to update the existing "DNR" guidelines.[7] Over the course of a year, the committee drafted guidelines intended to put into practice the principles underlying the recommendations of the DFT Report. These guidelines were then approved by the PUH Patient Care Committee and subsequently by the Executive Committee.

BASIC PRINCIPLES

The fundamental and guiding principle of the guidelines is patient autonomy—that is, decisions about health care are the prerogative of the patient (III.1*). This is so both when a patient is terminally ill and when a patient is expected to return to the premorbid condition. This is also a guiding principle whether a patient is refusing treatment or consenting to it (II.1). It is both a fundamental ethical principle and a legal one.[8] However, because it may be foreign to the tradition of the doctor-patient relationship[9] and is only gradually becoming accepted in contemporary medical practice, this principle must be clearly stated at the outset and reiterated for emphasis.

The right to decide is an empty one unless a patient has the information necessary to make an intelligent decision. Thus, the guidelines require as a necessary corollary of patient autonomy that patients be provided with adequate information about diagnosis, prognosis, and reasonably available therapeutic options, and about the risks, benefits, nature, and purpose of those options (III.1, III.2.b, III.4).

Information is a means toward an end; it is not an end in itself. Even as patients are entitled to adequate information so that they can make an intelligent and rational decision, they are not required to do so. If medical

---

*Parenthetical references are to sections of the guidelines. (See Appendix A.)

decision making were a purely objective matter, there would be no need for or value to patient autonomy. Rather the notion of patient autonomy is grounded in part on the assumption that in making decisions about any important matter, health or otherwise, people bring to bear not only objective information (e.g., about treatment options) but also their own values, goals, needs, and desires—all necessarily subjective.[10] This decision making involves weighing alternatives, assigning costs and benefits to the alternatives, and deciding whether the "game," and which "game" if any, is "worth the candle." This is an inherently subjective enterprise when undertaken by a patient, and it is no less so when performed by a physician on behalf of a patient. However, because it is the patient who ultimately must bear the pain and pay the cost of any choice, it is also the patient's prerogative to decide.

Although patient autonomy—and the provision of information to patients to further that goal—is a fundamental principle of the guidelines, it is not an absolute imperative. The right to be informed must be tempered by other considerations. Thus, while the guidelines state that "there is a strong presumption that all information needed to make an appropriate decision should be provided" (III.5.a), they recognize two situations in which that presumption may be overcome.

First, information may be withheld if its disclosure would harm the patient (III.5.c). Harm is narrowly defined as "an immediate threat to the patient's health or life." It does not include upsetting the patient by disclosing unpleasant information. Nor does it include the possibility that the patient may be harmed by declining treatment as a consequence of being told about the treatment, especially about the side effects or the possibility that the treatment will not be successful[11] (III.5.b). This exception to the usual disclosure requirements, known in law as the "therapeutic privilege,"[12] is based on the ethical principles of beneficence (or more accurately in this context, nonmaleficence) and of respect for persons.

Second, a patient might wish not to be provided with information. If patients clearly make known that they do not want information, as long as they are aware of their right to be informed, information should be withheld (III.5.d). Similarly, a patient who has been adequately informed may wish to allow others to decide on his or her behalf or to have others, especially family members and care givers, participate in the decision making.

COLLABORATIVE DECISION MAKING

Making decisions about health care almost always involves some party other than the patient. Only rarely—for instance, when one first decides to seek professional attention—will such a decision be made in isolation. One party to such decisions is ordinarily a physician. Decision making about health care, then, should be a process of collaborative decision efforts[13] (III.2). Even in its most reductionist form, the legal doctrine of informed consent assigns a role to the physician as well as to the patient—namely, the provision of information. In its more sophisticated renditions, the doctrine recognizes that decision making is a process, not an event.[14]

A patient who is "informed" by being given a shopping list of therapies from which to choose—even when told about their risks and benefits, nature, and purpose—is ordinarily in no position to exercise his or her autonomy intelligently. Patients often need and want professional advice as well as information; they may need to ask questions, based in part on that advice and information; they may be too frightened or intimidated to ask the questions that bother them and may need to be encouraged to do so. They may not understand their options very well even after explanation, questions, answers, and discussion. There may also be the need for the passage of time, and perhaps the reiteration of the process, or a part of it, before they are able to make a decision. The guidelines recognize that the process of decision making is an interactive not a linear one; that it requires the physician as well as the patient to play an active role; that it is a time-consuming process and not an abrupt event (III.4.e).

Although acting in the service of the patient, the physician too has needs and rights worthy of consideration and respect. Thus, the guidelines acknowledge that, for reasons of conscience, a physician may decline to participate in the limitation or withdrawal of therapy requested by a patient (II.6, III.3). Although largely a moral precept, this principle may have a medical component as well. Thus, a patient who chooses to forego (or, indeed, to undergo (III.3.c)) a therapy on the basis of what the physician believes is a mistaken understanding of its efficacy or of its side effects may decline to support the patient's choice. In other words, a patient cannot compel a physician to engage in what the physician deems to be professionally irresponsible conduct.

This does not mean, however, that the physician may refuse to accept a patient's choice because of a disagreement with the patient's subjective preferences (goals, values, needs, wishes). When the patient's choice does strain the outer limits of moral or medical acceptability, the physician is still obligated to attend the patient until care can be transferred to another physician. Prior to that time, however, the physician should (without being coercive) attempt to reason with the patient, explain his or her own position, and make an effort to dissuade the patient from what the physician considers a morally unacceptable course (III.5).

The same principles that apply to making decisions to forego life-sustaining treatment also apply to decisions to undergo such treatment. Indeed, at the outset, we must start with the assumption that we do not know whether a patient wishes to undergo or forego a particular therapy. In order to make the decision, information must be provided. Only then can the patient decide, on the basis of such information and his or her own values, goals, needs, and desires, what course is best for him or her. Thus, until it is clear that the patient (or surrogate) has decided otherwise, the wish to be treated must be presumed (II.1).

WHAT CONSTITUTES "TREATMENT"

The President's Commission in its DFT Report takes the position that there is no significant ethical distinction between stopping treatment already begun and not starting treatment in the first place. The Commission recognized, however, that once treatment is begun, expectations are often created in patients, family, and care givers that it will be continued, so that it may be psychologically more difficult to terminate treatment than not to begin it.[15] Accepting the position of the President's Commission, the guidelines refer to "foregoing" life-sustaining treatment. This term is intended to include decisions to terminate treatment, to limit treatment, and to withhold treatment that may be, but has not yet been, initiated (I.2).

Although what constitutes "treatment" may seem self-evident, this is not necessarily so, at least not in the context of making decisions about life-sustaining treatment of the hopelessly ill patient. Perhaps because existing policies in many hospitals deal exclusively or primarily with foregoing cardiopulmonary resuscitation, many physicians and other health care personnel may unconsciously assume that the guidelines are intended to apply only to CPR—that is, that they are essentially a "do not resuscitate" policy. Because of the common usage of the terms "ordinary" and "extraordinary" treatment both within the health professions and without, and the parallel assumption that only "extraordinary" therapies may be foregone,[16] it must be clear that these guidelines implicitly reject such a dichotomization. Instead, they substitute an analytic process (increasingly accepted by the courts)[17] that requires the weighing of the benefits and burdens of therapy (III.2.b, c). The emphasis is thereby transferred from the therapeutic technique to the condition of the patient and to the probability of altering that condition significantly.[18]

Finally, litigation has raised some concern about whether, when it comes to deciding about foregoing treatment, therapies are essentially interchangeable. Although much of the earlier concern in court cases dealt with foregoing mechanical ventilation,[19] there has been a gradual shift of concern to other therapies such as dialysis,[20] antibiotics,[21] chemotherapy,[22] and most recently food and water.[23]

The guidelines adhere to the position of the President's Commission that what treatments may and may not be foregone should not be made in accordance with the "ordinary/extraordinary" treatment categories, but rather should be made on the basis of benefit or burden to the patient.[24] Ethically sound practice requires that patients (or the surrogates of incompetent patients) be able to reject any intervention without regard to its nature. What is ethically relevant, in the view of the guidelines and the President's Commission, is whether the treatment "has at least a reasonable chance of providing benefits to the patient, which benefits outweigh the burdens attendant to the treatment."[25] Thus the guidelines provide that "life sustaining-treatment... encompasses all health care interventions that have the potential effect of increasing the life span of the patient," not only ventilators, dialysis, intravenous fluids, and "all the paraphernalia of modern intensive care medicine," but physical therapy and special feeding procedures "provided that one of the anticipated effects of the treatment is to prolong the patient's life" (I.1).

If a decision is made to forego a particular procedure, however, the patient must still be provided with all other therapy that is routine for such a patient or that has otherwise been ordered and not specifically foregone (II.3). This is both in keeping with the fundamental presumption of the guidelines in favor of providing treatment (II.1) and in recognition of the dignity of the individual, which must be preserved through appropriate nursing care, hygienic care, comfort care, and analgesia (II.4). In other words, patients who have made a decision to forego a particular life-sustaining therapy are still alive and must not be relegated to a second-class status. They remain fully deserving of whatever care they (or their surrogates) have not specifically declined.

DECISION MAKING FOR INCOMPETENT PATIENTS

To this point, we have assumed that patients facing a decision to undergo or forego life-sustaining treatment are capable of participating in the kind of decision-making process described. The guidelines, following both the legal presumption of competency and the ethical principle of respect for persons, require that patients be presumed to be capable of decision making (IV.1). In fact, the same circumstances that render a person critically ill may (but will not always) limit or eliminate one's capacity to make decisions.[26] However, patients lacking such capacity have the same substantive rights under the guidelines that competent patients do (IV.2). Thus, whenever the guidelines refer to a decision made by a "patient," they include that of the surrogate for a patient who lacks decision-making capacity (II.5). Although one court has held in the case of persons who have never been competent that a surrogate does not have authority to decline life-sustaining treatment on behalf of such patients,[27] the guidelines do not make this distinction. It may be premature to claim the emergence of a legal trend, but two courts have permitted the withholding or withdrawal of life-support from never-competent patients.[28]

Of necessity, the procedures for making decisions for incompetent patients must differ even if the underlying substantive right to forego life-sustaining therapy is the same. Obviously, someone other than the patient will have to make decisions for the patient. Following the President's Commission, the guidelines refer to such a person as a "surrogate." This term is intended to include a person chosen by the patient ("proxy"), a person appointed by a court (a "guardian," "guardian ad litem," or a "surrogate"), as well as a person selected by someone other than the patient, such as a physician or social worker.

When decision-making capacity is an issue, the first step is to assess whether or not it exists. As previously mentioned, the starting point is a presumption of competency, but this is often called into question by the patient's medical condition. An unconscious or comatose patient clearly lacks decision-making capacity. However, other conditions, such as delirium, dementia, depression, mental retardation, psychosis, intoxication, or stupor, may impair decision-making capacity to a greater or lesser degree without eradicating or even necessarily compromising related capacities, such as the ability to communicate. Therefore, these conditions should trigger an inquiry into a patient's decision-making capacity, though their existence is not determinative of a lack of capacity (IV.1.d). Neither does the refusal of treatment determine a lack of decision-making capacity, even in the case of treatment that most patients accept. However, a refusal of such treatment might reasonably prompt an assessment of the patient's capacity[29] (IV.1.e).

The guidelines make assessment of capacity the responsibility of the attending physician. In cases in which the attending physician believes there is a need for special expertise in performing the assessment, a psychiatric consultation may be sought (IV.3). Such consultation, however, should not be routine because the determination of incapacity ordinarily calls for no special skills.[30]

Similarly, it is the responsibility of the attending physician to select a surrogate to make decisions on behalf of a patient who lacks decision-making capacity. When a patient, while competent to do so, has designated another to act as his or her surrogate in the event of future incompetency, a strong presumption should exist in favor of selection of that person (IV.4.d). Otherwise, the surrogate should generally be a close family member. A close friend may be appointed surrogate if no family member is available.[31] In some cases, it may even be more consonant with the incompetent patient's presumed desires to appoint a close friend over a family member, such as where the close friend is the functional equivalent of the patient's spouse, a practice that the guidelines approve (IV.4.b).

In the case of patients having no friends or family, or at least no readily present and involved friends or family, the attending physician or another member of the health care team may act as surrogate, in consultation with the Ethics and Human Rights Committee, but only if the patient has so designated while still competent (IV.4.e). The tremendous variation in and subtlety of circumstances from case to case dictate that a great deal of discretion be placed in the hands of the attending physician in the selection of a surrogate. Thus, the guidelines are intentionally ambiguous and noncategorical about this issue. In the case of intractable conflict among family members and/or close friends over who ought to serve as surrogate, or if there is no one to serve, judicial appointment of a surrogate must be sought (IV.4.f).

The decision of a properly designated surrogate is to be accorded the same presumption of validity as the decision made by a competent patient. However, that validity is presumptive only, and there may be compelling reasons why a surrogate's decision should not be honored. First, the surrogate himself or herself may lack decision-making capacity. This is more likely to be the case where the surrogate has been appointed by the patient; if the staff appoints a surrogate there will be a better opportunity to discern lack of capacity before the selection is made.

Second, even if the surrogate is competent to make a decision, not all decisions must be accepted by the attending physician. As is the case with the patient, a decision with which the attending physician cannot comply for strong reasons of conscience ultimately requires that the attending physician transfer the patient to the care of another physician if possible (III.3). Also, the guidelines require the surrogate to attempt to replicate the decision that the patient would have made for himself or herself (IV.2). Thus, a surrogate's decision that the attending physician has good reason to believe would be contrary to the wishes of the patient need not be honored.

THE PRESUMPTION AGAINST JUDICIAL INVOLVEMENT

The guidelines rely heavily on informal, hospital-based decision-making procedures rather than on formal, judicial procedures. In their formulation, it was consciously decided to avoid resort to the judicial system for resolution of problems regarding (1) assessment of patient competency, (2) appointment of a surrogate, (3) review of the surrogate's decisions about treatment, and (4) determination of the validity of an advance directive. Only when there is intractable conflict among participants in the process over any of these issues, or when a judicial determination is otherwise clearly required by state law, should there be resort to the judicial system (II.8, IV.4.f, V.4.).

This presumption against judicial decision making finds support in several sources. First, in many jurisdictions there is no clear legal requirement that such matters be determined judicially. Second, courts often defer to the customary practices of a profession in determining whether a particular course of conduct is legally acceptable. It is fair to say that physicians have traditionally resolved issues of these kinds without routine resort to the courts.[32] Physicians customarily assess their patients' decision-making capacity. Usually this is done so routinely and reflexively that it appears to be an unconscious process.

In addition, judicial resolution of such issues means that what are inherently private decisions will be made publicly, thus inflicting additional suffering (and probably financial cost) on those who are already involved in an extremely painful situation. Furthermore, the routine submission of such issues to the courts will likely add a tremendous administrative burden to health care providers and to the courts alike, in terms of both delay and cost.[33] There are some jurisdictions in which courts have been insistent on judicial review of at least some aspects of the decision-making process, such as the determination of incompetency[34] or the review of a guardian's decision.[35] Most courts that have dealt with this issue, however, have taken the position that while they are available to assist in the decision-making process, a rule requiring judicial involvement is unnecessary to protect the patient's well-being and might prove too cumbersome.[36]

ADVANCE DIRECTIVES ("LIVING WILLS")

In further recognition of the importance of patient autonomy and of the importance of clarity regarding what types of therapy to limit in a life-threatening situation, the guidelines address the issue of written advance directives.[37] An advance directive is a written manifestation of an incompetent patient's wishes concerning health care made while still competent. Such directives are popularly known as "living wills," but such a term really applies only to one form of advance directive, known as an instruction directive, which gives instructions about one's health care.[38] Another form of advance directive is a proxy directive, by which a patient, rather than giving instructions, designates another person to do so for him or her in the event of future incapacity[39] (V.1).

A number of organizations such as "Concern for Dying," "Euthanasia Educational Council," and "The Society for the Right to Die" have, for quite a few years, served as advocates of advance directives to insure against unwanted treatment in a final illness. The legal status of these advance directives, however, has never been certain. Developments in recent years have substantially reduced the uncertainty surrounding advance directives: (1) the willingness of several courts to enforce oral declarations of now-incompetent patients made while they were still competent,[40] (2) the enactment of "natural death acts" in a number of states,[41] (3) the use of durable powers of attorney as a vehicle for recording a patient's directives in advance of becoming incompetent,[42] and (4) the explicit approval given to written advance directives by the Florida Supreme Court.[43] Although questions about the validity and enforceability of advance directives have not been definitively resolved, enough progress has been made in that direction that the drafters of the guidelines felt comfortable providing for their use.

The guidelines accord such directives the same effect as an oral declaration from a competent patient (V.2). They should be followed to the extent that they do not request a physician to engage in any conduct that is criminal, that violates the physician's personal or professional ethical responsibilities, or that violates accepted standards of professional practice. Such a directive is presumed to be valid unless evidence is presented to the contrary (V.3). It is filed along with other pertinent information in the appropriate section of the patient's medical record (V.3,5).

THE ROLE OF THE ETHICS COMMITTEE

The issues raised by undertaking or foregoing life-sustaining treatment place patients, families, and care givers on the horns of a medical, moral, psychological, and financial dilemma. In the absence of a well-established tradition for the resolution of these issues, new arrangements need to be developed.[44] This accounts for the drafting of guidelines such as those that are the subject of this chapter. But no cookbook is adequate for such a complicated and often subtle task. For the purpose of fine-tuning the guidance provided by the guidelines, the Ethics and Human Rights Committee is also available to assist in applying its general dictates to the complexities of particular cases (III.7). Cases will also arise in which there are no serious disagreements about discontinuing treatment, yet a residuum of psychological discomfort exists in the family or members of the health care team. In such a situation, one of the discomfited parties may seek a consultation with the Ethics and Human Rights Committee. Such a consultation, depending upon the particulars of the case, may seek to determine that all relevant information has been made available or to acquire additional information. A consultation may also correct misunderstandings, provide psychological support, or serve as a forum for those who may believe that their opinions have not been adequately heard and considered. The role of the Committee is not to make decisions about undertaking or foregoing treatment, but to make certain that procedures have been followed to aid in ensuring that the decision reached by others is voluntary, informed, and just.[45]

WRITING ORDERS AND KEEPING RECORDS

There is a need for good communication not only between physician and patient, but also between the attending physician and others on the health care team. Other care givers will often be called on to effect decisions to forego or undergo treatment and thus need to know what those decisions are. Therefore, orders need not only be written, but written in such a way that they can be carried out with reasonable fidelity (V.1). This means that a progress note must be entered into the medical record explaining the basis for the order (VI.2), and a (VI.3). However, the guidelines do recognize three categorical orders physicians may use if they do not wish to individualize the order (V.3a,b,c). The attending physician also should initiate discussion about the written order to increase the likelihood that its intended consequences will not be misunderstood (VI.1).

Discussion of the order with the health care team will also have the salutary effect of providing an opportunity for any member of the team who is uncomfortable either with the order or the way in which the decision to write it was made to express that view. In light of the fact that the only reported criminal prosecution for discontinuing life-sustaining treatment (which was ultimately resolved favorably to the accused physicians) was instigated by a member of the health care team, the importance of such discussion takes on added significance.[46]

CONCLUSION

The guidelines are written primarily to direct hospital policy and decision making about foregoing life-sustaining treatment, but they serve as a reminder to all who use them of the frailty of human existence. Persons privileged to participate in a decision that leads to an end to life do, after all, have a moral obligation. Within the current technologic, research-oriented, hospital-based context in which this process will most likely take place, devoting more medical resources is not necessarily better than devoting less. Careful, compassionate, and informed reasoning about how we want to die may be difficult and unpleasant for both patient and physician to discuss.[47] However, it cannot be avoided, nor should it be unduly postponed.

NOTES

1. ETHICAL AND SOCIAL ISSUES IN BIOMEDICINE 1-12 (R. Wertz ed. 1973); R. STEVENS, AMERICAN MEDICINE AND THE PUBLIC INTEREST 417-528 (1971).
2. Matter of Conroy, 486 A.2d 1209 (N.J. 1985); Grenvik, *Terminal Weaning: Discontinuance of Life-Support Therapy in the Terminally Ill Patient*, CRITICAL CARE MED. 394-95 (1983).
3. PRESIDENT'S COMMISSION FOR THE STUDY OF ETHICAL PROBLEMS IN MEDICINE AND BIOMEDICAL AND BEHAVIORAL RESEARCH, MAKING HEALTH CARE DECISIONS: THE ETHICAL AND LEGAL IMPLICATIONS OF INFORMED CONSENT IN THE PATIENT-PRACTITIONER RELATIONSHIP (1982).
4. P. STARR, THE SOCIAL TRANSFORMATION OF MEDICINE 380 (1982).
5. Rescher, *The Allocation of Exotic Life Saving Therapy*, 1 ETHICS, 173-86 (1969).
6. PRESIDENT'S COMMISSION FOR THE STUDY OF ETHICAL PROBLEMS IN MEDICINE AND BIOMEDICAL AND BEHAVIORAL RESEARCH, DECIDING TO FOREGO LIFE-SUSTAINING TREATMENT (1983).
7. Grenvik, et al., *Cessation of Therapy in Terminal Illness and Brain Death*, 6 CRITICAL CARE MED. 284-90 (1978).
8. *Supra* note 3; T. BEAUCHAMP & J. CHILDRESS, PRINCIPLES OF BIOMEDICAL ETHICS (1979).
9. J. KATZ, THE SILENT WORLD OF DOCTOR AND PATIENT (1984).
10. *Supra* note 3, at 42-45.
11. Canterbury v. Spence, 464 F.2d 772 (D.C. Cir. 1972).
12. Meisel, *The "Exceptions" to the Informed Consent Doctrine*, WIS. L. REV. 413-88 (1979).
13. *Supra* note 3.
14. Lidz & Meisel, *Informed Consent and the Structure of Medical Care*, in PRESIDENT'S COMMISSION FOR THE STUDY OF ETHICAL PROBLEMS IN MEDICINE AND BIOMEDICAL AND BEHAVIORAL RESEARCH: MAKING HEALTH CARE DECISIONS: THE ETHICAL AND LEGAL IMPLICATIONS OF INFORMED CONSENT IN THE PATIENT-PRACTITIONER RELATIONSHIP 317-410 (1982).
15. *Supra* note 6, at 73-77.
16. *Id.* at 62.
17. Conroy, *supra* note 2; Barber v. Superior Court, 147 Cal. App.3d 1006, 195 Cal. Rptr. 484 (1983); Matter of Hier, 464 N.E.2d 959 (Mass. Ct. App. 1984); Foody v. Manchester Memorial Hosp., 482 A.2d 713 (Conn. Super. 1984).
18. Paris & Reardon, *Court Responses to Withholding or Withdrawing Artificial Nutrition and Fluids*, 253 J. A.M.A. 2243-45 (1985).
19. Matter of Quinlan, 355 A.2d 647 (N.J. 1976); Satz v. Perlmutter, 326 So.2d 160 (Fla. Ct. App. 1978), *aff'd*, 379 So.2d 359 (Fla. 1980); Matter of Eichner, 420 N.E.2d 64 (N.Y. 1981).
20. Matter of Spring, 405 N.E.2d 115 (Mass. 1980); Matter of Lydia E. Hall Hosp., 455 N.Y.S.2d 706 (Sup. Ct. Nassau County 1982).
21. Matter of Tweed, No. 1983-663 (Northampton County, Pa.; filed Oct. 10, 1984).
22. Superintendent of Belchertown State School v. Saikewicz, 370 N.E.2d 417 (Mass. 1977).
23. Conroy, *supra* note 2; Barber v. Superior Court, *supra* note 17; Matter of Hier, *supra* note 17.
24. *Supra* note 6.
25. Barber v. Superior Court, *supra* note 17, 195 Cal. Rptr. at 491.

26. Jackson & Youngner, *Patient Autonomy and Death with Dignity*, 301 NEW ENGL. J. MED. 404-08 (1979).
27. Matter of Storar, 420 N.E.2d 64 (N.Y. 1981).
28. Matter of Hier, *supra* note 17; Matter of Hamlin, 689 P.2d 1372 (Wash. 1984).
29. *Supra* note 3, at 123.
30. *Id.*
31. *Id.* at 126-27.
32. *Id.* at 125.
33. *Id.* at 126.
34. Conroy, *supra* note 2.
35. Saikewicz, *supra* note 22.
36. John F. Kennedy Memorial Hosp. v. Bludworth, 452 So.2d 921 (Fla. 1984).
37. Clouser, *Allowing or Causing To Die: Another Look*, 87 ANN. INTERN. MED. 622-24 (1977).
38. *Supra* note 6, at 156.
39. *Id.* at 158.
40. Matter of Eichner, *supra* note 19; Matter of Lydia E. Hall Hosp., *supra* note 20; Lane v. Candura, 376 N.E.2d 1232 (Mass. Ct. App. 1978); Leach v. Akron Medical Center, 426 N.E.2d 809 (Common Pleas, Summit County, Ohio, 1980).
41. John F. Kennedy Memorial Hospital *supra* note 6, at 141-45.
42. *Id.* at 145-47.
43. *Supra* note 36.
44. Fost & Cranford, *Hospital Ethics Committees—Administrative Aspects*, 253 J. A.M.A. 2687-2692 (1985).
45. *Supra* note 8, at 160-70.
46. Barber v. Superior Court, *supra* note 17; *see also* Saunders v. State, 492 N.Y.S.2d 510 (Sup. Ct. Nassau County 1985).
47. Black, *Clinical Problems in the Use of Brain Death Standards*, 143 ARCH. INTERN. MED. 121-23 (1983); Pinkus, *Families, Brain Death and Traditional Medical Excellence*, 60 J. NEUROSURG. 1192-94 (1984).

Appendix A

Presbyterian-University Hospital Guidelines on Foregoing Life-Sustaining Treatment

I. INTRODUCTION

These Guidelines are applicable to all kinds of life-sustaining treatment and are not limited to decisions to forego cardiopulmonary resuscitation. The term "life-sustaining treatment," as used in the Guidelines, encompasses all health care interventions that have the potential effect of increasing the life span of the patients. Although the term includes respirators, kidney machines, intravenous fluid and all the paraphernalia of modern intensive care medicine, it also includes, for instance, physical therapy and special feeding procedures, provided that one of the anticipated effects of the treatment is to prolong the patient's life. (See Section III.2.b)

The term "forego" is used to include both stopping a treatment already begun as well as not starting a treatment because there is no significant ethical distinction between failing to institute new treatment and discontinuing treatment that has already been initiated. A justification that is adequate for not commencing a specific treatment is also sufficient for ceasing that treatment.

Approved by PUH Executive Committee - May 30, 1985.
Source: Reprinted with permission of Presbyterian-University Hospital, 1985.

II. STATEMENT OF GENERAL PRINCIPLES

1. Presumption in Favor of Treatment

It is the policy of PUH to provide high quality medical care to its patients with the objective of sustaining life and practicing in conformity with traditional and current ethical and medical standards. It is imperative that the professional staff remain committed to this objective by maintaining a presumption in favor of providing treatment to all patients. However, this commitment must recognize the right that patients have in making their own decisions about their health care and in continuing, limiting, declining, or discontinuing treatment, whether life-sustaining or otherwise.

2. Right to Refuse Treatment

As a general rule, all adult patients who do not lack decision making capacity may decline any treatment or procedure. There is sometimes, however, a reluctance to apply this rule to patients who seek to forego life-sustaining treatment. Thus, the Guidelines are adopted and promulgated to deal specifically with decisions to forego life-sustaining treatment.

3. Decisions to Forego Are Particular to Specific Treatments

A decision to limit, decline, discontinue or otherwise forego a particular treatment or procedure is specific to that treatment or procedure and does not imply that any other procedures or treatments are to be foregone unless a specific decision is also made with respect to them.

4. Preservation of Patient Dignity

The dignity of the individual must be preserved and necessary measures to assure comfort must be maintained at all times by the provision of appropriate nursing care, hygienic care, comfort care, and analgesics to all patients, including those who have elected to forego a specific life-sustaining therapy.

5. Surrogates and Patients

In these guidelines the term "surrogate" decision maker is defined as specified in the informed consent policy of the hospital. Unless otherwise indicated, the term "patient" includes the surrogate of a patient who lacks decision making capacity.

6. Physicians' Rights

It is the ethical and legal right of individual physicians to decline to participate in the limitation or withdrawal of therapy. However, no physician may abandon his or her patient until care by another physician has been secured. (See Section III.3)

7. Availability of Guidelines to Patients

These guidelines must be freely available to all patients (and their families), who upon admission to PUH will be given a general explanation of the existence and content of these guidelines (e.g., through an introductory brochure) and be given the opportunity to name a surrogate decision maker in writing. Patients (and their families) will be able to obtain copies of the guidelines at each patient unit station.

8. Presumption Against Judicial Review

Families and health care professionals should work together to make decisions for patients who lack decision making capacity. Recourse to the courts should be reserved for the occasions when adjudication is clearly required by state law or when concerned parties have disagreements that they cannot resolve over matters of substantial import. (See Section V)

III. GENERAL PRINCIPLES GOVERNING DECISION MAKING

1. Right to Decide and To Be Informed

It is the ethical and legal right of each patient who possesses the capacity to make decisions regarding his or her health care to do so. Furthermore, it is the concomitant ethical and legal right of each patient to be provided with adequate information about the diagnostic and therapeutic options (including risks, benefits, nature and purpose of the options) which are reasonably available.

2. Collaborative Physician-Patient (or Surrogate) Decision Making

(a) Decisions to forego life-sustaining treatment should be made between the patient (or surrogate) and the attending physician after as thorough discussion of therapeutic options as is reasonably possible.

(b) When a patient is terminally ill and the treatment to be foregone is, in the professional judgment of the attending physician, unlikely to provide the patient with significant benefit, the patient (or surrogate) should be so informed, unless there is evidence that such disclosure would be harmful to the patient.

(c) A patient (or surrogate) may not compel a physician to provide any treatment which in the professional judgment of that physician is unlikely to provide the patient with significant benefit.

(d) If the patient (or surrogate) is unwilling to forego such treatment, the treatment may nonetheless be foregone (that is, either stopped or not started) after notice to the patient (or surrogate) that is sufficient to permit transfer of the patient's care to another physician or hospital.

3. Physicians' Rights

Any physician may decline to participate in the limitation or withdrawal of therapy. In exercising this right, however, the physician must take appropriate steps to transfer the care of the patient to another qualified physician. Such a decision should be made only for reasons of conscience and after serious efforts have been made to dissuade the patient (or the patient's surrogate) from the decision to forego treatment, and after adequate notice has been given to the patient that the physician will have to withdraw from the case.

4. Informing for Decision Making

(a) It is the physician's responsibility to provide the patient (or, in the case of a patient who lacks decision making capacity, the patient's surrogate) with adequate information about therapeutic and diagnostic options so that the patient or surrogate may make an informed decision.

(b) This information should include the risks, discomforts, side effects and financial costs of treatment, the potential benefits of treatment, and the likelihood, if known, that the treatment will realize its intended beneficial effects.

(c) The physician may, in addition to providing such factual information, also wish to provide advice about treatment.

(d) The physician should seek to elicit questions from the patient or surrogate, should provide truthful and complete answers to such questions, should attempt to ascertain whether or not the patient or surrogate understands the information and advice provided, and should attempt to enhance understanding when deficient.

(e) Understanding of options by the patient or surrogate will often increase over time. Therefore, decision making should be treated as a process, rather than an event. In order to provide adequate time to deal with patients before they lose their capacity to decide, the process of informing patients or surrogates should begin at the earliest possible time.

5. Withholding of Information from Patients (or Surrogates)

(a) There is a strong presumption that all information needed to make an appropriate decision about health care (including a decision to forego life-sustaining treatment) should be provided to the decision maker (i.e., the patient or surrogate).

(b) Information may not be withheld from a patient or surrogate on the ground that its divulgence might cause the patient or surrogate to decline a recommended treatment or to choose a treatment that the physician does not wish to provide. Nor may information be withheld because of the belief that its disclosure would upset the patient or surrogate.

(c) Only if, in the exercise of professional judgment, the physician believes that disclosure would lead to an immediate and serious threat to the patient's (or surrogate's) health or life, may it be withheld. In such cases, the least restrictive degree of withholding, consistent with the patient's (or surrogate's) well-being, should be practiced, i.e., disclosure of relevant information not presumed to be immediately and seriously harmful should be provided. Since the process of decision making will often take place over a period of time, such information should gradually be given to the patient or surrogate, when possible, so as to minimize the presumed harmful impact.

(d) Information may also be withheld from a decision maker who clearly makes known that he or she does not wish to have the information in question, as long as the decision maker has previously been informed of his or her right to have such information.

(e) When disclosure is purposely limited, the reasons therefor must be documented in the medical record.

6. Consultation with Family

Patients should be encouraged to discuss foregoing life-sustaining treatment with family members and (where appropriate) close friends. However, a patient's privacy and confidentiality require that his or her wish not to enter into such a decision or not to divulge to family members the patient's decision to forego life-sustaining treatment must be respected.

7. Ethics and Human Rights Committee Consultation

The attending physician, any member of the health care team, patient, surrogate or any family member may seek a consultation with representatives of the Ethics and Human Rights Committee at any time. Motive for consultation might include family-staff conflicts, conflicts between family members, staff-staff conflicts and unclear moral or legal status of any aspect, including a lack of clarity as to who should act as the patient's surrogate. The goal of such a consultation may include: correcting misunderstandings, helping in the acquisition of needed information, allowing ventilation of emotions and otherwise aiding in the resolution of disputes. In order for patients and surrogates effectively to exercise this prerogative, they must be made aware of the existence and purpose of the Ethics and Human Rights Committee.

IV. DECISION MAKING FOR PATIENTS WHO LACK DECISION MAKING CAPACITY

1. Presumption of Capacity; Decision Making Capacity in General

(a) Patients should be considered, in the first instance, to possess the capacity to make health care decisions.

(b) In the case of conscious and alert patients, the ethical and legal presumption of capacity will govern, unless countervailing evidence arises to call the presumption into question.

(c) A patient's authority to make his or her own decisions should be overridden only after a clear demonstration of lack of capacity.

(d) Inquiry into a patient's capacity may be initiated by such conditions as delirium, dementia, depression, mental retardation, psychosis, intoxication, stupor or coma.

(e) Refusal of specific treatment to which most patients would agree does not mean that the patient lacks decision making capacity, but may initiate inquiry into the matter of such capacity.

(f) Furthermore, decision making incapacity can be a transient condition and can be specific to a particular decision. Therefore, patients who suffer from any of the above conditions may not lack capacity at all times for all purposes and decision making capacity may need to be reassessed from time to time.

2. Rights of Patients Lacking Decision Making Capacity

Patients who lack decision making capacity have the same substantive ethical and legal rights as do patients who possess such capacity. The only distinction is that in the case of patients lacking decision making capacity, health care decisions must be made on their behalf by a surrogate decision maker. Decisions made on behalf of patients who lack decision making capacity should, when their wishes are known, replicate the decision that they would have made for themselves had they had the capacity to do so. If the patient has executed a "living will" or any other form of advance directive to a health care provider, this document should serve as strong evidence of the patient's wishes. (See Section V)

3. Formal Assessment of Capacity

The formal assessment of capacity is a process that ordinarily ought to be performed and documented by the attending physician. A psychiatric consultation may be indicated if psychological factors are thought to be compromising capacity. However, a consultation is not required if the attending physician is able to assess capacity without it.

4. Selection of a Surrogate Decision Maker

(a) In the case of a patient who, after proper assessment, is determined to lack decision making capacity, a surrogate must be chosen to make decisions on behalf of the patient.

(b) Ordinarily the surrogate should be a close family member but a friend may occasionally be the best choice.

(c) In the case of a patient who has several concerned and available family members, decisions should be made by consensus of those family members whenever possible.

(d) Where the patient, prior to losing decision making capacity, has designated a surrogate either formally or informally, the patient's choice must be respected.

(e) If the patient has no family or friends to serve and if the patient so requests while still possessing decision making capacity, the attending physician or another member of the health care team in consultation with the Ethics and Human Rights Committee, may serve as the patient's surrogate.

(f) In the case of intractable conflict among family members or when there is no appropriate person to serve as a surrogate and the patient has not previously designated a surrogate, the judicial appointment of a surrogate must be sought.

V. ADVANCE DIRECTIVES

1. Definition

An advance directive is any written document drafted by an individual either while a patient or prior to becoming one, that either (a) gives instructions to a health care professional or provider as to the patient's desires about health care decisions, or (b) designates another person (i.e., surrogate) to make health care decisions on behalf of the patient if the patient is unable to make decisions for himself or herself, or (c) both gives instructions and designates a surrogate. To meet this definition for purposes of these Guidelines, an advance directive need not comply with any particular form or formalities, as long as it is in written form, and it appears to be authentic and unrevoked. It may be handwritten by the patient or at the patient's direction, or it may be typewritten. It may but need not use a preprinted "living will" form or be in the form of a durable power of attorney pursuant to title 20 of Purdon's Pennsylvania Consolidated Statutes Annotated section 5603(h) or section 5604 or a similar statute (including a "Natural Death Act") of the state of which the patient was a resident at the time of the execution of the document. The document need not be witnessed.

2. Effect To Be Given Advance Directive

An advance directive is merely a written manifestation of a patient's wishes concerning health care decision making. It should therefore be accorded the same effect as an oral declaration from a competent patient. That is, it should be followed to the extent that it does not request a physician to perform or refrain from performing any act which is criminal, which violates that physician's personal or professional ethical responsibilities, or which violates accepted standards of professional practice.

3. Weight To Be Given Advance Directive

An advance directive should be accorded a presumption of validity. The fact that it is written in the handwriting of a person other than the patient, for example, should not necessarily invalidate the document, but should be taken into account in determining the weight to be accorded to the directive. Similarly, the fact that the patient who executed the advance directive may have lacked the capacity to make a health care decision at the time the directive was executed may be taken into account in determining the weight to be accorded the directive. In all cases in which an advance directive is to be disregarded, such a decision must be based on more than surmise or speculation as to the circumstances surrounding the execution of the document, and instead should be based on persuasive and credible evidence. A document that is notarized and witnessed, or complies with similar legal formalities for that particular type of document, ought to be disregarded for only the most compelling reasons. However, the failure to notarize or witness a document by itself should not invalidate the document.

4. Probate of an Advance Directive

Ordinarily, there should be no need to seek judicial review of the enforceability of a written advance directive any more than there ought to be routine judicial review of a patient's oral wishes to forego life-sustaining treatment. However, in extraordinary cases—such as where there is conflict between the written advance directive and the wishes of the patient's family, or where there is a substantial doubt as to the authenticity of the advance directive—judicial review should be sought.

5. Procedures for Recording the Advance Directive

A written advance directive must be filed in the appropriate section of the patient's medical record. Further, a notation must be made in the Progress Notes of the existence of the advance directive.

VI. DOCUMENTATION OF DECISIONS AND ENTRY OF ORDERS

1. Orders

When it has been determined that a particular life-sustaining procedure is to be foregone (i.e., limited, terminated or withheld, should it become needed) and the above procedures have been followed, the resulting order must be written into the patient's medical record by the attending physician or a designate as directed by the attending physician. A verbal or telephone order is not acceptable. Once the order has been entered, it is the responsibility of the attending physician to ensure that the order and its meaning are discussed with appropriate members of the hospital staff (including nursing staff and house staff) so that all involved professionals understand the order and its implications.

2. Progress Notes

At the time an order to limit life-sustaining treatment is written, a companion entry should be made in the progress notes, which includes at a minimum the following information:

a. diagnosis;

b. prognosis;

c. patient's wishes (when known) or surrogate's wishes (if patient lacks decision making capacity) and family member's wishes (where known);

d. the recommendations of the treating team and consultants with documentation of their names;

e. a description of the patient's decision making ability at the time the decision was made and the efforts made to ascertain the patient's capacity.

3. Acceptable Orders

Each situation is unique, necessitating individual consideration. Detailed orders are usually required in each specific case. However, if detailed orders are not provided, to facilitate communication when therapy is to be limited, one of the following categories should be indicated.

a) *All But Cardiac Resuscitation* – These patients are treated vigorously, including intubation, mechanical ventilation and measures to prevent cardiac arrest. However, should such a patient develop cardiac arrest in spite of every therapeutic effort, no resuscitative efforts are made and the patient is permitted to die. In those situations where patients are being monitored for arrhythmia control, cardioversion or defibrillation for ventricular tachycardia or fibrillation will be attempted once, unless specified not to by written order. Further, it is understood that a cardiac arrest of an "All But Cardiac Resuscitation" patient occurring unexpectedly, for example as an iatrogenic complication, may be treated with full cardiopulmonary resuscitation. However, this possibility should be discussed with the patient and/or family in advance.

b) *Limited Therapy* – In general, no additional therapy is initiated excepted for hygienic care and for comfort. Should cardiac arrest occur, no resuscitative efforts are made. Therapy already initiated will be limited by specific written order only. Exceptions may occur—for example, it may be appropriate to initiate certain drug therapy in a patient who had decided in advance against intubation, dialysis, etc.

c) *Comfort Measures Only* – These patients will only receive nursing and hygienic care and medications appropriate to maintain comfort as ordered. Therapy (e.g., administration of narcotics) which is necessary for comfort may be utilized even if it contributes to cardiorespiratory depression. Therapies already initiated will be reviewed by the physician and discontinued if not related to comfort or hygiene.

SUMMARY OF GUIDELINES ON FOREGOING LIFE-SUSTAINING TREATMENT

Purpose

The purpose of this summary is to provide access to information contained in the PUH Guidelines on Foregoing Life-Sustaining Treatment. It is not to be used as a substitute for those guidelines which should be referred to when specific medical-ethical dilemmas occur. Page numbers and appropriate sections of the guidelines are here included to facilitate this access.

Introduction

No ethically relevant distinction exists between failing to institute new treatment and discontinuing treatment that has already been initiated. Therefore, the term "forego" is used to include stopping treatment already begun as well as not starting a new treatment. These guidelines are applicable to all kinds of life-sustaining treatment and are not limited to decisions to forego cardiopulmonary resuscitation.

Statement of General Principles (Section II, pp 3-4) and General Principles Governing Decision Making (Section III, IV pp 4-7)

As a general rule, all adult patients who do not lack decision making capacity may decline any treatment or procedure. Patients who lack decision making capacity have the same ethical and legal rights as do patients who possess such capacity but health care decisions must be made on their behalf by a surrogate decision maker. It is the ethical and legal right of an individual physician to decline to participate in the limitation or withdrawal of therapy, if he or she considers this action inappropriate. However, no physician may abandon his or her patient until care by another physician has been secured. Further, a patient or his surrogate may not compel the physician to provide any treatment which in the physician's professional judgment is unlikely to provide the patient with significant benefit, i.e., the treatment is not medically indicated. Procedures for assessing decision making capacity, for selecting a surrogate decision maker and for Ethics Committee consultation are outlined in this section.

Advance Directives (Section V pp 7-8)

The definition of, weight to be given to, and procedures for handling advance directives (living wills) are outlined in this section.

Documentation of Decisions and Entry of Orders (Section VI, pp 9-10)

When it has been determined that a particular life-sustaining procedure is to be foregone, the resulting order must be written into the patient's medical record and an appropriate progress note written including information on diagnosis, prognosis, patient's or surrogate's wishes, the recommendations of the treating team and a description of the patient's decision making ability. It is the physician's responsibility to communicate this information to other members of the health care team.

Detailed orders are usually required but one of the following categories may be used:

A. *All But Cardiac Resuscitation.* These patients are treated vigorously, including intubation, mechanical ventilation and measures to prevent cardiac arrest. However, should such a patient develop cardiac arrest in spite of every therapeutic effort, no resuscitative efforts are made and the patient is permitted to die. In those situations where patients are being monitored for arrhythmia control, cardioversion or defibrillation for ventricular tachycardia or fibrillation will be attempted once, unless specified not to by written order. Further, it is understood that a cardiac arrest of an "All But Cardiac Resuscitation" patient occurring unexpectedly, for example as an iatrogenic complication, may be treated with full cardiopulmonary resuscitation. However, this possibility should be discussed with the patient and/or family in advance.

B. *Limited Therapy.* In general, no additional therapy is initiated except for hygienic care and for comfort. Should cardiac arrest occur, no resuscitative efforts are made. Therapy already initiated will be limited by specific written order only. Exceptions may occur—for example, it may be appropriate to initiate certain drug therapy in a patient who has decided in advance against intubation, dialysis, etc.

C. *Comfort Measures Only.* These patients will only receive nursing and hygienic care and medications appropriate to maintain comfort as ordered. Therapy (e.g., administration of narcotics) which is necessary for comfort may be utilized even if it contributes to cardiorespiratory depression.

Therapies already initiated will be reviewed by the physician and discontinued if not related to comfort or hygiene.

Index

A

Abruptio placenta, 70
Acute myocardial infarction (AMI), 99
Advance directives, 51–53, 175–176, 188–189
American Academy of Pediatrics, 77
American Association of Critical Care Nurses (AACCN), 8
American Bar Association, 123
American Board of Medical Specialties (ABMS), 1, 5, 6, 8
American Hospital Association, 76–77
American Medical Association, 79, 123
Anencephaly, 70, 71
Anxiety, 148
Application of President and Directors of Georgetown College, Inc., 35
Artificial feeding withholding, 45–47, 76, 77
Authority channels, 14–17

B

Baby Doe rule, 76–81
Baby Jane Doe case, 78–79
Barry, Andrew, In re Guardianship of, 67
Birth injury, 70
Bouvia case, 38
Brain injury, 112–113
Brieant, Charles, 79

C

Child abuse, 79–81
Child Abuse Amendments of 1984, 79–81
Children. *See* Critically ill infants; Pediatric treatment decisions
Children's Hospital National Medical Center, 77
Chromosomal abnormalities, 72–73
Cicero, In re, 76
Cluster analysis, 27
Competency determination, 39–41, 173
Conroy case, 45–47
Consent to treatment, 31–34, 166, 169, 184–185. *See also* Incompetency; Refusal of treatment; Withholding/withdrawing treatment
Critically ill infants
  ethics committee role, 81–82
  federal requirements, 76–81
  medical conditions, 68–76

195

uncertainty problems, 75–76
Custody of a Minor, 67

D

Dato's Law of Stress, 148
Deformation defects, 70
Department of Health and Human Services (DHHS), 76–79
Determination of death
  artificial life support and, 111–114
  conceptual approaches, 116–118
  criteria for, 114–116
  future trends, 125–128
  judicial decisions, 121–122
  legal rule formulation, 119–121
  organ transplantation and, 125
  overview, 109
  statutes, 122–127
  traditional standards, 110–111
  treatment termination and, 124–125
Diagnostic Related Groups (DRGs), 98
Dinnerstein, Matter of, 49
Disclosure of risks, 32–33, 169, 184–185
Down's syndrome, 72–73
Durable power of attorney, 53
Duty to act, 13–14

E

Easy risks, 14
Economics of care
  cost, 94–97
  cost reduction approaches, 99–100, 103
  effectiveness, 92–93
  growth, 87–92
  hospital financing changes, 97–99
  savings potential, 100–101
Eichner, Matter of, 44, 50–51
Emergencies, 33
Encephaloceles, 70–71
Engineering analyses, 23

Equipment
  incident analysis, 22–23
  liabilities, 3–5
  maintenance, 20
  modification, 21
  records, 21–22
  risk management, 19–23
Ethics committees, 48, 51, 81–82, 158–159, 176–177

F

Families
  case example, 142–144
  grief, 141–142
  responses of, 136–138
  staff interactions, 138–141
Feeding withholding, 45–47, 76, 77
Fetal-placental disorders, 70
Foregoing treatment. *See* Withholding/withdrawing treatment

G

Genetic disorders, 73–74
Gesell, Gerhard, 77
Green, Chad, 66
Green, In re, 67
Gregory S., In re, 66
Grief, 141–142

H

Hamilton, Pamela, 66
Handicapped infants. *See* Critically ill infants
Higher brain standard, 117, 124
Hofbauer, In re, 67
Hospital liabilities, 3–5, 9
Hydranencephaly, 70, 71
Hypoplastic left heart syndrome, 74–75

I

ICU psychosis, 134–136
Impaired newborns. *See* Critically ill infants
Incident reporting, 22–27
Incompetent patients
  advance directives, 51–53, 175–176, 188–189
  consent and, 33, 173
  determination of incompetency, 39–41, 173
  withholding/withdrawing treatment, 41–51, 62–65, 172–174, 186–187
Infant care review committees (ICRCs), 78, 79
Infants. *See* Critically ill infants
Informed consent, 31–34, 166, 169, 184–185
Intensive care units
  costs, 94–97
  effectiveness, 92–93
  efficiency improvement, 99–100
  family-related factors, 136–141
  growth of intensive care, 87–92
  hospital financing and, 97–99
  patient responses to, 134–136
  recommendations for, 101–104
  savings potential, 100–101
  staffing, 155–156
  stress factors in, 148–149
Intraventricular hemorrhage (IVH), 69–70

J

Jehovah's Witnesses, 35, 36, 38, 66
Joint Commission on Accreditation of Hospitals (JCAH), 155
Justice Department, 79

K

Karwath, In re, 66
Kennedy Memorial Hosp. v. Bludworth, 52

L

Liability principles, 2–5
Living wills, 52–53, 175–176
Locality rule, 2
Low birth weight, 68–70

M

McNulty, Karen Ann, 76
Maine Medical Center v. Houle, 75–76
Maintenance by exception, 20
Malformations, 70–72, 74–75
Medical neglect, 79–80
Medical records, 18–19
Medicare, 91, 96–98
Melideo, In re, 35, 36
Myelomeningoceles, 71–72

N

National Association of Children's Hospitals and Related Institutions, 77
National Conference of Commissioners on Uniform State Laws, 123
Natural Death Acts, 51–53
Neonatal intensive care. *See* Critically ill infants
Neural tube defects, 70–72
Newborns. *See* Critically ill infants
No-code orders, 49. *See also* Withholding/withdrawing treatment
Nontreatment. *See* Refusal of treatment; Withholding/withdrawing treatment
Norwood procedure, 74

Nurse specialists
  attitudes toward care, 156–157
  responsibilities, 16–17
  standard of care, 8–9
  stress, 149–152, 155, 161
  turnover rate, 156

O

Organ donation, 115, 120, 121, 125
Osborne, In re, 35, 37
Outliers, 24

P

Patient responses, 134–136, 142–144
Pediatric treatment decisions, 65–67. See also critically ill infants
People v. Eulo, 121–122
Persistent vegetative state, 113
Personnel. See Nurse specialists; Physician specialists; Staff
Phenylketonuria (PKU), 73–74
Physician specialists
  attitudes toward care, 156–157
  responsibilities, 15–16
  standards of care, 2–5, 7–8
  stress, 152–155, 160
  turnover rates, 156
Pipelining, 13–14
Placenta previa, 70
Positive feedback, 13
Power of attorney, 53
Prematurity, 68–70
Presbyterian-University Hospital
  foregoing treatment guidelines
    advance directives, 175–176, 188–189
    basic principles, 168–169, 182–183
    decisionmaking, 169–171, 183–186
    ethics committee role, 176–177
    incompetent patients, 172–174, 186–187

  judicial involvement, 174–175
  records, 177, 189–191
  summary, 191–193
  treatment definition, 171–172
President's Commission for the Study of Ethical Problems in Medicine and Biomedical and Behavioral Research, 36, 40, 47, 51, 52, 109, 113–114, 123, 124, 159, 167–168, 171
Products liability, 3–4, 22–23
Prospective payment system, 98
Psychosis syndrome, 134–136

Q

Quackenbush, In re, 35
Quinlan, In re, 42–43, 48, 62–64

R

Raleigh Fitkin-Paul Morgan Memorial Hosp. v. Anderson, 37–38
Records
  equipment, 21–22
  medical, 18–19
  withholding/withdrawing treatment, 177, 189–191
Refusal of treatment, 33–39, 62, 66–67. See also Withholding/withdrawing treatment
Rehabilitation Act of 1973, 76–79
Respiratory distress syndrome (RDS), 69
Respondeat superior, 3
Risk disclosure, 32–33, 169, 184–185
Risk management
  authority channel establishment, 14–17
  duty to act and, 13–14
  easy risk elimination, 14
  economics of, 12–13
  equipment-related incidents, 19–23

incident reporting system, 22–27
medical records system, 18–19
principles, 11–14
procedures, 19–20
Rotkowitz, In re, 67

S

Saikewicz case, 43–44, 48–49, 63–64
Schiller, In re, 40
Section 504, 76–81
Seiferth, In re, 67
Severns, In re, 46
Spina bifida cystica, 71–72
Sporadic malformations, 74–75
Spring, In re, 49–50, 65
Staff
 family interaction, 138–141
 professional interaction, 156–157
 responsibilities, 14–17
 unit staffing, 155–156
 See also Nurse specialists; Physician specialists
Standards of care
 consent related, 32–33
 establishment guides, 5–9
 hospitals, 3–5, 9
 nurse specialists, 8–9
 physician specialists, 4–5, 7–8
 problems of, 1–2
 scope of disciplines, 6
 traditional, 2–5
 training, 6–7
State Department of Human Services v. Northern, 40
Storar, Matter of, 44, 51
Stress
 concept of, 147–148
 ethical committee factors, 158–159
 intensive care environment, 148–149
 legal factors and, 157–158
 nurses, 149–152, 155, 161

physicians, 152–155, 160
 recommendations for alleviation, 160–162
 staffing and, 155–156
 staff interaction, 156–157
Strict liability, 3–4
Substituted judgment test, 42–44, 64–65
Superintendent of Belchertown State School v. Saikewicz, 43–44, 48–49, 63–64

T

Therapeutic Intervention Scoring System (TISS), 156
Therapeutic privilege, 33, 169
Training, 6–7, 20
Treatment decisions
 advance directives, 51–53, 175–176, 188–189
 determination of death and, 124–125
 incompetency determination, 39–41
 informed consent, 31–34
 pediatric, 64–67
 problems of, 31
 refusal of treatment, 33–39, 62
 See also Critically ill infants; Withholding/withdrawing treatment
Trisomy 13, 18, 21, 72–73

U

Uniform Anatomical Gift Act, 115, 125
Uniform Determination of Death Act (UDDA), 109, 123, 125–127
United States v. George, 35
University of California at Davis Medical School, 14

V

Vegetative state, 113

W

Whole brain standard, 117–118, 124
Withholding/withdrawing treatment
  advance directives, 51–53,
    175–176, 188–189
  attitudes toward, 156–157
  decision-making process, 62,
    169–171, 183–186
  determination of death and,
    124–125
  ethics committee role, 51, 176–177
  feeding, 45–47
  incompetent patients, 48–51,
    62–65, 172–174, 186–187
  judicial involvement, 48–51,
    64–65, 174–175
  legal standards, 42–45, 64–65
  overview, 41–42, 165–168
  principles of, 168–169, 182–183
  procedure guidelines sample,
    181–193
  records, 177, 189–191
  treatment definition, 171–172

Y

Yetter, In re, 39

About the Editors

KATHERINE BENESCH is a practicing attorney specializing in medical and hospital matters. She received her Master of Public Health degree from Yale University School of Medicine and her law degree from Duquesne University. Attorney Benesch is an Adjunct Assistant Professor of Anesthesiology and Critical Care Medicine at the University of Pittsburgh School of Medicine and has written and lectured extensively on medical and hospital liability, risk management, life support, informed consent, and medical staff privilege issues. She has served as in-house Legal Counsel at Presbyterian-University Hospital in Pittsburgh and has represented numerous hospital, physician, and health care clients with counseling and litigation needs.

NORMAN S. ABRAMSON is a Board Certified Emergency Medicine physician and an Assistant Professor of Critical Care Medicine/Anesthesiology at the University of Pittsburgh. After completing an Emergency Medicine residency at the University of Cincinnati and a Critical Care Fellowship at the University of Pittsburgh, he became a Research Associate at the Resuscitation Research Center, University of Pittsburgh. For the past six years he has been actively involved in research on cerebral resuscitation and is currently coordinator of an international randomized clinical trial of brain resuscitation after cardiac arrest. His other research interests include artificial perfusion after cardiac arrest, informed consent, and medicolegal aspects of resuscitation medicine.

AKE GRENVIK graduated from medical school at the Karolinska Institute and obtained his PhD degree at the University of Uppsala, Sweden. After speciality training in general and thoracic surgery he moved to the United States for further training in anesthesiology and critical care medicine. Dr. Grenvik is Director of Intensive Care at Presbyterian-University Hospital and Chief of the Critical Care Medicine Training Program at Pittsburgh's University Health Center. He is a founding member and past president of the

Society of Critical Care Medicine and has published extensively on CCM topics, including ethical issues in intensive care.

ALAN MEISEL is Professor of Law in the School of Law and in the Department of Psychiatry of the School of Medicine at the University of Pittsburgh. He served on the President's Commission for the Study of Ethical Problems in Medicine and Biomedical and Behavioral Research, where he was one of the authors of the reports *Making Health Care Decisions* and *Deciding to Forego Life-Sustaining Treatment*. He is also a coauthor of *Informed Consent: A Study of Decisionmaking in Psychiatry* (Guilford Press, 1984) and of *Informed Consent: Legal Theory and Clinical Practice* to be published by Oxford University Press. Professor Meisel is also of counsel to the Pittsburgh law firm of Berkman Ruslander Pohl Lieber & Engel.

About the Contributors

ALEXANDER M. CAPRON is Topping Professor of Law, Medicine, and Public Policy at the University of Southern California. He was formerly Executive Director of the President's Commission for the Study of Ethical Problems in Medicine and Biomedical and Behavioral Research; Professor of Law, Ethics, and Public Policy at Georgetown Law Center; Senior Fellow at the Kennedy Institute of Ethics at Georgetown University; and Professor of Law and Professor of Human Genetics at the University of Pennsylvania. He is currently a member of the Institute of Medicine and serves on the Council and Executive Committee of the Institute of Medicine of the National Academy of Sciences. He is also a Fellow of the Hastings Center and a member of its Board of Directors, a member of the Board of Directors of the American Society of Law and Medicine, and an Honorary Fellow of the American College of Legal Medicine. He is the author of numerous articles and books, including *Law, Science, and Medicine* (with Areen, King, and Goldberg) and *Catastrophic Diseases: Who Decides What* (with Jay Katz).

JOEL FRADER, MD, graduated from Columbia College (New York City), Tufts University School of Medicine, and the University of Pennsylvania (MA in Sociology). His interest in biomedical ethics and medical sociology grew out of his college work experience as a hospital orderly, his undergraduate studies, and the dilemmas he encountered during medical training. Dr. Frader is the author of many articles and book chapters in the field of medical ethics. He is currently Assistant Professor of Pediatrics at the University of Pittsburgh and the Children's Hospital of Pittsburgh, where he pursues interests in general academic pediatrics, bioethics and law and medicine.

WILLIAM A. KNAUS, MD, is a Fellow of the American College of Physicians. He is co-director of the Intensive Care Unit at The George Washington University Medical Center, where he is also founder and director of the ICU Research Unit. This unit aims at improving the evaluation of intensive care units by developing a severity of disease index for acutely ill patients and at improving patient prognosis by examining the relation between acute disease, intensive therapy and outcome.

JUDITH R. LAVE received her undergraduate training at Queen's University in Canada and her Ph.D. in economics from Harvard University. She has been a faculty member at Carnegie-Mellon University; director of Economic and Quantitative Analysis, Office of the Deputy Assistant Secretary for Planning and Evaluation, Department of Health and Human Services; and director of the Office of Research, Health Care Financing Administration (HCFA). She is currently professor of health economics at the Graduate School of Public Health, University of Pittsburgh. Dr. Lave has published extensively, has served as a consultant to both private and public agencies, and has served on a number of national committees. She is a member of the panel on Statistics for an Aging Society for the Committee on National Statistics and on the HCFA Technical Advisory Panel on the Evaluation of the Medicare Prospective Payment System.

ROSA LYNN PINKUS received her doctorate in history at the State University of New York at Buffalo in 1975. She has worked as a research fellow for the Pennsylvania Public Committee for the Humanities/Falk Medical Fund. Since 1979, Dr. Pinkus has been at the School of Medicine, University of Pittsburgh, where she teaches courses on medical ethics and acts as an ethics consultant for a neurosurgical intensive care unit. She has published articles on medical/ethical decision making, brain death, and neurosurgical topics.

KATHARINE C. RATHBUN, MD, MPH, received her undergraduate training in sociology at Rice University and the University of Colorado. After receiving her medical degree from the University of Michigan, Dr. Rathbun completed a Masters in Public Health at the University of Texas School of Public Health. Her specialty is preventive medicine, and she is currently Director of the San Antonio Metropolitan Health District. In addition to research on congenital syphilis, she has an ongoing interest in the legal constraints on medical practice.

NANCY K. RHODEN is an Assistant Professor of Law at Ohio State University. She is a 1974 graduate of Oberlin College and received her JD in 1977 from New York University. From 1979 to 1980 she was a postdoctoral fellow at the Hastings Center, and she has been writing in the area of bioethics and law since that time.

EDWARD P. RICHARDS, III, JD, MPH, received his undergraduate training in biology and behavioral science at Rice University. After conducting graduate work in medical physiology and pharmacology, he completed his legal training at the University of Houston and received his MPH from the University of Texas School of Public Health. Mr. Richards practices personal injury and medical law with the firm of Roberts, Markel & Folger in Houston. He also does extensive writing and research in the area of preventive law as an Affiliated Scholar at the Center for Preventive Law at the University of Denver College of Law. His special research and practice interests are the problems of high-technology medicine.

DEBORAH J. ROBINSON graduated from Allegheny College in 1971 and worked as a public health educator and administrator for the Onondaga County Department of Public Health in Syracuse, New York. In 1980, she graduated from the University of Pittsburgh School of Law and has practiced in Ann Arbor, Michigan since that time. She is currently an Associate with the firm of Dykema, Gossett, Goodnow, Spencer & Trigg in Detroit and Ann Arbor, and she specializes in health and hospital law.

ROBYN S. SHAPIRO is the Acting Director of the Bioethics Center at the Medical College of Wisconsin, Assistant Clinical Professor of Health Law at the Medical College of Wisconsin, coordinator of the Medical Ethics curriculum at the Medical College of Wisconsin, and a partner in the Menomonee Falls law firm of Barr & Shapiro. She serves on several institutional ethics committees and state governmental advisory committees. She has published numerous articles in the field of medical ethics.

JAMES V. SNYDER attended Thomas Jefferson University and then served at Akron City Hospital and in the Navy before his residency in Anesthesiology and his Fellowship in Critical Care Medicine at the University of Pittsburgh. Dr. Snyder is Professor of Anesthesiology and Critical Care Medicine and remains an attending physician in Intensive Care at Presbyterian-University Hospital.

GEORGE L. WALLACE-BARNHILL, PhD, CCMHC, is an Assistant Professor in Anesthesiology and Surgery at the University of Miami School of Medicine. He received his BS from Pennsylvania State University in 1964, his MS in Psychology from Millersville State College in 1972, and his PhD in 1981 from the University of Maryland. Dr. Wallace-Barnhill has his national board certification as a Clinical Mental Health Counselor and is a Licensed Mental Health Counselor in the State of Florida.